At the Core
and in the Margins

 LATINOS IN THE UNITED STATES SERIES

At the Core and in the Margins

INCORPORATION OF MEXICAN IMMIGRANTS IN TWO RURAL MIDWESTERN COMMUNITIES

JULIA ALBARRACÍN

Michigan State University Press • East Lansing

♻ The paper used in this publication meets the minimum requirements of ANSI/NISO Z39.48-1992 (R 1997) (Permanence of Paper).

 Michigan State University Press
East Lansing, Michigan 48823-5245

Printed and bound in the United States of America.

25 24 23 22 21 20 19 18 17 16   1 2 3 4 5 6 7 8 9 10

LIBRARY OF CONGRESS CATALOGING-IN-PUBLICATION DATA
Names: Albarracín, Julia.
Title: At the core and in the margins : incorporation of Mexican immigrants in two rural Midwestern communities / Julia Albarracín.
Description: East Lansing : Michigan State University Press, 2016. | Series: Latinos in the United States series | Includes bibliographical references and index.
Identifiers: LCCN 2015022488| ISBN 9781611862065 (paperback) | ISBN 9781609174927 (PDF) | ISBN 9781628952650 (ePub) | ISBN 9781628962659 (Kindle)
Subjects: LCSH: Mexican Americans—Cultural assimilation—Illinois. | Mexican Americans—Illinois—Statistics. | Mexican Americans—Illinois—Interviews. | Immigrants—Illinois—Social conditions. | Immigrants—Illinois—Statistics. | Social surveys—Illinois. | Beardstown (Ill.)—Ethnic relations. | Monmouth (Ill.)—Ethnic relations. | Illinois—Ethnic relations. | Illinois—Rural conditions. | BISAC: SOCIAL SCIENCE / Ethnic Studies / Hispanic American Studies. | SOCIAL SCIENCE / Sociology / Rural. | POLITICAL SCIENCE / Public Policy / Cultural Policy.
Classification: LCC F550.M5 A43 2016 | DDC 305.8968/720773—dc23 LC record available at http://lccn.loc.gov/2015022488

Cover and book design by Charles Sharp, Sharp Des!gns, Lansing, MI
Cover image is from the Mexican Independence Day Celebration, 16 September 2013, in Beardstown, IL. Photograph by Julia Albarracín.

green press INITIATIVE Michigan State University Press is a member of the Green Press Initiative and is committed to developing and encouraging ecologically responsible publishing practices. For more information about the Green Press Initiative and the use of recycled paper in book publishing, please visit *www.greenpressinitiative.org.*

Visit Michigan State University Press at *www.msupress.org*

To my dad. A mi papá.

Contents

Figures

Tables

RUBÉN MARTINEZ

Foreword

THE INCORPORATION OF LATINO IMMIGRANTS IS AND HISTORICALLY HAS BEEN A major challenge for American society. The first major Spanish-speaking peoples that became part of the United States in the mid-1840s were Spanish and Spanish-Indian peoples living in the northern provinces of New Spain. Mexico formally gained its independence from Spain in 1821, but it did not really have, as a nation, much influence on the peoples of the northern provinces, except for the military losses to Texans and then the United States, which reconfigured national boundaries. Twenty-seven years after its independence, Mexico had its northern region taken over by the United States. After a half century of tensions and struggles between *Tejanos, Hispanos,* and *Californios* with *los Americanos,* Mexicans began to immigrate to the United States in substantially increased numbers at the turn of the twentieth century.

The Spanish-speaking people that remained in what is today known as the Southwest, following the conquest of 1848, struggled to retain control of their lands while undergoing the process of proletarianization that attended the dispossession. These new citizens of the United States had stronger regional identities as *Hispanos* (New Mexico), *Californios* (California), and *Tejanos* (Texas) than as Mexicans, although the economic and cultural ties cannot be underestimated. Americans came to see these new citizens as Mexicans and later as Mexican Americans. The intergroup relations that developed between Mexican Americans set the stage for Spanish-speaking immigrants that came to the United States throughout the twentieth century.

Following the almost near dispossession of these early generations of Chicanos of their lands, relations between Americans and Mexican Americans were impacted by waves of Mexican immigrants that came at different times throughout that century. This often set in motion reactionary movements among Americans, who mounted repatriation and deportation movements in the 1930s, the 1950s, and more consistently at the turn of the twenty-first century. Indeed, because of these intergroup dynamics, today's immigrants from Central and South America are viewed by many Americans as Mexicans, which is the general stereotype by which Americans perceive Latinos—as poor, illiterate, unskilled, and (for the most part) hardworking. This stereotype is opposite to that which prevailed during the twentieth century, when Mexicans and Mexican Americans were perceived as lazy, indolent, and violent.

Relations between Latino immigrants today are embedded in those between Mexican Americans and Americans, which are embedded within the broader racial dynamics that have been part of the nation's history since its inception. These include Native Americans, African Americans, Chinese Americans, Puerto Ricans, and other racially oppressed peoples that have a history of a century or more in this nation. While the initial Spanish-speaking peoples of the Southwest were part of this nation as it experienced industrialization, today's immigrants are experiencing a neoliberal order that produced deindustrialization through policies that opened markets abroad through a series of trade agreements. Neoliberalism denies the existence of racism and structures of inequality (inequality is the result of individual talent and effort). Market expansion led to manufacturing plants running away to countries where companies could access cheaper labor and reduce their costs of production. The runaway plant phenomenon displaced millions of workers at home, while trade agreements displaced workers and small farmers in Mexico and other countries, forcing them to emigrate in search of better lives. Economic restructuring and the "manufactured" era of austerity engendered widespread uneasiness and poverty across the country, and provided fertile ground for the rise of political conservatism, especially among White Americans.

The downward mobility experienced by millions of White Americans produced, among other things, widespread scapegoating of immigrants, generally perceived as Mexicans, and political initiatives to "close the border" while deporting "undocumented immigrants." Myths arose that Mexican immigrants were and are taking jobs from American workers. More recently, presidential candidate Donald

Trump portrayed Latino immigrants as "Mexico's worst," calling them drug dealers and rapists. At the same time he has argued that Latinos love him, that he employs "thousands" of them. Trump's position reflects the contradiction that America experiences with Latino immigrants: Americans are hostile to the so-called Mexican immigrants at the same time that these immigrants are needed in the economy to perform the economic tasks that Americans will not perform. The latter group seeks better jobs in the economy. This contradiction finds expression in the daily lives of people in the nation's small town and cities.

This book by Julia Albarracín is important in that it examines the perceptions of Mexican immigrants in two small towns in west Illinois relative to intergroup relations, how they address exclusionary measures, and how they promote a sense of community among themselves. These towns are what today are called new destinations for Latino immigrants, with locals having little contact and experience with Spanish-speaking immigrants. Actually, in most cases, Latino immigrants and Americans had little experience with each other, with both groups having to accommodate and institutions having to develop capacity to incorporate the newcomers. Albarracín, an immigrant herself, brings a fresh perspective to the dynamics between Mexican immigrants and members of the host communities—the new destination sites. It is my pleasure to welcome her volume to the series on Latinos in the United States. I know that readers will have a better understanding of Latino/American relations in rural communities in the Midwest and other new destination towns.

Acknowledgments

This book went through a long gestation process and I'm indebted to many for their support. I'm thankful for the funding by Western Illinois University's Research Council. I received invaluable feedback from Philip Williams, my former adviser from the University of Florida, and from my current chair, Keith Boeckelman. I'm also grateful for the helpful comments by my sister, Dolores Albarracín, and my friend Jutta Helm. I want to acknowledge, as well, the instrumental feedback and guidance by anonymous reviewers and Rubén Martinez, the editor of the Michigan State University Press's series on Latinos in the United States.

I couldn't have done this work without the support of a number of students from Western Illinois University who helped me with the surveys and sources, including Alex Villar, Tracy Weiss, Dustin Hinrichs, Stephanie Howe, Jessica Cortés, and Tad Scott. I'm also thankful to the General Mexican Consulate in Chicago for allowing me to interview immigrants during the Mobile Consulates, and I'm indebted to Saint Alexius Church in Beardstown, Illinois, and the Immaculate Conception Church in Monmouth, Illinois. I couldn't have done this research without the help and support of Helena from the store La Pequeñita, who put up with us for countless hours while we interviewed immigrants and Martin from Beardstown, Illinois, who helped me with the recruitment of participants. Last but not least, I'm thankful for the support of my family and friends, and for Ben's company during innumerable hours of work.

Introduction

I sometimes wonder: if we are not well received in this society, why stay?
—Alejandra, interview with the author, November 26, 2011, Beardstown, Illinois

SINCE I MOVED TO THE MIDWEST IN 2005, I HAVE ATTENDED THE ILLINOIS STATE Fair in Springfield, and Heritage Days celebrations and other festivities in Macomb. These are the types of festivities I grew accustomed to early on. Yet in 2007, I was invited to give a talk at a Cinco de Mayo celebration in Monmouth, Illinois, a town of nine thousand people located in the west central part of the state, by the owner of a local Mexican store. I expected a modest number of people at the door of the Mexican store. Instead, a lively street party that included Mexican food, dance groups, and more than one hundred attendees awaited me. The celebration was entertaining, the food was delicious, and the occasion allowed me to meet many Mexican immigrants in the area.

Eighty miles south of Monmouth lies Beardstown, Illinois, a town of six thousand people that also celebrates Cinco de Mayo and Mexican Independence Day. The Latino communities in Beardstown and Monmouth account for 33 percent and 15 percent of the total population, respectively (U.S. Census Bureau 2013a). However, twenty years ago the Latino communities in these two towns were almost nonexistent. Further, in recent years the number of Latino children enrolled in schools has surpassed 40 percent in Beardstown and 30 percent in Monmouth, and school districts have responded by establishing language programs to accommodate the growing number of Latino students. What accounts for the arrival of Mexican immigrants in these two small towns in rural Illinois? What are the prospects for the legal, cultural, and political incorporation of these immigrants into Beardstown and Monmouth?

New Destinations

Out of the 308.7 million people living in the United States in 2010, 50.5 million (16 percent) were of Latino or Hispanic origin. In 2010, people of Mexican origin represented 63 percent of the Latino population and 55 percent of the foreign-born population in the United States (U.S. Census Bureau 2011). Latinos continue to be concentrated in the South and West (Massey and Capoferro 2008; Riosmena and Massey 2012). However, two developments in the geographic distribution of Latinos are notable. First, Hispanics are living in states outside of the West in growing numbers. Between 2000 and 2010, for instance, the largest growth in the proportion of Latinos occurred in regions outside the West (figure 1).

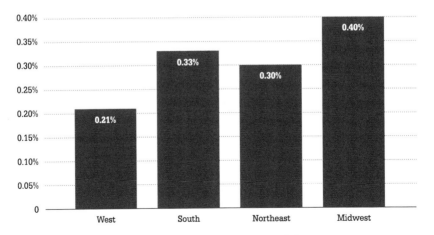

Figure 1. Growth of the Latino Population in U.S. Regions, 2000–2010

**Table 1. Proportion of Latinos in 2010 and Growth in the Proportion
of Latinos 2000–2010 in the Midwest Region**

State	2010 (%)	Growth 2000–2010 (%)	State	2010 (%)	Growth 2000–2010 (%)
Illinois	15.8	33	Minnesota	4.7	75
Kansas	10.5	60	Michigan	4.5	35
Nebraska	9.2	77	Missouri	3.5	79
Indiana	6.0	82	Ohio	3.1	63
Wisconsin	5.9	74	South Dakota	2.7	103
Iowa	5.0	84	North Dakota	2.0	73

Source: U.S. Census Bureau, American FactFinder. Census 2000 (2012a) and Census 2010 (2012b). Http://factfinder2.census.gov.

Second, Latinos are also settling in non-metropolitan and rural areas. Immigrants offer potential benefits for fading rural communities (Jensen 2006; Johnson and Lichter 2008). Between 2000 and 2005, for instance, 211 counties across the country experienced population increases only because Hispanic gains offset the population decline of non-Hispanics. Hispanic population growth also tempered the loss of population in 1,100 other counties, including large strips of the Great Plains, representing the first population growth in decades for some communities (Johnson and Lichter 2008).

The Midwest is experiencing unparalleled demographic changes (Aponte 1999; Baker and Hotek 2003; Kandel and Cromartie 2004; Massey and Capoferro 2008; Pérez Rosenbaum 1997; Saenz 2011; Sanderson and Painter 2011; Valdivia et al. 2008). In 2010, Illinois ranked fourth in the nation in its number of Latinos and first in the Midwest region. Between 2000 and 2010, the growth of the Latino population in the Midwest ranged from 33 percent to 104 percent (U.S. Census Bureau 2011) (table 1). Other states in the Midwest with important proportions of Latinos include Kansas (11 percent), Nebraska (9 percent), Indiana (6 percent), and Wisconsin (6 percent) (U.S. Census Bureau 2011) (table 1).

A number of factors have contributed to the dispersion of immigrants into new states and less-urban areas. The increasing diversity of immigrant destinations is bound up with the growing volume of immigration overall (Hirschman and Massey 2008). Other factors related to the geographic dispersion of immigrants include stricter border enforcement in the Southwest (Durand, Massey, and Charvet 2000; Kandel and Cromartie 2004; Massey and Capoferro 2008; Valentine 2005), labor market saturation and weak economies in such traditional urban destinations as Los Angeles (Kandel and Cromartie 2004), and the unintended consequences of the legalization of millions of immigrants by the Immigration Reform and Control

Act (IRCA) of 1986 (Kandel and Cromartie 2004; Massey and Capoferro 2008; Valentine 2005). In addition, the restructuring of U.S. agriculture and agro-industry has provided a demand for Latino labor (Aponte 1999; Gouveia and Saenz 2000; Haverluk and Trautman 2008; Jensen 2006; Kandel and Cromartie 2004; Lichter and Johnson 2006; Paral 2009; Valentine 2005).

An unintended consequence of the fortification of the border has been to help reverse the trend of settlement in places convenient for circular migration that was common in the past (Cornelius 2001; Harveluk and Trautman 2008; Valentine 2005). This policy made crossing the border more costly, but also forced many immigrants to increase their length of stay in the country and cross the border less frequently (Cornelius 2001). Labor market saturation and recession trends in Texas, California, and other parts of the Hispanic core region probably influenced the dispersion of immigrants as well (Durand, Massey, and Charvet 2000; Suro and Singer 2002). These push factors may have increased Hispanic interest in relocating to the South and Midwest. IRCA 1986 did not directly influence destinations, but the legalization programs contained in it made immigration a more permanent phenomenon (Kandel and Cromartie 2004; Valentine 2005). Instead of concentrating in border states, immigrants with their green cards in hand searched for better opportunities for themselves and their families in nontraditional destination states (Valentine 2005).

What types of jobs are immigrants finding in non-metropolitan and rural communities? Meatpacking is the main engine of immigration to the Midwest (Aponte 1999; Baker and Hotek 2003; Fennelly and Leitner 2002; Gouveia and Saenz 2000; Haverluk and Trautman 2008; Jensen 2006; Kandel and Cromartie 2004; Lichter and Johnson 2006; Paral 2009; Sanderson and Painter 2011; Valentine 2005). Formerly, meatpacking plants were located in urban centers and used unionized labor (Dalla, Ellis, and Cramer 2005). Because of the pressure for global production, the beef industry has shifted to highly mechanized plants that do not require skilled labor and has moved the production facilities to rural areas (Haverluk and Trautman 2008). This decision has allowed producers to hire cheaper, non-skilled labor, avoid places with a history of labor activism, and, at the same time, lower transportation costs. Now, meatpacking plants recruit laborers from nearby Mexico and faraway Asia (Dalla, Ellis, and Cramer 2005).

Why Study Beardstown and Monmouth, Illinois?

Immigrants in new destinations are transforming small town America. Whereas in 2010, the proportion of Latinos in Beardstown and Monmouth was 33 percent and 15 percent, respectively, ten years earlier those numbers were only 17.9 percent and 4.3 percent, respectively. In short, the proportion of the Latino population in Beardstown almost doubled and the Latino population in Monmouth more than tripled between the years 2000 and 2010. The largest group of immigrants in both towns comes from Mexico, followed by Puerto Rico and Cuba. In 2010, the Mexican population accounted for 78 percent of Latinos in Beardstown and 88 percent of this population group in Monmouth (U.S. Census Bureau 2013a).

Incorporation

In this book, I explore the legal, cultural, and political incorporation of immigrants in Beardstown and Monmouth. Based on a survey of 260 immigrants and forty-seven in-depth interviews, these issues are addressed using the concept of incorporation (Black 2011; Bean, Brown, and Rumbaut 2006; DeSipio 2011; Gidengil and Stolle 2009; Gerstle 2010; Hochschild and Mollenkopf 2009; Jones-Correa 2004; Mahler and Siemiatcki 2011; Mollenkopf and Hochschild 2010; Setzler and McRee n.d.). Incorporation can be defined as gaining a position in society that is secure (Hochschild and Mollenkopf 2009). Groups are neither incorporated nor unincorporated in a dichotomous sense (Segura 2013). The concept of incorporation draws attention to both actions by immigrants and political opportunities and barriers in the host society.

Formerly, immigrants and their offspring were expected to first acculturate and then seek entry and acceptance among the native-born for their social and economic advancement (Portes and Zhou 1993). Nowadays scholars agree that the incorporation of immigrants is a dynamic process that does not require immigrants to acculturate first and then get incorporated into the host society (Black 2011; Bean, Brown and Rumbaut 2006; DeSipio 2011; Gidengil and Stolle 2009; Gerstle 2010; Hochschild and Mollenkopf 2009; Jones-Correa 2004; Mahler and Siemiatycki 2011; Mollenkopf and Hochschild 2010; Setzler and McRee n.d.).

Gerstle (2010) defines three different dimensions of political incorporation used in this book: legal, cultural, and institutional or political. The first dimension is the legal one and refers to immigration status and the final attainment of citizenship as an important stage in the incorporation of immigrants (Bean, Brown, and Rumbaut 2006; DeSipio 2011; Gerstle 2010; Hochschild and Mollenkopf 2009; Jones-Correa 2004). The process of legal incorporation is to a large degree determined by the opportunities and constraints available in the host society (De Souza Briggs 2013; Portes and Böröcz 1989; Portes and Rumbaut 2001; Portes and Zhou 1993, 1994). More specifically, the government's rules for admission and naturalization of foreign citizens are major factors shaping the process of legal incorporation. The legal incorporation of immigrants can follow a progression that includes the obtainment of a work visa (going from undocumented to documented), a permanent residency permit (green card), and citizenship.

Becoming a citizen of the United States is important because citizenship grants immigrants the right to vote, sit on juries, and hold elective office (Gerstle 2010). Thus, citizenship allows immigrants to fully enjoy life in a democratic society. In combination with other factors, low levels of naturalization can also lead to weak political resources (Vega, Martínez, and Stevens 2011). Not all immigrants choose to become naturalized when this possibility is available to them (Bloemraad 2006). In principle, the U.S. Supreme Court and State Department directives allow multiple citizenships (Bloemraad, Korteweg, and Yurdakul 2008), but the citizenship procedure requires an oath renouncing all prior allegiances, and it is possible that this oath deters some immigrants from naturalizing.

Naturalization rates in the United States are lower than in other countries. Different factors influence naturalization rates, including the degree of complexity of the rules and bureaucratic procedures that immigrants need to follow (Bloemraad 2006), the benefits attached to naturalization (Bloemraad 2002, 2006; Freeman et al. 2002), and the levels of education and income of immigrants seeking naturalization (Algan, Bisin, and Verdier 2012; Bloemraad 2002, 2006; González-Barrera et al. 2013; Portes and Böröcz 1989; Schleef and Cavalcanti 2009). In addition, because they are a requirement for naturalization in the United States, English language skills also affect naturalization (González-Barrera et al. 2013).

Notably, many immigrants of recent arrival are undocumented (Baker and Hotek 2003; Kandel and Cromartie 2004; Lichter 2012). Not only are these immigrants denied the democratic rights of citizens or legal residents, but they are also likely to live significantly isolated and in fear of authorities. In addition, undocumented immigrants are also prone to obtaining lower-paying jobs. Until the decision by President Obama to grant legal status to immigrants who are the parents of American citizens and have been in the country for at least five years, the chances for undocumented immigrants to adjust their immigration status were slim.

The second dimension of incorporation is the cultural one and refers to the acculturative process through which immigrants come to feel part of the host society (Gerstle 2010; Schleef and Cavalcanti 2009; Setzler and McRee n.d.). This feeling develops through language acquisition, exposure to American culture and people, and socialization in different institutions in society. To a large degree, cultural incorporation involves a process of sustained interaction between newcomers and the societies in which they live. However, the opportunities and barriers present in society can also determine the level of incorporation. As Portes and Zhou (1993) explain, the values and prejudices of the host society are likely to influence the prospects for assimilation.

When immigrants first arrive in a society, they need to learn the local language (Ager and Strang 2008; Gerstle 2010; Padilla 2006; Padilla and Perez 2003; Schleef and Cavalcanti 2009). Language skills can be essential for work, house-hunting, the schooling of children, and, in general, getting by in society. Rates of English language fluency among first-generation immigrants in the United States are uneven. Immigrants from Latin America have the highest share of Limited English Proficient (LEP) individuals (64.7 percent), followed by immigrants from Asia (46.6 percent) and Europe (29.8 percent). However, immigrants today are learning English faster than the immigrants who came to the United States at the turn of the last century (Jiménez 2011).

Immigrants can learn the local language in different ways. One traditional way is by taking language courses, although not all immigrant destinations offer free language classes. Immigrants may also learn the local language outside of a classroom setting, for example through interactions with locals at work, church, and their children's schools. They can also acquire it by reading and watching television in the local language. Immigrants may face different obstacles when trying to learn the local language. For example, even if free language classes are available, work and family responsibilities may prevent immigrants from attending these classes. In addition, work settings and other institutions may be dominated by immigrants and not include Anglo-Americans with whom they can converse.

Immigrants can follow different acculturation strategies regarding how individuals relate to their original ethnic culture and the dominant culture of the majority (Algan, Bisin, and Verdier 2012). Upon arrival, individuals may have a sense of connectedness or commonality, which is usually associated, beyond the family, with the person's ethno-racial, national, or cultural group. Over time, however, immigrants can develop a sense of connectedness or commonality with the members of the dominant group. This sense of connectedness is referred to in the literature as "linked fates" (Dawson 2001; Kaufmann 2003; Sánchez 2008; Sánchez and Masuoka 2010). Although the role of connectedness in social incorporation with one's own ethnic group has been called into question (Putnam 2000), the relationships between immigrants and the host population are at the core of the incorporation process (Korhonen 2006).

Different factors in the host society interact with the process of immigrant incorporation. Sociologists and anthropologists refer to this dynamic as the context of reception (Portes and Böröcz 1989; Schwartz et al. 2010). The context of reception also includes the stance of the host government and of employers, the characteristics of preexisting ethnic communities, and discrimination by the host society (Portes and Böröcz 1989). Discrimination by the host population is a crucial factor because it influences immigrants' chances for a better life; perceptions of discrimination are also a major source of stress in the lives of immigrants (Schwartz et al. 2010). Unfortunately, dominant considerations regarding immigration have deteriorated in most societies from assistance and hospitality to rejection and hostility (Fekete 2001). This is also true of the United States.

The United States has become less welcoming of immigrants in the last few decades, concurrent with decades of neoliberal policies aimed at shrinking the welfare state by normalizing and naturalizing conditions such as free trade, flexible labor, public sector austerity, and low inflation (Varsanyi 2011). In the 1990s, the Clinton administration launched a series of initiatives aimed at preventing undocumented immigration at selected high traffic points (Ellis 2006) and restricting welfare services to mostly citizens (PRWORA). Ironically, these initiatives coincided with the approval of the North American Free Trade Agreement (NAFTA), intended to increase trade and cooperation among the United States, Mexico, and Canada. Despite President Clinton's predictions, neoliberal NAFTA increased immigration to the United States by displacing millions of peasants from Mexican rural areas (López 2011; Luckstead, Devadoss, and Rodríguez 2012; Nevins 2007). Further, this uprooting of peasants from their livelihoods also contributed to the growth of the drug cartels in Mexico, which, in turn, has been used as a reason to further restrict immigration from this country (Fryberg et al. 2012; McKenney 2013). Thus, the increased cooperation with Mexico after NAFTA has not translated into more receptive immigration policies.

Authors debate whether neoliberalism and immigration restrictions are at odds with each other (Albarracín 2004; Sassen 1996; Varsanyi and Nevins 2007) or whether immigration restrictions are inherent in the logic of the neoliberal state (Ackerman 2011; Cisneros 2015; Hiemstra 2010; Gill 1995; Inda 2013). On the one hand, Saskia Sassen (1996) argues that states have a double standard: a liberal one for trade and goods, and a restrictive one for people. She believes states should reconcile the conflicting requirements of border-free economics and border controls to keep immigrants out. On the other hand, David Cisneros (2015) believes immigration restrictions are inherent in the logic of neoliberalism. He explains how the neoliberal ideology has influenced the politics of immigration in different ways, including an increased emphasis on responsibility as a marker of the "good" citizen-subject, making only immigrants who embrace the neoliberal subjectivity (entrepreneurialism, responsibility, and U.S.-style multiculturalism) worthy of the nation of immigrants. For some, repression can therefore be considered a central feature of the neoliberal state because it must tackle the effects of its retraction regarding social protection (Ackerman 2011).

The terrorist attacks of September 11, 2001, led to an increased militarization of the border and the creation of the Department of Homeland Security, placing the former Immigration and Naturalization Services (INS) within the umbrella of this security agency (Romero 2004). As a result, immigration and immigrants after September 11 became increasingly criminalized (Fryberg et al. 2012; Jeong et al. 2011; Woods and Arthur 2014). Public attitudes and the media also turned more anti-immigration after September 11. For instance, the percentage of Americans who believed that "immigration should be decreased" rose from 41 percent in June 2001 to 58 percent in October 2001 (Woods 2011, 222). Following the September 11 attacks, the media coverage of immigration also became more negative. More specifically, "while the negative framing rate fluctuated between 30 percent and 40 percent throughout much of the 1980s and 1990s, the post–September 11 news era saw a range between 40 percent and nearly 60 percent" (Woods and Arthur 2014, 437). Thus, the September 11 attacks had important implications for receptiveness toward immigrants.

The emergence in 2007 of the Tea Party, a political organization with characteristics that resemble European anti-immigration right-wing parties like the National Front in France, tilted the immigration debate toward the restrictive side, as well. Supporters of the Tea Party are predominantly White, male, Republican, and conservative (Arceneaux and Nicholson 2012). The Tea Party is characterized by a resentment of perceived federal government "handouts" to "undeserving groups," the definition of which seems heavily influenced by racial and ethnic stereotypes (Blee and Yates 2015; Williamson, Skocpol, and Coggin 2011). Immigrants, especially those who are undocumented, are seen as undeserving groups. Several states have passed restrictive immigration bills in recent years. Although these measures affect only the immigrants living in the respective states, the passage of Arizona's SB 1070 in 2010, which allowed state authorities to check the immigration status of suspected undocumented immigrants, marked the return of immigration to center stage in American politics. Not coincidentally, the Tea Party was behind this bill (Barreto et al. 2011).

Another factor that has often contributed to the rise of public opinion against immigration is fear associated with economic insecurity (Espenshade 1995; Stephan, Ybarra, and Bachman 1999; Zick, Pettigrew, and Wagner 2008). The recent economic crisis of 2008 may have therefore increased the negative public opinion surrounding immigration. Concerns with immigrants' undesirable cultural traits have also made public opinion less welcoming of immigration (Huntington 2004; Stephan, Ybarra, and Bachman 1999). Finally, as mentioned before, the implementation of NAFTA led to an increased number of immigrants from Mexico. Public opposition to immigration may have been related to these rising numbers of immigrants (Dovidio et al. 2010).

Prejudice and discrimination provide the context for the incorporation of immigrants. Prejudice is an "antipathy based on a faulty or inflexible generalization" (Allport 1954 in Quillian 2006). This definition implies both a negative affective feeling toward the target group and a poorly founded belief about the members of the target group (a stereotype). Discrimination happens when an exterior manifestation of prejudice materializes and produces an unequal treatment of the target group (Quillian 2006). Discrimination can take place at the individual and institutional levels. Whereas ethnic prejudice is universal, discrimination is not (Berry 2001).

Discriminatory practices occur in different contexts, including labor markets (Blau 1980; Brettell 2011; Butcher and DiNardo 2002; Cornelius 1981; Hersch 2011; Mason 2004; Rivera-Batiz 1999; Sánchez and Brock 1996; Valdivia and Flores 2012), retail and services (Brewster 2012), housing markets (Brettell 2011; Dion 2002; Ondrich, Ross, and Yinger 2000; Ondrich, Stricker, and Yinger 1999; Williams 2006; Yinger 1998), and education (Goodwin 2002; Oxman-Martínez et al. 2012; Portes and MacLeod 1999). Immigrants are also victims of racial profiling (Arnold 2007; Romero 2006) and face discrimination in the criminal system (Dovidio et al. 2010; Stowell, Martínez and Cancino 2012). At the same time, discrimination can have lasting consequences on health (Mossakowski 2003; Rumbaut 1994; Stein, González, and Huq 2012; Viruell-Fuentes, Miranda, and Abdulrahim 2012) and life satisfaction in general (Safi 2010).

Authors speculate as to whether discrimination levels differ between traditional and new destinations of immigration (Hirschman and Massey 2008). On the one hand, many immigrants settle in areas unaccustomed to seeing large numbers of immigrants, and this can lead to xenophobia and prejudice among the host population, who perceive them as threatening competition for resources, group identity, and power (Fennelly 2008). On the other hand, these new areas of immigration can be free of the prejudices common in traditional areas of immigration like California (Massey and Capoferro 2008). In addition, populations in these new areas of immigration may be grateful that immigrants help offset population losses. Thus, in some cases immigrant arrivals can lead to the formation of pro-immigrant coalitions of local citizens (Fennelly 2008).

The third dimension of political incorporation is the institutional or political one (Gerstle 2010). Participation and engagement in the political system are indicators of the political incorporation of immigrants (Black 2011; DeSipio 2011; Hochschild and Mollenkopf 2009; Jones-Correa 2004; Schleef and Cavalcanti 2009). Participation is essential for democratic life because through it, people can have input into the political system. Besides voting and holding office, immigrants participate in society in different ways, and this participation can predispose citizens to voting (Verba, Schlozman, and Brady 1995). Further, active and engaged members of society foster efficient governments (Albarracín and Valeva 2011; Putnam 1993). In addition, the involvement of immigrants in the political arena can make the political system responsive to their needs. In this sense, political incorporation can be defined as "the extent to which group interests are effectively represented in policy making" (Hochschild and Mollenkopf 2009, 15).

Upon arrival in a country, immigrants are presented with a number of opportunities to participate in different social activities that can in turn support the process of incorporation. Churches, for example, offer various advantages to newly arrived immigrants, in that they provide spiritual support and social networks immigrants can rely on for their incorporation into the host society. Because many immigrants have school-age children, schools are also one of the first institutions with which immigrants come into contact. Schools encourage parents' involvement in school life through their participation in PTAs and volunteer activities. Further, decades of research suggest that parent involvement is linked to student retention and achievement (Kuperminc, Darnell, and Álvarez-Jiménez 2008; Shah 2009). Finally, immigrants' networks of trust and support with co-ethnics can also have an impact on their incorporation into the host society (Jackson 2009; Lim 2008; Ramakrishnan and Viramontes 2010; Rocha and Espino 2010; Staton, Jackson, and Canache 2007).

Latinos are the largest minority group in the United States and represent a key voting bloc (Djupe and Neiheisel 2012). Political participation can be defined as an activity that has the intent or effect of influencing government action (Verba, Schlozman, and Brady 1995). Citizens and noncitizens alike can have input into the political system. To be sure, voting is reserved for citizens, but noncitizens can participate in the political system in many ways. For instance, people can contact a public official for different reasons, including filing a report, expressing concerns, or supporting or opposing a potential government decision or bill. People with clear political preferences may participate in political campaigns, either by volunteering time or contributing money. Others can participate in public meetings of a city council, board of county commissioners, or other governing body, or can join in a protest or demonstration. Finally, those who are citizens can vote, and in some cases run for office.

Studies attempting to understand the factors that make people more likely to participate have shaped the political-science literature for decades. For instance, most scholars agree that individuals with higher income and higher education levels (Socio-Economic Status Model [SES]) are more likely to participate in society in different social and political activities (Barreto and Muñoz 2003; Downs 1957; Jang 2009; Junn 1999; Leighley and Nagler 1992; Leighley and Vedlitz 1999; Tam Cho 1999; Verba and Nie 1972; Verba, Schlozman, and Brady 1995; Wolfinger and Rosenstone 1980). Certain individual attitudes can influence both social and political behavior (Abrahamson and Aldrich 1982; Albarracín and Valeva 2011; Bevelander and Pendakor 2009; Brehm and Rahn 1997; Cook and Gronke 2005; Espinal, Hartlyn, and Kelly 2006; Guterbock and London 1983; Hetherington 1999; Verba, Schlozman, and Brady 1995). For example, the degree to which people believe the government can be trusted to do what is right can affect their participation (Guterbock and London 1983; Hetherington 1999; Leal 2002; Marshall 2001).

The extent to which people pay attention to politics and government affairs influences their level of participation as well. Thus, being politically interested or knowledgeable enhances the chances that an individual will be active in political activities (Albarracín, Wang, and Albarracín 2012; Leighley and Vedlitz 1999; Verba, Schlozman, and Brady 1995). Other attitudes like party identification and ideology can influence the likelihood of a person's participation (Albarracín and Valeva 2011; Beck 2002; Weisberg 2002). Also, people's awareness of their disadvantaged group status can affect their participation (Verba and Nie 1972). Finally, social capital, defined as "features of social organization, such as trust, norms and networks that can improve efficiency of society by facilitating coordinated actions" (Putnam 1993, 167), can also enhance participation (Brehm and Rahn 1997; Halpern 2005; Putnam 1993, 2000).

Trust in government institutions can also be a measure of the level of political incorporation in society (Doerschler and Irving Jackson 2012; Maxwell 2010b). Commentators in advanced democracies are concerned that people have become more cynical about the government since the 1960s (Hetherington 1998; Michelson 2003; Putnam 2000). Major corruption scandals like Watergate, controversial wars like Vietnam, and a more recent general distrust of government institutions promoted by Reaganomics have contributed to this trend. Trust is a "basic evaluative orientation toward the government founded on how well the government is operating according to people's normative expectations" (Hetherington 1998, 791). Political trust is essential for democracy because it links citizens to the institutions that are intended to represent them. It also enhances the legitimacy of democratic governments in that the more people trust the government, the more likely they are to accept the institutions of government and the people occupying them (Mishler and Rose 2001).

A number of socio-demographic factors are likely to influence political trust. For example, younger persons tend to trust the government more than older ones (Abrajano and Álvarez 2010; Hetherington 1998; Wilkes 2015). The role of income and education in predicting trust is less understood. On the one hand, higher levels of income and education may make people trust the government less because the more they know about politicians the less they may trust them (André 2014; Hetherington 1998; Wilkes 2015). On the other hand, a deterioration of the economic circumstances people face can be linked to negative sentiments about the government (Citrin and

Green 1986). Still, even if the position of immigrants in society is not ideal, they may still trust the government in the host society more because they feel that they are better off than they were in their country of origin (Maxwell 2010a).

Some works have analyzed the effect of acculturation on trust in government (Michelson 2003, 2007; Wenzel 2006). Specifically, these works argue that acculturation erodes trust in government (Michelson 2003; 2007; Wenzel 2006). As immigrants acculturate, they may go from the point of view of a newcomer looking forward to being a member of mainstream society to that of a person who has been denied full membership in this society (Michelson 2003; Wenzel 2006). Thus, those who are more acculturated may be more aware of discrimination and may become more cynical about the government (Michelson 2007). Also, as immigrants assimilate into mainstream American society, they may acquire the more cynical views of this group.

People who pay attention to politics and government affairs are more likely to participate in politics (Verba, Schlozman, and Brady 1995). However, do those who pay more attention to politics and government affairs trust the government more or less than those who pay less attention? A cynical view of politics would argue that the more people know about politics, the more they tend to distrust those involved in it. Conversely, a more psychological outlook may expect the people who like politics to be more politically engaged and exhibit higher levels of trust in government (Catterberg and Moreno 2006).

Perceptions about the existence/importance of discrimination and personal experiences with discrimination can also shape political trust. More specifically, those who feel discrimination is a major problem and those who have had a close experience with discrimination may be likely to distrust the government (Abrajano and Álvarez 2010; Michelson 2003, 2007; Schildkraut 2005). It is also likely that a personal or close experience with discrimination may be more influential on the level of political trust than the mere perception that discrimination is a major problem. The reason behind this is that those who have experienced discrimination may project this experience onto government institutions (Brehm and Rahn 1997).

Most of the research on immigrants' political attitudes and behavior focuses on post-arrival factors (for example, see Abrajano and Álvarez 2010; Albarracín and Valeva 2011; Barreto and Muñoz 2003; Barreto et al. 2009; Benjamin-Alvarado, DeSipio, and Montoya 2009; De La Garza, Falcon, and García 1996; DeSipio 2011). However, it is possible that the political views immigrants hold were acquired before migration. "Immigrants don't enter the United States as political blank slates" (Wals 2011, 2). Instead, pre-migration political experiences may shape or modify the effect of post-migration factors (Wals 2011). In addition, it is possible that trust in institutions originates in longstanding and deep-seated beliefs about people that are rooted in cultural norms and communicated through early-life socialization (Mishler and Rose 2001). Overall, authors agree that trust in government has important implications for social and political life.

Incorporation and Assimilation

Although the term "assimilation" has been widely criticized, the concept is still helpful for the study of the incorporation of immigrants and their descendants (Alba and Nee 1997). The Chicago School of sociology took as a major subject the understanding of immigrant assimilation in that city (Waters and Jiménez 2005). Robert E. Park, Ernest Burgess, and W. I. Thomas trained a cadre of graduate students to study the experiences of immigrants in Chicago (Waters and Jiménez 2005). The work of Robert E. Park has been widely influential in the study of immigrant assimilation. Park (2000) defined race relations as the "relations existing between peoples distinguished by marks of racial descent, particularly when these racial differences enter into the consciousness of the individuals and groups, and by doing so determine in each case the individual's conception of himself as well as his status in the community" (105).

The theory of race relations was applied in the study of assimilation, defined as "a process of interpenetration and fusion in which persons and groups acquire the memories, sentiments, and attitudes of other persons and groups and, by sharing their experience and history, are incorporated with them in a common cultural life" (Park and Burgess 1969, 735). A close reading of this definition of assimilation shows that it does not require what many critics of assimilation assume, "namely, the erasure of all signs of ethnic origin" (Alba and Nee 2003, 19). Park believed that social contact initiated interaction and that assimilation was the "final perfect product" (Park and Burgess 1969, 736) of the cycle of contact, competition, accommodation, and eventual assimilation (Alba and Nee 1997). Nowadays, being bicultural is considered an asset (Padilla 2006), but Park considered it a liability, a feature of his depiction of the "marginal man" (Park 1928).

For Park, assimilation was also a process that was "apparently progressive and irreversible." Competition is the initial consequence of contact between groups that struggle to gain advantages over one another (Alba and Nee 1997). Eventually, competition gives way to a more stable stage of accommodation, where unequal relationships among groups and a settled understanding of group positions comes into being. In assimilation, "the process is typically unconscious: the person is incorporated into the common life of the group before he's aware and with little conception of the course of events which brought this incorporation about" (Park and Burgess 1969, 736). Park was criticized by later writers for appearing to portray assimilation as an inevitable outcome of multiethnic societies (Alba and Nee 1997). Nonetheless, Park and his associates laid the foundations of assimilation theory.

This study uses a modified version of the stages of assimilation developed by Park and Burgess (1969) and classifies them as contact, conflict/negotiation, incorporation, and full incorporation. This framework is not the only way to portray the different stages the process of integration/incorporation may entail. However, it seems appropriate for understanding the process of immigrant incorporation. For example, I consider that these four stages/degrees of incorporation are cyclical in nature, and a person can encounter periods of adjustment continuously as he or she moves from one situation to another. In addition, an immigrant group may live in the United States for a long time and never progress to full incorporation. Upon arrival, immigrants first get in touch with the new society, start learning about it, and begin assessing the opportunities and constraints for their incorporation. They bring with them certain resources and beliefs and attitudes about the host society and its people. The other stages of incorporation—namely, conflict/negotiation, incorporation, and full incorporation—vary in the extent to which immigrants command the use of English; believe they are linked to other Latinos and Anglos; interact with Anglos and neighbors, as well as other members of society; participate in social and political activities; and acquire the political attitudes of the host society. In addition, to achieve the higher degrees of incorporation, immigrants need to at least be documented.

The progression through different stages also depends on a number of individual and social factors. At the risk of oversimplifying, this study considers the effects of social class (Algan, Bisin, and Verdier 2012; Portes and Böröcz 1989; Schleef and Cavalcanti 2009), length of stay in the country (Cabassa 2003), immigrants' attitudes and beliefs (Alba and Nee 2003; De Souza Briggs 2013; Waters and Jiménez 2005), and the opportunities and constraints encountered in society (De Souza Briggs 2013; Portes and Böröcz 1989; Portes and Rumbaut 2001; Portes and Zhou 1993, 1994).

If the attitudes and beliefs of a group of immigrants are not conducive to incorporation—for example, because most of the members of this group want to go back to their home country in the short term, or they have highly negative attitudes and beliefs about the host society and local population—this group of immigrants will likely be in a process of conflict and negotiation of this conflict with the host society. This process will occur regardless of the opportunities for, and constraints on, incorporation that society has to offer. As the attitudes and beliefs of a group of immigrants become more conducive to incorporation into the host society, the group can make progress toward the process of full incorporation. The highest degree of incorporation can be achieved when the greatest number of the members of an immigrant group hold positive attitudes and beliefs about the host society and the prospects of incorporation, and when the opportunities for incorporation are abundant and the constraints to incorporation are not significant. Immigrant groups do not necessarily go through all these stages, and they can even live in the United States for decades without getting out of the stage of conflict/negotiation.

Determinants of Incorporation

The framework proposed here pays attention to both actions by immigrants and opportunities and barriers in the host society that influence immigrants' incorporation into the host society. It considers a variety of factors, including individual ones like SES (Algan, Bisin, and Verdier 2012; Portes and Böröcz 1989; Schleef and Cavalcanti 2009) and beliefs and attitudes of the population. In addition, this framework includes the opportunities and constraints present in the host society.

Incorporation is a process that relates to different circumstances affecting immigrants, including their class and social status (Schleef and Cavalcanti 2009). The structuralist approach states that differences in socioeconomic opportunities can be associated with differences in social integration among immigrant and minority groups. Limited access to health care, education, power, and privilege affects immigrants' ability to integrate (Algan, Bisin, and Verdier 2012). In turn, these disadvantages can lead to persistent ethnic disparities in the level of educational attainment, occupational achievement, and income. The length of stay in the country can also influence the process of incorporation, although the effect of length of stay is not absolute. As mentioned before, the different stages of incorporation are cyclical, and a group of immigrants may never progress through all the stages.

Whereas people have little control over their social class and its influence on the process of assimilation, agency is also involved in the process of incorporation into a new society (Alba and Nee 2003; De Souza Briggs 2013; Hochschild 2013). For example, the attitudes and beliefs about the host country, about the people in the dominant and minority cultures (Maxwell 2013; Padilla and Pérez 2003; Teske and Nelson 1974), and about learning English, to mention just a few, will influence the behaviors involved in the process of incorporation into society. Attitude "is a psychological tendency that is expressed by evaluating a particular entity with some degree of favor or disfavor" that can affect behavior (Albarracín, Johnson, and Zanna 2005, 4).

An attitude can be cognitive (based on evaluation of information) or affective (based on emotions more than objective information). For example, incorporation can require a positive orientation toward the out-group (Teske and Nelson 1974).

Belief is the perceived likelihood that an attribute is associated with an object (Albarracín, Johnson, and Zanna 2005). Although beliefs are not always based on evaluation of objective information, they are falsifiable. For example, I may believe that Anglo-Americans are very different from me, and this belief can influence my incorporation into society. In sum, the term "attitude" is reserved for evaluative tendencies, which can be both inferred from, and have an influence on beliefs and behavior.

Contextual factors that are beyond the control of individuals also affect the process of assimilation into society (De Souza Briggs 2013; Portes and Böröcz 1989; Portes and Rumbaut 2001; Portes and Zhou 1993, 1994). This is to say, immigrants are not always free to choose the integration strategy they want to pursue, but are limited by the availability of ways for supporting their adaptation and achieving integration into society (opportunities) as well as by the factors deterring these processes (obstacles/constraints). Contextual factors include government policies for acquiring the necessary papers to work, and measures for fostering integration into society (language courses, dual language programs for schoolchildren, etc.). They also include residential patterns (segregation versus integration) and the existence of a community of co-ethnics (Portes and Rumbaut 2001; Portes and Zhou 1993, 1994).

The availability of services and resources in society also influences the process of incorporation. Finally, the beliefs and expectations that society has of newcomers will affect their process of adaptation; if discrimination and the social stigma attached to immigrants are widespread, this will affect the selection of strategies for integration by immigrants and their chances of integration into society altogether (Teske and Nelson 1974; Padilla and Pérez 2003; Portes and Rumbaut 2001; Portes and Zhou 1993, 1994). Thus, discrimination can function as a barrier to incorporation (Ager and Strang 2008).

Why Study New Destinations?

Most of the literature on incorporation focuses on traditional areas of immigration. The process of incorporation of immigrants in new destinations is unique, however, because of several characteristics of the destinations themselves and the type of immigrants arriving in them. Thus, studying this process seems essential. First, immigrants moving to new destinations face distinct opportunities and challenges. For example, many new destinations selected by immigrants in the Midwest are small-size counties, with low proportions of Latinos and negative population growth rates. Therefore, in addition to avoiding the disadvantages of large urban centers like crowding, traffic, and crime, immigrants moving to these destinations may face lower competition for jobs. However, the new destinations' lack of experience with immigration may present new challenges to communities and immigrants alike. For instance, governments may not offer bilingual services, and school systems may not be prepared to accommodate non-native speakers.

Further, services to immigrants provided by nonprofit organizations can be nonexistent in non-metro areas, giving immigrants in rural destinations of immigration little access to services that would help their incorporation into society. Finally, some characteristics of immigrants arriving in new areas of immigration can also make their incorporation into the new destinations' societies more challenging. For example, immigrants in newly established settlements tend to be disproportionally undocumented (Baker and Hotek 2003; Kandel and Cromartie 2004; Lichter 2012), and their recent arrival can make their language skills poorer than those of immigrants in traditional destinations. In addition, immigrants in new destinations tend to be less educated and poorer than immigrants in other destinations (Donato et al. 2008). For these reasons, immigrants in new destinations can be in a vulnerable position and living in a society that is not prepared to receive them. Thus, developing insights into the incorporation of immigrants into new destinations seems crucial.

Research Methodology

The dataset contains the responses from surveys conducted face-to-face in 2006 and 2011 among 260 Mexican immigrants (eighteen years or older) living in West Central Illinois, in the towns of Beardstown and Monmouth. For a full description of the questions, see the appendix. My sample was not randomly selected, but was chosen in a way consistent with methods and techniques that help identify potential members of this type of targeted community (Wampler, Chávez, and Pedraza 2009). I located participants in different venues where members of the Hispanic community gathered together, such as local churches that offered Spanish services, Mexican grocery stores, a soccer field where men played soccer on weekends, and two programs of the Mexican Consulate General in Chicago.

All of the interviewers were bilingual college students and, whenever possible, of Mexican ancestry. Interviewers invited all respondents who seemed to be of Latino or Mexican ancestry to participate in the survey. If respondents agreed, they were given the choice of taking the survey in either Spanish or English, thus mitigating the effect of a potential language barrier. Interviewers asked the questions in the language chosen by respondents. The response rates ranged from 60 to 90 percent. No compensation was offered for participating in the survey.

All the answers to the survey were fixed-response, with the exception of age and length of stay in the United States. The survey included questions regarding place of birth, length of stay in the country, citizenship status, and standard demographic variables; political topics like interest in politics, trust in institutions, participation in social and political activities, party preference, and voting; the sense of connectedness with Anglos, African Americans, and other Latinos; the importance attributed to the maintenance of the respondents' original culture; feelings of acceptance by Anglo-Americans, and opinions and experiences of discrimination; knowledge and use of Spanish and English; and gender beliefs.

For the separate sample of interviews, this study used the same recruitment venues and also a snowballing network sampling approach. Immigrants who answered the questions were asked if they had friends who might be interested in participating. Participants were offered twenty dollars for their participation because of the longer time commitment involved. The interviews took around forty-five minutes. Respondents were asked if and how and why they were learning English; the reasons why they felt what happens to Anglos in their community or other Latinos in the country had or did not have to do with their lives; why they did or did not trust their neighbors; if they attended social functions with Anglos, and why and how they attended these functions if they did; if they had personal experiences with discrimination and in what situations; about the obstacles to participating in different social and political activities; and if they trusted the government, and why or why not. In addition, immigrants were asked about their immigration history and efforts to obtain papers to work in the United States. All of the interviews were conducted and translated by the author.

CHAPTER 1

Case Studies
The Cases of Beardstown and Monmouth, Illinois

This small town is OK because there are no gangs.
—Romulo, interview with the author, July 31, 2011, Monmouth, Illinois

ILLINOIS RANKED FIFTH IN THE COUNTRY IN ITS PROPORTION OF LATINOS IN 2010
(U.S. Census Bureau 2011). Large metropolitan areas in Illinois have traditionally
attracted immigrants. More recently, immigrants have been increasingly moving
to non-metro areas as well. Table 2 shows the sixteen counties with the largest
proportions of Latinos in Illinois, ranging from 8 to 31 percent. Most of these
counties are located in metropolitan areas. For instance, Kane, Cook, Will, Kendall,
DuPage, McHenry, and DeKalb Counties are part of the Chicago-Aurora-Joliet
Metropolitan Division. Boone, Winnebago, and Ogle counties belong to the Rockford
Metropolitan Statistical Area. Lake County is part of the Lake County-Kenosha
County, IL-WI Metropolitan Division. Finally, Rock Island County constitutes part
of the Quad Cities Metropolitan Area, also known as the Davenport-Moline-Rock
Island Metropolitan Statistical Area.

Some of the counties with high proportions of Latinos listed in table 2, however,

■ 1

Table 2. Proportion of Latinos in Illinois in 2010: Top Sixteen Counties

County	Percentage of Latinos	Metro/Non-Metro Area	County	Percentage of Latinos	Metro/Non-Metro Area
Kane County	30.7	Chicago Metro	Rock Island County	11.6	Quad Cities Metro
Cook County	24.0	Chicago Metro	McHenry County	11.4	Chicago Metro
Boone County	20.2	Rockford Metro	Whiteside County	11.0	Non-Metro
Lake County	19.9	Milwaukee Metro	Winnebago County	10.9	Rockford Metro
Cass County	16.8	Non-Metro	DeKalb County	10.1	Chicago Metro
Will County	15.6	Chicago Metro	Kankakee County	8.9	Non-Metro
Kendall County	15.6	Chicago Metro	Ogle County	8.4	Rockford Metro
DuPage County	13.3	Chicago Metro	Warren County	8.0	Non-Metro

Source: U.S. Census 2010

are located in non-metro areas. The two counties where Beardstown and Monmouth are located, Cass and Warren, are among them. The proportion of Latinos in these two counties in 2010 was 17 percent and 8 percent, respectively (table 2). As explained later, the proportion of Latinos in the towns themselves was even higher.

New immigrant destinations in the Midwest share a number of characteristics. Table 3 shows a selection of twenty non-metropolitan counties in this region that in 2010 had at least 5 percent Latinos.[1] The proportion of Latinos in these counties ranged from 5 percent in Putnam County, Ohio, to 47 percent in Finney, Kansas. Almost without exception, counties drawing immigrants had sizable meatpacking plants. Beardstown and Monmouth; Storm Lake and Denison, Iowa; Sioux City and Garden Island, Nebraska; Garden City and Dodge City, Kansas; McDonald and Sullivan Counties, Missouri; and Frankton, Indiana, all have meatpacking plants or related food-processing industries. Further, the only county from table 3 that did not have a meatpacking plant within thirty miles was Pulaski, Missouri. The meatpacking industry has gone through a process of mergers and acquisitions, and just a few corporations today hold most of the market share. For example, at least nine of the counties selected in this study had processing plants belonging to the Tyson group, two to Farmland Foods, Inc., and two to JBS USA LLC.

The counties selected by immigrants had relatively small populations, ranging from 13,642 in Cass County, Illinois, to 102,228 in Walworth County, Wisconsin (table 3). Research shows that the movement of Hispanics to small cities reflects their desire for lower crime rates, fewer street gangs, and greater tranquility in general (Parrado and Kandel 2008). Several of these advantages became apparent during this research. For example, Romulo explained, "This small town is ok because there

Table 3. Demographic Data for Selected Small-Size Counties in the Midwest, 2010*
(Counties with Towns with More Than 5 Percent Latinos)

County	Town with High % Latinos	Total Population	Latinos (%)		Median Household Income ($)		Population Growth Rate since 2000 (%)
			2010	2000	by Town	by State	
Cass, IL	Beardstown	13,642	16.8	8.5	45,734	56, 797	0.00
Warren, IL	Monmouth	17,707	8.4	2.7	43,536		−0.05
Cass, IN	Logansport	38,966	12.6	7.1	41,940	48,248	−0.05
Clinton, IN	Frankfort	33,224	13.2	7.3	48,953		−0.02
Buena Vista, IA	Storm Lake	20,260	22.7	12.5	46,951	51,843	−0.01
Crawford, IA	Denison	17,096	24.2	8.7	46,548		0.01
Finney, KS	Garden City	36,776	46.7	43.3	47,945	51,332	−0.09
Ford, KS	Dodge City	33,848	51.2	37.7	51,178		0.04
Oceana, MI	Hart	26,570	13.7	11.6	40,023	48,411	−0.01
Van Buren, MI	Covert	76,258	10.2	7.4	45,129		0.00
Nobles, MN	Worthington	21,378	22.5	11.2	48,208	59,836	0.03
Watonwan, MN	Saint James	11,211	20.9	15.2	49,698		−0.06
McDonald, MO	Anderson	23,083	11.2	9.4	37,997	47,380	0.06
Pulaski, MO	Waynesville	52,277	9.0	5.8	49,820		0.27
Dakota, NE	Sioux City	21,006	35.3	22.6	47,069	51,672	0.04
Hall, NE	Grand Island	58,607	23.3	14.0	48,712		0.09
Defiance, OH	Defiance	39,035	8.7	7.2	47,593	48,308	−0.01
Putnam, OH	Ottawa	34,449	5.5	4.4	61,192		−0.01
Jefferson, WI	Jefferson	83,686	6.6	4.1	53,454	52,413	0.13
Walworth, WI	Lake Geneva	102,228	10.3	6.5	54,020		0.09

* North and South Dakota were excluded because they did not have counties with more than 5 percent Latinos in 2010.

Source: U.S. Census 2010 (total population and percentage of Latinos); U.S. Census Bureau, American Community Survey, Five-Year Estimates, 2009–2013 (median household income); and U.S. Census 2000 and 2010 (estimates for population growth rate)

are no gangs."[2] Helena agreed that Monmouth is free of crime, and that parents can be confident their kids are fine.[3]

Counties selected by immigrants also tended to be poorer than the average county in their respective states. As table 3 shows, 80 percent of the counties surveyed had median household incomes below their respective state medians. Thus, communities receiving increased numbers of immigrants may be economically more depressed than the average community in the Midwest. This circumstance may contribute to affordable housing and a lower cost of living in general (Dalla, Ellis, and Cramer 2005; Parrado and Kandel 2008), helping to attract immigrants to augment the local workforce. In turn, immigration can bring economic vitality to these communities.

Most of the communities (60 percent) selected by immigrants had either negative population growth or population growth rates close to zero (Donato et al. 2008; Gouveia and Saenz 2000; Jensen 2006; Johnson and Lichter 2008; Lichter and Johnson 2006). Young people in these communities tend to leave to pursue an education or in search of better jobs. Thus, immigration gains offset population losses (Donato et al. 2008). These fading communities may offer the possibility of finding jobs to younger newcomers.

Having a large community of co-ethnics is usually a "plus." These communities can help newcomers find housing and jobs, and keep their culture alive. A small community of co-ethnics, however, can also be an advantage because of the decreased competition to find jobs.[4] To be sure, the counties in table 3 each had a significant proportion of Latinos in 2010, but ten years earlier this proportion was much smaller. For this group of counties, the growth of the Latino population between the decennial censuses of 2000 and 2010 ranged from 25 percent (Putnam, Ohio) to 266 percent (Crawford, Iowa). Therefore, even though the proportion of Latinos in these counties is increasing, these counties had historically lower proportions of Hispanics than most traditional areas of immigration.

Having less exposure to Latino immigrants can make the local population relatively unprejudiced against this group (Fennelly 2008; Kandel and Cromartie 2004). This is not to say that immigrants in new destinations face no prejudice and discrimination. "I sometimes wonder," mused Alejandra, "if we are not well received in this society, why stay?"[5] Immigrants seem to be trying to move away from areas of high prejudice and anti-immigration sentiments, such as California, Arizona, and New Mexico.

Beardstown and Monmouth

The growth of the Latino population in Beardstown and Monmouth is fairly recent. As table 4 shows, the proportion of Latinos in these two towns in 2000 was 18 percent and 4 percent, respectively. However, the population in Beardstown almost doubled, and in Monmouth it more than tripled between the years 2000 and 2010. Further, in 1980, the Latino population in both towns was almost nonexistent: Latinos in Beardstown accounted for 0.9 percent and in Monmouth for 1.5 percent of the total

Table 4. Latinos in Beardstown and Monmouth, IL, by Gender and Place of Origin

Population	2000				2010			
	Beardstown	%	Monmouth	%	Beardstown	%	Monmouth	%
Total Population	5,766		9,841		6,123		9,444	
Total Hispanic	1,032	17.8	428	4.3	1,994	32.5	1,358	14.3
Male	620	60.0	212	49.5	1,116	55.9	740	54.5
Female	412	40.0	216	51.5	878	44.1	618	45.5
Mexican	898	87.0	370	86.4	1,553	77.8	1,200	88.3
Puerto Rican	4	0.4	6	1.0	125	6.2	9	0.1
Cuban	11	1.0	1	0.1	98	4.9	10	0.1
Other Hispanic	119	11.5	51	11.9	218	10.9	139	10.2

Source: U.S. Census 2000 and U.S. Census 2010

population in that year (U.S. Census Bureau 1983). Obviously, the Latino immigration to these two towns is a recent occurrence. The largest group of Latino immigrants in these two towns is Mexican, followed by Puerto Rican and Cuban (table 4). The Mexican immigrant population, the focus of this book, accounts for 78 percent of Latinos in Beardstown and 88 percent of this population group in Monmouth.

Immigrants in Beardstown and Monmouth find jobs in services, farms, and construction, among other sectors. However, the main drivers of immigration to these two towns are their hog processing plants. Beardstown is home to Excel (now Cargill), the largest hog processing plant in the state, which employs 2,300 workers (Jensen 2006). The major employer of immigrants in Monmouth is Farmland Foods, which employs 1,500 workers (Farmland n.d.). This plant was bought by Farmland Foods in 1993.[6] It may be that the difference in size between these two plants explains the difference in size of the Latino populations in these two towns (1,994 versus 1,358). Many employees in the Farmland Foods plant work six days a week.[7] In 2009, Excel (Beardstown) started demanding that its employees work on Saturdays.[8]

The meatpacking industry has attracted large numbers of undocumented immigrants. These plants supposedly hire only documented workers because they require a Social Security number. In practice, however, many immigrants working at these plants are undocumented and use others' names and Social Security numbers. In 2007, Beardstown had a number of Immigration and Customs Enforcement (ICE) raids. On one occasion, enforcement agents burst into the Cargill factory, arresting sixty undocumented immigrants who worked for a cleaning company hired by Cargill.[9] Many of these immigrants were deported, leaving close to fifty children without their parents. Raids like this one became common in Beardstown.

Besides high proportions of Latinos, these plants also employ Whites and minorities and immigrants from different parts of the world. For example, about eight hundred West Africans from countries like Togo, Senegal, Cameroon, the Democratic Republic of Congo, and Benin live mainly in Beardstown and Rushville, but also in Springfield and Jacksonville, Illinois.[10] Several interviewees reported working with Anglo-Americans. Floriberto and Jorge, from Beardstown, stated that more than 40 percent of the employees in their department at the plant were Anglo-Americans.[11] Further, Rosa, also from Beardstown, mentioned her department was 90 percent Anglo-American.[12] Many immigrants spoke of having built friendships with Anglos at work.

Schools in the area have high proportions of Latino students, and school districts in both towns have made efforts to respond to their changing populations. For example, the school district in Beardstown had 40 percent Latino students in 2011.[13] For Monmouth, this number was 32 percent in 2009.[14] Beardstown established a dual language program in the mid-2000s. Within this program, students take classes both in English and Spanish, switching throughout the day. The program is optional and available for native and non-native speakers alike. In turn, Monmouth set up a bilingual kindergarten program and has recently hired a bilingual teacher to teach first graders.[15] In addition, both districts offer ESL (English as a Second Language) classes. Thus, both towns have responded to the needs of growing bilingual populations.[16]

Churches offer different advantages to newly arrived immigrants, in that they provide spiritual support and social networks immigrants can rely on for their incorporation into the host society. Saint Alexius Catholic Church and Immaculate Conception Catholic Church, in Beardstown and Monmouth respectively, offer Masses in Spanish, thus providing an important opportunity for immigrants who lack English language skills. Further, the priest in Beardstown made efforts to integrate the Hispanics and Anglos who attend the local Catholic Church.[17] Other churches serve the Latino communities in Beardstown and Monmouth as well. For example, the churches Nazarene, De Restauración Cristo te Ama, Ebenezer Encuentro con Dios, and Nueva Vida offer services for Spanish speakers in Beardstown. The church Solid Rock offers Spanish services in Monmouth.

My research revealed that immigrants in Beardstown had better access to health care than those in Monmouth. The Cass County Health Department in Beardstown offers a full-service primary care clinic, as well as discounted rates on all of their services for uninsured patients. The Warren County Health Department in Monmouth offers only immunizations, smoking-cessation programs, breast-cancer awareness outreach, and cardiovascular-health awareness outreach. In sum, whereas immigrants in Beardstown can access primary care physicians in town at discounted rates, immigrants in Monmouth need to drive fifteen miles to the nearby town of Galesburg, Illinois, to do so.

Discrimination seems to be an issue in both towns. Latino-Anglo relationships deteriorated in Beardstown after a Latino killed an Anglo at El Flamingo bar and this Latino bar on the square was burned in retaliation.[18] Nonetheless, these relationships have improved since then. Monmouth's history of relationships is not as rocky as the one in Beardstown, but discrimination seems to be common in this town as well. Being a Latino living in Beardstown or Monmouth seems far from ideal. Some immigrants, however, feel optimistic about their prospects for incorporation into society. "The more united we are, the easier will be our integration in this country,"[19] Jorge stated. This book will offer a snapshot of the lives of these immigrants and their degrees of incorporation into their communities.

Characteristics of the Sample in Beardstown and Monmouth

Appendix 2 compares my sample with a sample of the 2004 Pew Hispanic Center's National Survey of Latinos. My sample contained 131 cases from Beardstown and 129 cases from Monmouth. Most immigrants came from the Mexican states of Mexico, Michoacán, Durango, Guanajuato, Guerrero, Veracruz, and Chihuahua. The mean number of years in the United States was close to eleven. Thus, the typical subject of this study was of more recent arrival than in the one by the Pew Hispanic Center. This study gave the option of answering questions in English or Spanish (appendix, no. 5). Whereas 98 percent of the respondents chose to answer the questions in Spanish, this number for the Pew sample was 86 percent.

The gender (56 percent male) distribution (appendix 2) was comparable to the gender distribution for Latinos in Beardstown and Monmouth in 2010 (appendix, no. 6; table 4). The higher proportion of men is not uncommon in places of recent immigration because many men first move alone and only later bring their families to the United States. The mean age was 32.20 for this study's sample and 36.46 for the Pew sample (appendix, no. 7; appendix 2). The results for race are somewhat puzzling (appendix, no. 9). Whereas only 5 percent of this study's sample described themselves as White, this number for the Pew sample was 43 percent. Moreover, 95 percent and 37.6 percent respectively reported their race as Hispanic. Considering that the question asked by Pew was the same one this study used, this finding requires further research. It may be that Mexican immigrants who have been in the country longer identify themselves as White in larger numbers.

This study's respondents were more likely to be married or living with a partner (92 percent) than the Pew subjects (66 percent) (appendix, no. 10; appendix 2). It may be that most single men choose bigger urban centers as their destination. Also, most respondents in the Illinois sample had children and were likely to live in a household with more than four people (appendix, no. 12; appendix 2). The number of immigrants who worked full-time was 68 percent for the Illinois sample and 52 percent for the Pew one (appendix, no. 13). This finding seems to indicate that the competition for jobs in Beardstown and Monmouth may be less intense than in the average immigrant destination.

The income level of respondents in the Illinois sample was significantly lower than that of those in the Pew sample (appendix, no. 14; appendix 2). For instance, 71 percent of the former made less than $30,000 year, compared to 53 percent of the latter. This is even more striking considering that a larger proportion of immigrants in Illinois worked full-time. The education level among respondents in Illinois was decidedly low, with 66 percent of them having an education of middle school level or less (appendix, no. 15).[20] Finally, an overwhelming majority of the respondents in our sample were Catholic (83 percent), a small number were Protestant (6 percent), a comparable proportion had another religion (7 percent), and a lower but not negligible number professed no religion (4 percent) (appendix, no. 17). Those numbers for the Pew sample were 79 percent, 4 percent, 4 percent, and 11 percent respectively.

As this comparison shows, national surveys of Latinos may miss the reality of towns of recent settlement such as the ones studied here. The Mexican immigrant population of Beardstown and Monmouth had been in the country for fewer years, was only comfortable responding to questions in Spanish, had a higher proportion of men, and was of a younger age than that of the national sample. This population also overwhelmingly identified itself as Latino and not as White, and was more likely to be married than the national sample. Finally, even though the average Mexican immigrant in Beardstown and Monmouth was more likely to be employed full-time than his counterpart in the national sample, he received a wages that was substantially lower. This latter finding indicates that even after accounting for cost-of-living differences, the poverty rates in these towns may be considerably higher than the average immigrants destination.

CHAPTER 2

Legal Incorporation
Immigration Status and Citizenship

I just want to be able to get a job, any job.

—Karen, interview with the author, September 15, 2013, Monmouth, Illinois

THE RULES STATING UNDER WHICH CONDITIONS IMMIGRANTS ARE ADMITTED into a country significantly influence their lives. Having the necessary documents to immigrate to the United States affects a person's chances for having a decent quality of life and avoiding the constant fear of deportation. However, an estimated 11 million immigrants are undocumented (Pew Hispanic Center 2013). The rules for admission of foreign citizens impact the lives of immigrants in Beardstown and Monmouth. Their life stories reveal the hardships immigrants go through after coming to the United States.

Gabriela is twenty-two years old and lives in Monmouth. She came to the United States with her family when she was nine years old. The family's original plan was to come for four years to learn English; however, they ended up staying. Gabriela has five siblings, but one, a brother, was left behind in Mexico when the family moved to the United States. This brother is still in Mexico and Gabriela thinks he is around thirty-three years old, but she's not sure. When her mother and father divorced in 2010, her father returned to Mexico to take care of his flower business there.

Many immigrants to new destinations first settle in a traditional area of immigration (Leach and Bean 2008). Upon their arrival in the United States, Gabriela and her family first went to Sacramento, California. After two weeks, they moved to Monmouth because her mother had a cousin in this town who helped the family get settled. Gabriela's mother and father found jobs at Farmland, the local hog processing plant. Gabriela then started her schooling in 2000. Because the Latino population in Monmouth was already growing, the school had started English as a Second Language (ESL) classes.[1] Therefore, Gabriela had a bilingual teacher who helped in her transition. In fact, most of the kids in her class spoke Spanish.

Gabriela has a dental assistant diploma, is now married, and has a child named María. She speaks Spanish to María, as does her mother-in-law. However, María's uncles and father speak to her in either English or "Spanglish." Gabriela still celebrates Mexican Independence. A day after the interview took place she, her husband, and some friends were going to celebrate September 16 by watching the Canelo vs. Mayweather fight. However, she has never felt like going back to Mexico. Further, her mother has been there only once since 2001.

Gabriela feels integrated into society. She has not faced discrimination either in Monmouth or in Virginia, where she lived for seven years. She believes that one has to work hard to succeed in life. However, she acknowledges the problems many immigrants face: "Many doors shut down for you when you are an immigrant," she stated.[2] Gabriela explained that undocumented workers cannot find jobs at the local meatpacking plant any longer, and that it is a challenge for them to find suitable jobs. She also reported that some immigrants are now moving to Peoria, Illinois, to find jobs.

Growing up, Gabriela saw her father very little because he was constantly traveling to the United States to work. However, these trips put Gabriela in a much better situation than most interviewees in this study because her family neither walked through the border nor paid for a people smuggler (*coyote*). Gabriela's father had been in the country before 1986 and was able to get his papers through the 1986 Immigration Reform and Control Act (IRCA). This act approved a general "amnesty" for undocumented workers and was specifically designed for agricultural laborers. Three million immigrants applied to these "amnesty" programs (Calavita 1994). Fortunately, Gabriela will be able to apply for naturalization once she studies the questions on U.S. history and government for the citizenship test (Congressional Budget Office 2006).

María Isabel lives in Beardstown. She came to the United States in 2000, along with her sixteen-year-old son, Oscar Norberto. However, she left her two other, younger children, Victor Alfonso and Carlos Omar, in Mexico. María Isabel used a *coyote* to cross the border through Aguaprieta-Douglas and had to walk through the desert for three days and two nights. "Thank God, it was raining and it wasn't too hot,"[3] María Isabel stated. She and her son spent two days without drinking water. As a result, Oscar Norberto was delirious when they arrived in Arizona and María Isabel's legs were "bleeding from the inside."[4] A truck finally picked them up and the driver took them to a house in Arizona where they were fed beans, bacon, hot dogs, and coffee.

After this, María Isabel and Oscar Norberto were transferred to another house in Arizona and then taken to a Greyhound station. The *coyote* left them there with two tickets to Conyers, Georgia, and ten dollars. María Isabel and Oscar Norberto did not have enough money to eat and were cold. They felt hopeless. A janitor at the Greyhound station gave them a jacket that somebody had left there. Luckily, María Isabel found ten dollars in the jacket's pocket. "We finally had money to eat,"[5] María Isabel said, weeping. In addition, Oscar Norberto was able to wear the jacket.

María Isabel and Oscar Norberto went to Conyers, Georgia, because María Isabel had a cousin there. Like many other immigrants, she used her existing family network to get settled in the United Sates (Cornelius and Tsuda 2004). María Isabel and her son lived with her cousin for two years and in their own apartment another four. María Isabel found a job at a local restaurant and her son found one at IHOP. In her free time, María Isabel cleaned houses. Today, María Isabel works at a local hog farm, where she castrates, feeds, inseminates, and vaccinates hogs. According to her, this is a rough job that no one wants. At one point her manager broke a wall with his fist out of frustration that the hog farm was running behind by one day.

María Isabel likes to make Anglo friends, but she explained that Anglos and Hispanics only interact during lunch breaks at the hog farm. "I miss Georgia because I used to befriend the persons I worked for when I was cleaning houses there."[6] María Isabel believes one has to have a good command of the English language to make Anglo friends. For this reason, she attended free English classes for two years, but stopped attending because she felt the instructor was more concerned with politics than with teaching English. Today, María Isabel feels pretty comfortable speaking English and can read it fairly well.

María Isabel lacks the necessary papers to work in the United States. She says she spoke with an immigration lawyer who recommended that she wait for the "amnesty" that immigration reform may bring about. María Isabel has a partner who is a lawful permanent resident, Jorge, who does not want to marry her. As a result, María Isabel has not seen her two younger kids since she left Mexico, and has not seen the older one, Oscar Norberto (who was recently deported), in five years. María Isabel hopes that Congress will approve immigration reform sometime soon. As these life stories show, immigration policies greatly impact the lives of immigrants.

Immigration Policy in the United States

The United States is defined as a country of immigrants. Between 1820 and 2004 it accepted 66 million legal immigrants (Martin 2004). However, the United States has not reached a consensus on three major questions regarding immigrants: "How many? From where? In what status should newcomers arrive?" (Martin 2004, 52). The door for immigration opened in the United States in 1791 to offset the "scarcity of hands" (Calavita 1994, 56). In fact, the Declaration of Independence identified British barriers to immigration as a major grievance (Ogletree 2000). This era was characterized by the government's active encouragement of immigration. The first restrictions to immigration were passed in the late nineteenth century to exclude the Chinese, those likely to become a public charge, those with prearranged work contracts, the criminal, the diseased, and the politically undesirable (Calavita 1994; McCabe and Meissner 2010; Ogletree 2000). With these policies in place, immigrant arrivals averaged 1 million a year (Calavita 1994).

In 1924, the U.S. Congress approved the Immigration and Nationality Act (INA) of 1924, which established the quota system (Ogletree 2000). The intent of this policy was to ensure that Northern and Western Europeans would be more numerous than other groups, such as Jews, Italians, Slavs, and Greeks (Ogletree 2000). INA allotted each country an annual quota of immigrants based on the proportion of people from that country present in the United States in 1920 (Calavita 1994). In addition, it established a ceiling of 150,000 immigrants from the Eastern Hemisphere, but set no limit for immigrants from the Western Hemisphere. This type of restriction based on ethnicity and national origin was common among other liberal states at the time (Cook-Martin and FitzGerald 2010). In 1965, Lyndon Johnson and a liberal Congress amended INA in key aspects by reducing the differential treatment of Western and Eastern Hemisphere immigrants and eliminating the quota system (Calavita 1994). In addition, they established the categorical preference system that structures U.S. immigration policy today, giving preference to relatives of U.S. citizens and lawful permanent residents, and to immigrants with job skills deemed useful to the United States (Congressional Budget Office, 2006).

The policies established in 1965 are still essentially in place today (Congressional Budget Office 2006). In 1986, the U.S. Congress decided to address the issue of undocumented immigration through the Immigration Reform and Control Act

(IRCA). This reform tightened enforcement and created new pathways to legal immigration. For the first time, this reform imposed sanctions on employers hiring undocumented immigrants (Calavita 1994; Congressional Budget Office 2006). Finally, this law created two legalization programs for undocumented immigrants, one for agricultural workers and one for undocumented workers in general. The Immigration Act of 1990 added a category of admission based on diversity (USCIS 2006), known as the "Visa Lottery," created to benefit Italian and Irish immigrants (Law 2002). In addition, it increased the ceiling for immigration from 290,000 to 700,000 per year for the first three years and 675,000 thereafter (Joppke 1999).

Immigration from Mexico

Immigration from Mexico became significant in the pre–World War I period (Bickerton 2001). By this time, European immigrants had developed a reputation as troublemakers because of their involvement in labor movements and strikes (Calavita 1994). Thus Mexican labor offered certain advantages over European immigrants, noted by the Dillingham Commission on Immigration in 1911: "The Mexican immigrants are providing a fairly adequate supply of labor . . . while they are not easily assimilated, this is of no very great importance as long as most of them return to their native land" (quoted in Calavita 1994, 58). This "flexibility" of Mexican immigration became evident when the government deported thousands of Mexican immigrants during the Great Depression (Calavita 1994).

Even though the 1917 Immigration and Nationality Act (INA) appeared to be highly restrictive, it contained a loophole to allow certain workers, including agricultural ones, to come to the United States to perform seasonal work (Bickerton 2001). Mexican immigrants were also exempt from the quota system. The Bracero program, a series of bilateral agreements that provided laborers to agriculture in the Southwest, institutionalized the desired temporary nature of Mexican immigration (Bickerton 2001; Calavita 1994). In addition, the informal policies of this period contributed to the increase in undocumented immigration that characterizes the contemporary movement (Calavita 1994). The U.S. Border Patrol usually escorted immigrants to the border, had them step to the Mexican side, and brought them back as legal *braceros* (Calavita 1994). Overall, the Immigration and Naturalization Service directors turned a blind eye to undocumented immigration.

The Mexican government recognized the advantages of the program, but also had some concerns (Bickerton 2001). For example, it was unclear whether the shortage of labor was real or if growers in the Southwest simply were seeking cheap labor. The government also feared that, if the economy worsened, Mexico could face the mass reverse migration from the United States that occurred during the Great Depression. Mexico was also concerned with the possible discrimination Mexicans could face in certain southern states. Finally, it feared that a mass exodus of people could threaten the development of the Mexican economy. Despite these concerns, a total of 818,454 *braceros* came to the United States between 1942 and 1952 (Calavita 1994). During the same period, however, the INS apprehended over two million undocumented immigrants, most of whom were from Mexico. By the time the Bracero program ended in 1964, Mexican laborers had established a symbiotic relationship with U.S. employers.

Current Policies for the Admission of Foreign Citizens

The policies for admission of foreign citizens determine the legal incorporation of immigrants (De Souza Briggs 2013; Portes and Böröcz 1989; Portes and Rumbaut 2001; Portes and Zhou 1993, 1994). Noncitizens can enter the United States lawfully in two ways: under a permanent (or immigrant) status, or a non-permanent (or non-immigrant) one. Immigrants admitted as "permanent" are registered as lawful permanent residents (LPRs) and granted a green card (Congressional Budget Office 2006). Foreigners admissible as lawful permanent residents include relatives of U.S. citizens and lawful permanent residents, and workers with specific job skills. Some people with extraordinary abilities, outstanding professors and researchers, and those who may benefit the national interest can also qualify to be admitted as permanent residents without having a "sponsor." The second path is temporary admission, which is granted to foreign citizens who seek entry to the United States for a limited time and for a certain purpose (such as tourism, diplomacy, temporary work, or study) (Congressional Budget Office 2006).

If the person lacks a relative in the United States but has skills and a college degree, this person can apply for a green card and later citizenship only if his or her employer is willing to file the paperwork. In this case also, the petitioner needs to prove that there was no other resident or citizen willing to take the job (labor certification). If the employer is not willing to file the paperwork for the green card, then the person can only come to the United States for a maximum of six years, after the approval of an H-1B visa. However, these visas have a cap of eighteen thousand a year.

If the person lacks a college degree but has either exceptional skills or one million dollars to invest, he or she can become a resident and later a citizen. Among persons with exceptional skills are those with "extraordinary abilities" and those who qualify to request "national interest waiver." These two categories require neither a sponsor nor labor certification. The extraordinary ability category is reserved for those immigrants with extraordinary ability in the sciences, arts, education, business, or athletics (USCIS 2011). Examples include Nobel Prize winners and notable athletes. In the case of national interest waiver, "the responsibility lies on the applicant to provide enough documentary proof along with a written explanation stating why his/her being granted an immigrant visa is in the best interests of the country—national interest" (USCIS n.d). As these categories show, getting a green card without having a relative or a college degree is highly difficult. Further, these strict immigration policies have contributed to the high number of undocumented immigrants, estimated at 11 million (Pew Hispanic Center 2013; White House n.d.).

On June 15, 2012, the Obama administration announced a program called Deferred Action for Childhood Arrivals (DACA). This measure allows people who came to the United States as children and who were under the age of thirty-one in June 2012 to avoid deportation by acquiring "legal presence," making them eligible to apply for a work visa, renewable after two years. In addition, because of Congress's inability to pass immigration-reform legislation, President Obama announced a sweeping immigration reform on November 20, 2014. The centerpiece of this reform would allow unauthorized immigrants who have children born in the United States and who have lived in the country for at least five years to apply for a work permit, provided they pass a background check and pay taxes (DAPA). An estimated four million people would benefit from this reform. In addition, this measure removed the age limit for DACA, allowing a substantial number of immigrants who came to the United States before the age of sixteen to temporarily regularize their immigration status.

Many immigrants decide to take their legal incorporation a step further by naturalizing. Naturalization is the process by which an immigrant becomes a U.S. citizen (Congressional Budget Office 2006). In general, any lawful permanent resident who has maintained a period of continuous residence in the United States can apply for naturalization. This period varies among the different paths to residency. For example, whereas the person who marries an American citizen can apply for naturalization after three years of permanent residency, the person who becomes a permanent resident through employment has to wait for an additional two years. Applicants for naturalization need to have good moral character, knowledge of U.S. history and government, proficiency in the English language, and an inclination to support and defend the United States and the Constitution (Congressional Budget Office 2006).

Because immigration procedures can be cumbersome, immigrants wanting to become residents and citizens need to hire attorneys. Immigration attorneys can be expensive and their fees can range from $800 to $15,000, depending on the lawyer and the complexity of the paperwork. Usually, filing a petition through relatives is cheaper than filing a petition through an employer. However, the poor in this country, including immigrants, generally lack access to legal services. It is estimated that 90 percent of attorneys in the United States serve 10 percent of the population (Langford 2004). This fact strongly impacts the immigrant community because a correlation exists between poverty and contemporaneity of arrival.

For example, fewer than half of the individuals who appeared before immigration judges between 1998 and 2002 had legal representation. Because of the economic difficulties in hiring attorneys, some immigrants resort to notaries, who are not authorized by law to represent immigrants. In addition, although not reflected in their high fees, sometimes notaries are unaware of the immigration laws or uninterested in following them. Thus, the use of notaries can jeopardize an immigrant's chances of staying in the United States (Langford 2004).

Immigration Enforcement

Immigration control policies can be classified into two types: ex-ante and ex-post (Cox and Posner 2007). Under an ex-ante approach, a nation-state decides whether to accept a particular immigrant on the basis of pre-entry information, such as education level or any other characteristic. In contrast, an ex-post approach selects immigrants on the basis of post-entry information, such as avoidance of criminal activity or employment in the host country. The ex-ante approach can lead to a system of exclusion, whereas the ex-post one can lead to a system of deportation. Cox and Posner (2007) argue that although the U.S. de jure system is highly ex-ante, the U.S. de facto system is predominantly ex-post.

U.S. border apprehension and deportation practices began in the 1920s (De Genova 2002), a decade in which major qualitative and quantitative restrictions on immigration were imposed (Ngai 2003). However, the U.S. border has become increasingly militarized in the last two decades (Arnold 2007). In the 1990s, the United States started a major initiative using enhanced border control to reduce undocumented immigration (Cornelius 2001). The Clinton administration increased the budget of the Immigration and Naturalization Service (INS), especially the funds allocated to border enforcement. Another key decision by the Clinton administration was to concentrate resources along points of the border most traditionally used to cross illegally. Even though the number of apprehensions rose steadily after these policy changes (Cornelius 2001), the number of undocumented immigrants continued to increase (Cornelius 2004).

Together with border enforcement, another preferred policy of the United States in recent years has been to focus on incarcerating alien smugglers and deporting immigrants who have committed crimes or other violations (Kobach 2008). As a result, more people have been deported under Obama's presidency than any other presidency in the history of the United States (Marchevsky and Baker 2014). Further, in 2012 the United States reached a record deportation number of 419,384 (González-Barrera et al. 2013; Pew Hispanic Center 2014). Since September 11, immigration has increasingly become entangled with criminal enforcement and national security (Kanstroom 2004). George W. Bush cemented this relationship when he placed the Immigration and Naturalization Service (INS) under the new Department of Homeland Security (Marchevsky and Baker 2014).

Delegation of Immigration Responsibilities

A trend toward devolution of immigration responsibilities to local levels has characterized immigration policy in recent years. Between 2005 and 2011, as many as 370 local governments proposed or implemented policies addressing issues related to undocumented immigration in their communities (Walker and Leitner 2011). The 1996 Illegal Immigration Reform and Immigrants Responsibility Act (IIRIRA)[7] authorized the devolution of immigration policy enforcement (Varsanyi et al. 2012). In addition, some local policies regarding immigration are grassroots responses to the presence of immigrants (Walker and Leitner 2011). Some scholars, however, believe that immigration policy is an aspect of foreign policy and is therefore intrinsically federal (Olivas 2007).

The nature of the policies enacted by state and local government varies a great deal. Some ordinances, which I term exclusionary in this study, limit or control immigration and immigrants' rights. The inclusionary ones, on the other hand, create better conditions and opportunities for immigrant incorporation. Examples of exclusionary ordinances are abundant in Southern states, including Alabama, Georgia, South Carolina, and North Carolina (Walker and Leitner 2011). For instance, some policies derived from IIRIRA focus on immigration policing and enforcement. Others include grassroots policies such as limited cooperation ordinances, employer sanctions, and the more recent "Illegal Immigration Relief Acts" passed by cities like Hazleton, Pennsylvania. Finally, other state and local policies focus on land use, housing, and nuisance ordinances that do not strictly focus on immigration but have the ultimate goal of controlling it through the "back door" (Varsanyi et al. 2012, 142). Examples of inclusionary ordinances are more common in big cities such as San Francisco, Oakland, and Santa Cruz. Nearly one hundred cities, for instance, proposed or established immigrant sanctuary ordinances, including measures stating that local authorities will not check residents' immigration status, extending local voting rights to noncitizens, and accepting the Mexican *matrícula consular* ID cards as a form of identification (Walker and Leitner 2011).

What can state and local authorities do to enforce immigration policies? State and local authorities can check a person's immigration status, report him or her to Immigration and Customs Enforcement (ICE), or both when a person is arrested for a violent crime or when he or she is involved in a traffic violation. Whereas 85 percent of sheriff and police departments surveyed by a study reported checking the immigration status of a person arrested for a violent crime, only 21 percent of them do so when a person is involved in a traffic violation (Varsanyi et al. 2012). However, the announcement by President Obama on November 20, 2014, called for an end to a program called Secure Communities, which allowed local authorities to cooperate with ICE by detaining and deporting immigrants stopped for minor offenses like traffic violations. Under the new rules, local police in some states would no longer be asked routinely to detain immigrants without papers when they are stopped for traffic violations.

In addition, the rules establishing procedures to apply when immigrants are stopped are far from transparent. For instance, less than 40 percent of the sheriffs and chiefs of police reported having a written policy to deal with these situations. Such street-level discretion is "worrisome when questions of rights and membership of community members may depend on which particular officer may arrive at the scene" (Varsanyi et al. 2012, 146). Consequently, many of these decisions have resulted in racial profiling (Romero 2006; Varsanyi et al. 2012). Evidence suggests that racial profiling may be occurring in Beardstown and Monmouth.

Documented or Not?

The first dimension of incorporation is the legal one, which refers to authorization to live and work in the United States and the eventual final attainment of citizenship (Bean, Brown, and Rumbaut 2006; DeSipio 2011; Gerstle 2010; Hochschild and Mollenkopf 2009; Jones-Correa 2004). However, many immigrants of recent arrival are undocumented (Baker and Hotek 2003; Kandel and Cromartie 2004; Lichter 2012). Not only are they thus deprived of their basic democratic and other rights, but they are also likely to live isolated and in fear of authorities. In addition, undocumented immigrants are also prone to obtaining lower-paying jobs and having lower incomes than other immigrants. Overall, the lives of immigrants who lack documents can be highly stressful (Samers 2001).

Legal incorporation can follow a progression that includes the acquisition of a work visa (going from undocumented to documented), a permanent residency permit (green card), and citizenship. The legal incorporation of immigrants depends both on the attitudes and actions by immigrants and on the government policies that rule immigration, also called context of reception (Bloemraad 2002, 2006). However, no one wants to suffer the uncertainty and lack of opportunity of being undocumented. Whereas immigrants may decide to never become citizens of the country where they reside, it is unlikely that an undocumented person would turn down the opportunity to get a visa or permanent residency.

The survey used in this study asked respondents about their citizenship status rather than their immigration status. More specifically, it asked the 260 respondents if they were citizens, applying for citizenship, planning to apply for citizenship, or not planning to apply for citizenship. I believed that a question about immigration status (documented versus undocumented) would be too intimidating for survey respondents with whom the researchers interacted for only twenty minutes.

In the forty-seven in-depth interviews, however, the researcher established an open dialogue with immigrants. Many of them were forthcoming about their undocumented status, and explained how they crossed the border, how much they paid the *coyotes*, how many times they were able to go back to Mexico, and how they managed to work without papers. I believe this information is reliable. This section explores the findings of these interviews and provides a snapshot of the lives of the immigrants interviewed. It pays particular attention to their immigration status, the places where and the ways in which they crossed the border, the different places where they lived, the jobs they had before arriving in the towns under study, and the ways in which they were planning to acquire or have acquired their immigration papers. This reveals some hardships immigrants go through when moving to the United States.

Fifty-five percent of immigrants in the sample of interviewees were documented and 45 percent were undocumented. Importantly, several of the documented immigrants had originally crossed illegally. Thirty-three percent of the interviewees crossed the border through Tijuana-San Ysidro (San Diego), 17 percent through Ciudad Juarez-El Paso, 11 percent through Aguaprieta-Douglas, and 11 percent through another crossing point (figure 2). However, some immigrants crossed the border legally. For instance, 28 percent of the interviewees arrived in the United States by plane.

Fifty-five percent of the immigrants interviewed used a *coyote* to cross the border. Although the ways in which immigrants crossed varied, most of them crossed the border on foot. For example, María Isabel,[8] mentioned above, walked through Aguaprieta-Douglas (Arizona), a desert area, for three days and two nights without water. Gustavo walked through Tijuana-San Ysidro (San Diego); the Border Patrol caught him and released him back in Tijuana, but he crossed back into the United States again that same night.[9] "The *coyote* was directing people because he knew

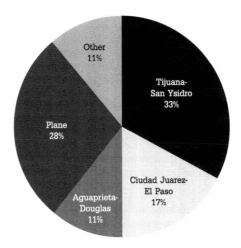

Figure 2. Immigrant Crossing Points: Sample of Forty-Seven Interviewees in Central Illinois

where the patrols were," he said.[10] Gustavo explained that the *coyotes* made them cross between patrol shifts, during the fifteen minutes when there was no one at the security checkpoint.[11]

In turn, Floriberto made three attempts to cross through Tijuana-San Ysidro until he finally made it.[12] Jorge took a little longer to cross. He spent two weeks in Tijuana trying to cross through the fence, making two attempts every night until he finally succeeded.[13] "We would leave at 10:00 at night, cross around 11:30 and they [Border Patrol] would send us back soon after that; we would try again at 4:00 in the morning and the patrol would send us back by 7:00. One night we got lucky and crossed." As these stories show, crossing the Mexico–United States border illegally is not easy.

Other immigrants tried different ways to cross. For example, Isabel paid a *coyote* and crossed the border in the trunk of a car.[14] Karen crossed the border pretending to be somebody's daughter.[15] Isabel and Karen were lucky that they safely crossed the border because, as Gustavo explained, *coyotes* can be sexually abusive.[16] "I saw how some women who were alone were taken to the 'hills' by the *coyotes*; I think they were being abused. The same thing happened in the houses where we were staying until we could reach our final destination."[17] As this comment shows, crossing the border illegally can have a high cost, beyond the financial.

Only thirty-three of the forty-seven immigrants interviewed came straight to Beardstown or Monmouth. The rest of them went to other places first (Leach and Bean 2008). These places included different locations in California, Kansas, Arizona,

Iowa, and Missouri. Marshall, Missouri, came up during the interviews several times. Twenty-two percent of our interviewees, all of them from Beardstown, went to Marshall first. As it turns out, Marshall had a meatpacking plant, also run by Cargill, which closed in 2001. At that time, the plant managers offered immigrants who were working there a chance to transfer to Beardstown. Many immigrants took advantage of this opportunity and got jobs at the Cargill plant in Beardstown.

What kinds of jobs do immigrants get? The meatpacking industry has had an important role in attracting immigrants to new nonmetropolitan and rural destinations in the South and Midwest (Aponte 1999; Gouveia and Saenz 2000; Haverluk and Trautman 2008; Jensen 2006; Kandel and Cromartie 2004; Lichter and Johnson 2006; Paral 2009; Valentine 2005). However, immigrants still get jobs in agriculture, carpet manufacturing, oil extraction, timber harvesting, and construction, among others (Kandel and Cromartie 2004). Before coming to Beardstown and Monmouth, immigrants held different jobs. Some immigrants worked in other meat processing plants, including beef and pork plants.[18] Others worked in agriculture, for example, harvesting strawberries and oranges in California. The rest of them worked in construction, manufacturing, and the service industry.

Another question this research set out to answer was how immigrants who were authorized to work in the United States had acquired their immigration papers. As mentioned before, IRCA included two legalization programs, one for farm workers and another one for other workers. Consequently, 60 percent of the documented interviewees were able to get a permanent residency thanks to IRCA (figure 3). These interviewees either qualified directly, or benefited indirectly through a parent who obtained a residency. An additional 30 percent of the documented interviewees, all of whom were women, became documented through marriage with a United States resident or citizen. Finally, the other 10 percent had a parent who had been born in the United States.

How were the undocumented immigrants planning to become documented? None of this study's interviewees had regularized or was planning to regularize his or her immigration status through an employer. The main employers, Farmland and Excel, allegedly think immigrants are already documented because they use Social Security numbers (which they buy) to work. Although this is their official position, this study found evidence that these employers know some immigrants are undocumented. For example, one of the interviewees was able to regularize her immigration status through her husband and was afraid of telling her manager. When she finally told her manager, he instructed her to go to human resources in a very discreet way and not to discuss it with anyone. Another interviewee explained that managers at the plant usually know who is undocumented and who is not. Thus, probably in order to protect themselves from accusations of knowingly

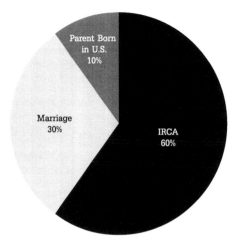

Figure 3. Paths to Legalization

hiring undocumented workers, employers were unlikely to help immigrants "get their papers."

Although the interviews predated President Obama's 2014 announcement of DAPA, a substantial number of the immigrants interviewed for this study who have children who are U.S. citizens and have been in the country for at least five years may be able to work legally in the United States if recent challenges to DAPA in courts fail to halt its implementation. In addition, those immigrants who came to the United States as children may also be able get a work visa under DACA, now that the age restrictions have been loosened. However, a large number of immigrants who do not have children who are U.S. citizens, came to the United States less than five years ago, and/or came to the country after the age of sixteen still will not be able to get work visas. Overall, the measures announced by President Obama will only benefit a portion of the undocumented immigrants living in the United States.

How do immigrants obtain Social Security numbers? Several of the interviewees explained that they purchased Social Security numbers to be able to work. According to one interviewee, one can find out where to get a Social Security number from other employees at the plant.[19] The Social Security numbers immigrants use are of two types: some are real numbers that belong to somebody else, and some have one's own name on them. However, the second type of number cannot stand minimum scrutiny. Immigrants can purchase a Social Security number for $60. Driver's licenses are also for sale. The 2013 decision by Illinois to allow undocumented workers to get Temporary Visitor Driver's Licenses in the state will make it unnecessary for immigrants to buy a driver's license.

Finally, immigration creates several challenges to families. One of these challenges is that families are separated for several years, if not forever. This theme became apparent during the interviews. Floriberto, for example, applied for the IRCA legalization in 1987, but his family only came to the United States in 2000.[20] Gustavo has ten siblings, but only a few came to the United States. In addition, his mother came to the United States seven years after her husband. Today, Gustavo's parents live half of the time in Mexico and half of the time in the United States. His father has heart problems and travels to the United States every month for his doctor's visits.[21]

Rosa came to the United States after crossing the border illegally in the late 1990s. She and her daughters then went back to Mexico because of a family emergency in 2001. After this, it took Rosa two years to reunite with her husband, who had remained in the United States.[22] If she wanted to regularize her immigration status through her husband, she would have to go back to Mexico for a few years because she was caught crossing illegally once.[23] Similarly, Alejandro came to the United States in 2000 with his parents and siblings.[24] Because his mom and four younger brothers failed to adapt to the United States, they went back to Mexico.[25] Another interviewee, Alejandra, got married in Mexico and had to wait three years before she could come to the United States with her daughter.[26] María Isabel may never see her children again. As these stories show, immigration can have distressing consequences for the families involved.

Who Is Planning to Become a Citizen?

Becoming a citizen of the United States is important because it grants immigrants the right to vote, to sit on juries, to advance in the military, and to hold elective office (Gerstle 2010). Other rights are also attached to citizenship. For instance, the Personal Responsibility and Work Opportunity Reconciliation Act (PRWORA) of 1996 restricted welfare services to citizens (with a few exceptions) (Hagan et al. 2003; Sainsbury 2006). The naturalization rates in the United States are low in comparison with other countries. For example, three-quarters of the foreign-born in Canada had a Canadian passport in 2001 (Bloemraad 2006); however, just two out of five immigrants were naturalized in the United States in 2000 (Bloemraad 2006).

Different factors influence a person's likelihood of becoming naturalized. Some European authors emphasize that differences in laws and bureaucratic procedures influence naturalization rates among the foreign-born in a country (Bloemraad

2006). This is to say, stricter rules for naturalization and more complicated processes to apply for citizenship usually translate into lower citizenship acquisition rates. This reasoning may partly explain lower naturalization rates in the United States. At the same time, the benefits attached to naturalization also influence these rates. More specifically, higher numbers of immigrants take advantage of the opportunity for naturalization when more benefits are attached to it (Bloemraad 2002, 2006; Freeman et al. 2002).

A change in the benefits attached to naturalization may explain changes in naturalization rates within the same country. For example, fear of losing welfare benefits after the PRWORA partly explained a surge in citizenship applications in the United States during the 1990s (Freeman et al. 2002). Also, opportunities for dual citizenship can increase naturalization rates (Bloemraad, Korteweg, and Yurdakul 2008). In the United States, Supreme Court decisions and State Department directives permit multiple citizenships. However, the oath that would-be citizens are required to swear still contains a promise to renounce prior allegiances (Bloemraad, Korteweg, and Yurdakul 2008). Mexico, the country of origin of this study's interviewees, allows for dual citizenship.

This study assesses the extent to which the process of incorporation is shaped by social class. Specifically, it argues that immigrants who have higher levels of education and live above the poverty line may be more likely to become naturalized (Algan, Bisin, and Verdier 2012; Bloemraad 2002, 2006; González-Barrera et al. 2013; Portes and Böröcz 1989; Schleef and Cavalcanti 2009). Different causes might explain variations in naturalization rates among people with different socioeconomic status. For example, those who have higher levels of education may also have better access to information on how to apply for citizenship. At the same time, income may influence naturalization rates because the naturalization process can require legal assistance and this assistance can be costly.

In addition, I analyze how length of stay in the country (Cabassa 2003) and gender influence the process of legal incorporation. Finally, English language skills are a requirement for naturalization. Thus, those who have better language skills are also more likely to become naturalized (González-Barrera et al. 2013). Language skills can also be an indicator of the degree of integration into the host society (Michelson 2003). Thus, I examine the impact of these individual factors on naturalization rates and intentions to naturalize among immigrants in Beardstown and Monmouth.

Immigrants' attitudes and beliefs also influence the process of legal incorporation (Alba and Nee 2003; De Souza Briggs 2013; Waters and Jimenez 2005). To measure the predispositions toward legal incorporation, the survey asked respondents, "Now we would like to ask you about your U.S. citizenship; are you: a citizen (1), processing your citizenship (2), planning to process your citizenship (3), or not planning to

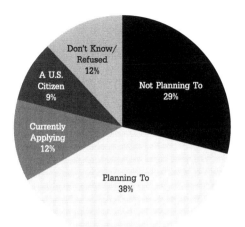

Figure 4. Citizenship Status and Plans to Apply for Citizenship: Sample of 260 Interviewees in Central Illinois

process your citizenship (4), don't know (5), refused (6)." These value labels were later reverse-coded so that a higher value meant an increased closeness to citizenship.

As figure 4 shows, only 9.4 percent of the respondents were already citizens. This number is low in comparison with the 40 percent general naturalization rate among immigrants in the United States (U.S. Census Bureau 2013b). It is also low compared to the 26 percent naturalization rate for Mexican immigrants living in the United States in 2012 (U.S. Census Bureau 2013c). The recent arrival of most immigrants in this sample may explain the difference between these last two numbers. An additional 11.6 percent of the respondents were in the process of applying for citizenship, and 38.2 percent of them were planning to apply. As this number shows, even though immigrants may face language and other barriers when trying to apply for citizenship, their attitudes toward the acquisition of citizenship seemed positive. Finally, for whatever reasons, 28.8 percent of immigrants were not planning to apply for citizenship. Thus, almost one third of immigrants in the sample may never achieve full legal incorporation.

The regression model included immigrants' length of stay in the country (appendix, no. 4) (Cabassa 2003), gender (appendix, no. 6), education (appendix, no. 15), employment status (appendix, no. 13), and income (appendix, no. 14) (Algan, Bisin, and Verdier 2012; Portes and Böröcz 1989; Schleef and Cavalcanti 2009) as control variables. It indicated that only income was associated with the citizenship variable (table 5) (Bloemraad 2002, 2006). That is, those with higher incomes were

Table 5. Linear Regression Model for Citizenship Acquisition Process: Sample of 260 Interviewees in Central Illinois

Key Factors Variable	Standardized Beta (Standard Errors in Parentheses) Plan to Become Citizen
Length of Stay in United States	0.03 (0.01)
Gender	0.04 (0.58)
Education	0.05 (0.16)
Employment Status	0.06 (0.19)
Income	0.20 (0.16)[†]
R Square	0.05

$* p < 0.1$ $† p < 0.05$ $‡ p < 0.01$

more likely to be closer to acquiring their citizenship. None of the other variables representing social class—namely, education and employment status—showed a significant association with the citizenship variable. However, these variables' standardized coefficients had a positive sign in the model, indicating that those with higher levels of education and full-time jobs may be more likely to apply for citizenship or to already be a citizen. Neither of the other two control variables—namely, length of stay in the country and gender—showed a significant correlation with the citizenship variable.

What factors explained the citizenship variable? Consistent with previous research, three of the language variables used in this study—namely, comfort speaking English ($r = 0.15$, $p < 0.05$), ability to read English ($r = 0.26$, $p < 0.01$), and language used to watch TV or listen to the radio ($r = 15$, $p < 0.05$)—were significantly associated with the citizenship variable (González-Barrera et al. 2013). In other words, those who had better language skills and were more likely to watch TV in English were also more likely to be planning to become citizens, to have applied for citizenship, or to already be citizens (Bloemraad 2006; González-Barrera et al. 2013). This finding makes sense considering that a person needs to have knowledge of the English language to be able to become a citizen.

What Have We Learned about the Legal Incorporation of Immigrants in Beardstown and Monmouth?

The legal incorporation of immigrants is strongly determined by the opportunities and constraints created by the rules for admission of foreign citizens (De Souza

Briggs 2013; Portes and Böröcz 1989; Portes and Rumbaut 2001; Portes and Zhou 1993, 1994). All interviewees were looking forward to acquiring green cards (Alba and Nee 2003; De Souza Briggs 2013; Waters and Jimenez 2005), but as of November 2014, the United States' immigration system poses various obstacles for those undocumented immigrants who lack a child who is a citizen, have less than five years of residence, have a criminal background, and/or came to the United States after they were sixteen years of age.

Almost half of the sample interviewees were undocumented, implying that the level of legal incorporation of immigrants is less than optimal. However, it is important to draw a distinction between immigrants who will benefit from the recent immigration policy changes and those who will not. More specifically, the recent changes in immigration policy may allow some of these persons to acquire temporary relief from deportation and to work legally in the United States. The rest of the immigrants, however, may remain in a legal limbo until a comprehensive immigration reform that benefits all undocumented immigrants is passed.

The number of immigrants who were citizens in this sample was only 9.4 percent, 16.6 percent lower than the naturalization rate for the Mexican population in the United States (U.S Census Bureau 2013b). This low number may be partly explained by the recent arrival of the immigrants in the sample. About one-third of the immigrants surveyed, however, were not interested in applying for naturalization, and these immigrants may spend their whole lives in the United States without achieving full legal incorporation. Income was associated with citizenship acquisition, implying that either those with higher incomes have fewer difficulties acquiring their citizenship or that the acquisition of citizenship can lead to a better standard of living (Algan, Bisin, and Verdier 2012; Bloemraad 2002, 2006; González-Barrera et al. 2013; Portes and Böröcz 1989; Schleef and Cavalcanti 2009). Finally, those with better language skills were also more likely to be closer to citizenship acquisition (González-Barrera et al. 2013).

CHAPTER 3

The Culture of Incorporation
Language Use, Identity, and Social Connectedness

Contact with any human being is important.
—Diana, interview with the author, July 30, 2011, Monmouth, Illinois

MOVING TO A NEW COUNTRY REQUIRES A NUMBER OF CULTURAL ADAPTATIONS.
In Beardstown and Monmouth this is reflected in immigrants' language acquisition,
sense of identification, and connectedness with other groups in society. Although no
single theoretical framework describes every path to incorporation (Jones-Correa
2004), the life stories reviewed below give a sense of how immigrants are negotiating
their incorporation into Beardstown and Monmouth.

Martín is a Mexican man from the state of Mexico who lives in Beardstown with
his wife and three children. He decided to leave Mexico because there he made in
one day the money he could make in the United States in one hour. He paid a coyote
to cross the border through Tijuana in 1989, and his crossing went without problems
because border control at the time was less strict than in the present (Massey and
Capoferro 2008). Like most immigrants in new destinations, he did not come directly
to Beardstown but settled in California first, a traditional area of immigration (Leach

and Bean 2008). A friend of his helped him get a job there. Irma, Martín's fiancée from his hometown, stayed in Mexico until they got married in 1996. The couple stayed in California until 1999, when they moved to Marshall, Missouri. Martín got a job at Cargill and he and his family stayed there until the plant closed in 2001. Cargill then offered Martín a job in Beardstown, and the family settled there.

In 2007, an immigration raid at Beardstown's Cargill plant resulted in the deportation of several immigrants. Martín, who is undocumented, was fortunate enough to avoid deportation. However, the raid had lasting consequences for the life of Martín and other immigrants. Until 2007, it was easy for immigrants to work at Cargill without the necessary papers. To be sure, Cargill required a Social Security number to work there, but the immigration status of employees was only superficially verified. After the raid, however, working at Cargill without papers became much more difficult. Because of this, many immigrants either were fired or left, and some of them moved to nearby meat processing plants, including the one in Monmouth. In June 2012, Martín's supervisor at Excel (formerly Cargill) asked Martín to provide further proof that he was authorized to work in the United States. Unable to do this, Martín resigned from his position on June 25, 2012. Martín now works in construction and is making 40 percent of the money he once made at Excel.

Martín is hoping to regularize his immigration status through his daughter. Given President Obama's recent executive action granting temporary legal status to immigrants who have children born in the United States, Martín may be able to obtain a work visa. Despite his personal circumstances, Martín feels he is fairly well incorporated into society. Like many other immigrants, Martín believes learning English is crucial for successful incorporation into American society. Free English language classes are available in Beardstown. At the time of the interview, however, Martín was renovating his house and did not have time to attend language classes. Despite this, Martín is pleased with the language skills he has acquired over the years and has a reasonable command of the English language.

Cultural incorporation also requires learning the local culture (Schleef and Cavalcanti 2009). However, scholars now believe that immigrants need not abandon their culture of origin (Black 2011; Bean, Brown, and Rumbaut 2006; Gerstle 2010; Jones-Correa 2004; Portes and Zhou 1993). Martín feels the process of cultural incorporation needs to include a negotiation between his ethnic culture and the dominant culture of the majority. For example, Martín stated, "I was once invited to a wedding by somebody at work but I didn't attend because I was going to be the only Latino and I didn't want to feel like an intruder . . . I only socialize with Anglo-Americans who are respectful of my culture; otherwise, I don't socialize."[1] As this comment shows, Martín hopes that his cultural incorporation in the United

States will not require him to renounce his own culture. Further, he would like locals to respect it.

María Luisa is an immigrant from the state of Veracruz who came to the United States in 2007 to join her husband of thirteen years in Monmouth. In turn, her husband had chosen this town because he had a sister who already lived there (Gidengil and Stolle 2009). Crossing the border was not easy, and María Luisa spent fifteen days trying every night until she finally succeeded. She and a group of eleven people crossed with the help of a coyote. On one occasion, for example, they had crossed the border but were unable to find the truck that was supposed to pick them up. When they finally succeeded, María Luisa joined her husband in Monmouth. María Luisa found a janitorial job at the local meatpacking plant, Farmland, where her husband was already working.

María Luisa and her husband lack the necessary papers to work in the United States. They both work the night shift and this is "not a problem" because María Luisa and her husband do not have children. Still, she believes daily life is challenging and explained, "My husband and I sleep a few hours in the morning and a few hours in the afternoon. Between those times, I'm so tired I barely leave the house."[2] Recently, María Luisa's husband was arrested when the local police stopped him for not wearing a seat belt. As the next chapter will show, the Monmouth police have become highly unfriendly toward immigrants. María Luisa's husband had to appear before a court in Chicago and was given a year to find an immigration attorney. He was fortunate enough to avoid deportation. María Luisa hopes that if immigration reform is passed into law, she and her husband will find better jobs and be able to visit their families in Mexico for the first time in seven years.

Residentially, neighborhoods in Beardstown and Monmouth are integrated. Due to the lack of segregation in Monmouth, María Luisa has the opportunity to meet Anglo-Americans in her neighborhood. María Luisa remarked, however, "I'm surrounded by Americans and I haven't had much interaction with them other than an occasional hello and goodbye."[3] Like Martín, María Luisa also believes that learning English is crucial.

Workplaces can also provide opportunities for interaction with people outside of the immigrant's close circle of friends and family. Anglo-Americans, however, tend to work in higher-paying positions, as opposed to lower-end jobs such as cleaning. "I work in cleaning and everyone else is Hispanic,"[4] María Luisa stated. Therefore, she has made no Anglo friends at work. Churches can also have an important role in the socialization of immigrants, as well as other groups. Catholic churches in Beardstown and Monmouth offer services in both English and Spanish. Usually, Latinos attend the Mass in Spanish, but they can meet Anglo-Americans at social gatherings like picnics and other festivities. María Luisa reported meeting Anglo-Americans at church, but her interaction with them was limited.

As these immigrants' stories show, becoming part of the host society involves learning the local language, negotiating cultures of origin and settlement, settling into a new neighborhood, and establishing new social relationships, among others (Schleef and Cavalcanti 2009). Through these processes, immigrants come to feel part of the host society (Gerstle 2010). Some individual behaviors like learning the language seem important in the process of incorporation. However, to a large degree, incorporation also involves a process of sustained interaction between newcomers and the communities in which they live, through socialization in neighborhoods, churches, schools, and other settings. Despite the numerous obstacles to incorporation reviewed here, incorporation occurs more rapidly in the United States than in many Western European countries (Mollenkopf and Hochschild 2010). This chapter investigates the cultural incorporation of immigrants in Beardstown and Monmouth.

The linear regression analyses used seven dependent variables: language preferred to watch TV or listen to radio, English reading skills, spoken English skills, linked fates with Latinos, linked fates with Anglo-Americans, trust in neighbors, and attendance of social functions with Anglo-Americans. Each section of this chapter provides details on the dependent variables, and the original questions are included in the appendix. All the analyses included the following as independent variables: length of stay in the country gender, education, employment status, and income.[5]

Language Use among Immigrants in Central Illinois

When immigrants arrive in a country, they need to learn the local language, and their ability to communicate effectively is crucial for incorporation (Ager and Strang 2008; Gerstle 2010; Padilla 2006; Padilla and Perez 2003; Schleef and Cavalcanti 2009). Rates of English language fluency among first-generation immigrants are uneven. Immigrants from Latin America have the highest share of Limited English Proficient (LEP) individuals (64.7 percent), followed by immigrants from Asia (46.6 percent) and Europe (29.8 percent). However, immigrants today are learning English faster than the immigrants who came to the United States at the turn of the last century. Whereas fewer than half of all immigrants who arrived in the United States between 1900 and 1920 spoke English within the first five years after arriving, more than three-fourths of those who arrived between 1980 and 2000 did so (Jiménez 2011).

This study included three variables reflecting language skills: the choice of language used when watching TV or listening to the radio, reading skills, and comfort with the use of spoken English. The language chosen to watch TV or listen to radio is an important indicator of the level of cultural incorporation of immigrants. To assess this choice, the question asked was "In what language are the news programs you usually watch on TV or listen to on the radio?" and the possible responses were "only Spanish (1), mostly Spanish (2), both the same (3), more English than Spanish (4), and only English (5)" (figure 5). Fewer of this study's respondents used only English or mostly English to watch TV or listen to the radio (9.6 percent) than did those of the 2004 Pew Research Hispanic Center Study (12.4 percent). In addition, fewer interviewees used only Spanish or mostly Spanish (51.5 percent) than did those of the Pew study (57.2 percent) (figure 5). Overall, the choice of media language in both groups seemed comparable.

The reading skills among the respondents, however, were somewhat lower than those of the Pew interviewees. Respondents were asked, "Would you say you can read a book or newspaper in English? Not at all well (1), just a little well (2), pretty well (3), or very well (4)." Whereas almost 80 percent of the Central Illinois respondents could read a book or newspaper in English just a little well or not at all well, this number for the Pew respondents was close to 66 percent (figure 6). As these numbers show, the reading skills among the Mexican immigrants in the sample were not optimal.

The last question reflecting language skills measured the level of comfort with spoken English and asked interviewees, "How much do you agree with the following statement? 'I feel comfortable speaking English,'" and the possible answers were "strongly disagree (1), somewhat disagree (2), somewhat agree (3), and strongly agree (4)." Because no question in the Pew questionnaire was easily comparable, only the

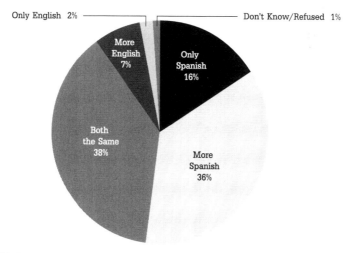

Figure 5. Media Language Use: Sample of 260 Interviewees in Central Illinois

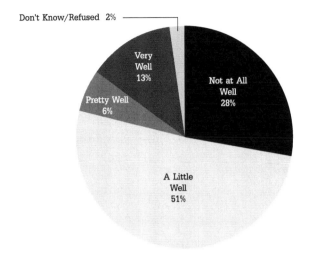

Figure 6. Reading Skills for Newspaper or Book in English: Sample of 260 Interviewees in Central Illinois

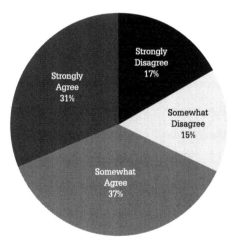

Figure 7. Agreement with the Statement "I Feel Comfortable Speaking English": Sample of 260 Interviewees in Central Illinois

findings for the Central Illinois sample of Mexican immigrants are reported. Almost 32 percent of the respondents strongly disagreed or somewhat disagreed with the statement "I feel comfortable speaking English." The other 68 percent reported somewhat agreeing or strongly agreeing with this statement (figure 7). Thus, it seems that Mexican immigrants in Central Illinois may not read English well, but at least feel comfortable communicating in spoken English. Therefore, their spoken English skills may help them get by in their everyday lives.

A major purpose of this research was to investigate whether social class (education, employment status, and income), the length of stay in the country, and gender explained cultural incorporation (table 6). Two of the language variables, namely, reading skills and comfort with spoken English, correlated positively with income and education (Algan, Bisin, and Verdier 2012; Portes and Böröcz 1989; Schleef and Cavalcanti 2009). In this sense, more educated participants who had higher incomes tended to have better English reading skills and felt more comfortable speaking English. In addition, education also correlated positively with the language used to watch TV or listen to the radio, with more educated people being more likely to watch TV or listen to the radio in only English versus only Spanish (Algan, Bisin, and Verdier 2012; Portes and Böröcz 1989; Schleef and Cavalcanti 2009). Therefore, this study found support for the contention that the level of language use is positively associated with social class (Algan, Bisin, and Verdier 2012; Portes and Böröcz 1989; Schleef and Cavalcanti 2009).

Not surprisingly, length of stay in the country was positively associated with language of TV and radio use and with English reading skills; people who had been in the country longer were more likely to watch TV or listen to the radio in English only versus Spanish only and had better English reading skills. This finding makes sense considering that a longer stay in the United States provides immigrants with additional time and opportunities to learn English. However, length of stay in the country showed no significant association with comfort speaking English. As for

Table 6. Linear Regression Models for Cultural Incorporation Variables: Sample of 260 Interviewees in Central Illinois (Standard Errors in Parentheses)

Variable	Standardized Beta					
	Length of Stay	Gender	Education	Employment Status	Income	R Square
Language TV	.18 (.01)[†]	−.20 (.14)[‡]	.20 (.14)[‡]	−.05 (.16)	−.05 (.15)	.11
Can Read Book or Newspaper	.18 (.01)[‡]	.01 (.12)	.31 (.12)[‡]	.07 (.14)	.19 (.13)[‡]	.19
Comfortable Speaking English	.07 (.01)	−.20 (.16)[‡]	.13 (.15)*	−.06 (.18)	.16 (.17)[†]	.09
Linked Fates with Latinos	.03 (.01)	−.04 (.16)	.20 (.15)[‡]	.031 (.18)	.05 (.16)	.05
Linked Fates with Anglos	−.04 (.01)	−.12 (.15)	.06 (.15)	.01 (.17)	.12 (.16)*	.04
Trust in Neighbors	.01 (.01)	−.17 (.14)[†]	.02 (.13)	−.02 (.16)	.09 (.14)	.04
Attends Social Functions with Anglos	.05 (.01)	−.02 (.17)	.24 (.16)[‡]	−.22 (.18)[‡]	.18 (.17)[‡]	.13

* $p < 0.1$ [†] $p < 0.05$ [‡] $p < 0.01$

gender, women were more likely to watch TV in only Spanish versus only English and to have poorer reading skills. The data were analyzed to see if women had lower levels of education, but this was not confirmed ($r = 1.03$, $p = 0.60$). It may be that men are more likely to work outside the home and therefore have more opportunities and pressure to learn English.

My framework contends that attitudes and beliefs about the different outcomes considered as part of the incorporation process will influence these behaviors (Albarracín, Johnson, and Zanna 2005; Alba and Nee 2003; De Souza Briggs 2013; Waters and Jiménez 2005). Thus, attitudes and beliefs related to learning English can determine the time and effort immigrants will invest in learning the language and ultimately influence immigrants' language skills. In general, people's attitudes toward learning English were positive, and most of the interviewees believed learning the language of the host society was important. Further, only one person said learning English was not important to her life. Benita and Úrsula were among them.[6] Úrsula went even further to state, "Without English you are nothing." In a similar vein, Walter expressed that "a person who knows English is worth two people."[7] Thus, immigrants were conscious of the importance of learning English for their satisfactory incorporation into the United States.

What were immigrants' beliefs regarding learning English? Several respondents felt that learning English would help them communicate better in general. For instance, Luis stated, "Learning English would help me communicate better in society"[8] and Estela said, "Learning English would help me get by better and communicate more."[9] Other interviewees had more specific beliefs associated with learning the language. Zacarias and Gabriel, for example, thought that learning more English could help them find better jobs.[10]

Florencia and Alberta said learning English was important to communicate with health providers and schoolteachers.[11] Last but not least, Hilda stated that learning English could help her understand her children better.[12] As these comments show, Mexican immigrants in Central Illinois believe learning English is a crucial step for their incorporation into the United States. Overall, this study found no support for the popular belief that immigrants do not want to learn English, with one minor exception. In this vein, Estela noted, "Why do I have to learn English if my husband's English is good? I don't need to."[13] This isolated comment by Estela shows a certain resignation to the lack of language skills that was uncommon in the sample of interviewees.

It is argued that the availability of opportunities and resources to immigrants, or the lack thereof, can shape their process of incorporation into society (De Souza Briggs 2013; Portes and Böröcz 1989; Portes and Rumbaut 2001; Portes and Zhou 1993, 1994). The availability of free English classes in Beardstown and Monmouth provided an opportunity for immigrants to learn English. Many interviewees reported having attended classes, or were doing so at the time of the interviews. However, society itself can provide opportunities for learning English as immigrants are faced with real-life situations that force them to learn the language. Several of the respondents reported learning English without taking formal classes. For example, Hugo said, "I learned English reading newspapers, interacting at work, and helping my children with their homework."[14] Benita stated, "I learned English at work, asking questions, and listening to the radio."[15] In turn, Hilda and Sandro learned English from watching TV.[16] As these comments show, immigrants found opportunities to learn English both inside and outside a classroom setting.

However, immigrants also faced some obstacles when trying to learn the language. Some respondents had difficulty attending English classes. Luis noted that he worked two jobs and was left with little time for English classes.[17] Several other men faced a similar situation. For instance, Martín explained that he was working on some home renovation projects after work and did not have time to attend English classes.[18] As for the women, several of them were too busy taking care of their children to find time to attend English classes. Hilda, for example, stated that she was busy with the children and did not have the money to pay for a babysitter, and Florencia had stopped attending English classes after she had children.[19] Thus, even though English classes were available in both towns, some immigrants had difficulty finding the time to attend them.

Ethnic Identity

Most scholars agree that immigrants need not abandon their ethnic identity and allegiance to their country of origin to successfully incorporate into American society (Black 2011; Bean, Brown, and Rumbaut 2006; Gerstle 2010; Jones-Correa 2004; Portes and Zhou 1993). Immigrants can follow four possible acculturation strategies in terms of how individuals relate to their original ethnic culture and the dominant culture of the host country (Algan, Bisin, and Verdier 2012). The first strategy, integration, entails a strong sense of identification with both the original and the host cultures. The second one, assimilation, requires a strong relationship with the host culture but a weak one with the original culture. The third, separation, implies a weak connection with the host culture but a strong one with the original culture. Finally, marginalization involves a weak link with both the host and the original cultures. These different strategies can be used when incorporating into the host country and balancing cultures of origin and settlement.

Upon arrival, individuals may have a sense of connectedness or commonality, which is usually associated, beyond the family, with the person's ethnoracial, national, or cultural group. However, especially as a person stays in a country longer, a sense of connectedness or commonality with the members of the host group can develop or strengthen. This sense of connectedness is called "linked fates" (Dawson 2001; Kaufmann 2003; Sánchez 2008; Sánchez and Masuoka 2010). Previous applications of this concept were limited to a sense of connectedness with members of the same ethnic group (Dawson 2001; Sánchez and Masuoka 2010), but this research extends its application to incorporate relationships between Latinos and Anglos as well.

The relationship between immigrants and the host population are at the core of the incorporation process (Korhonen 2006). This section examines the extent to which immigrants believed what happens to other Latinos in other parts of the country had implications for their own lives, the extent to which they believed what happens to Anglos in their community had implications for their own lives, and the extent to which social class and other factors influenced these senses of connectedness.

To capture the extent to which Mexican immigrants felt connected to other Latinos in the rest of the country, this study used the question, "To what extent does what happens to Latinos in other parts of the country have to do with your life?," and the possible answers were "not at all (1), not much (2), some (3) and a lot (4)." This variable also reflects the idea of bonding social capital, the norms and networks that are inward-looking and tend to enforce exclusive identities and homogenous groups (Putnam 2000). Recorded answers showed that 71 percent of the respondents said that what happens to other Latinos in other parts of the country had some or a lot to do with their lives (see figure 8). Moreover, only 13 percent of the interviewees stated that what happens to other Latinos in other parts of the country has nothing to do with their lives. As a basis for comparison, the number of Latinos reporting no linked fate with other Latinos in the 2006 Pew Research Hispanic Center's National Survey of Latinos was 20 percent (Sánchez and Masuoka 2010). These findings show that immigrants in Beardstown and Monmouth felt their lives were linked to the lives of other Latinos in the country in a significant way.

One purpose of this research was to determine if social class affected the cultural incorporation of immigrants in Central Illinois, and if a connection existed between cultural incorporation and gender or length of stay in the country. Regression analysis showed that the extent to which immigrants felt that what happens to other Latinos in the country had implications for their own lives was not significantly associated with employment status or income (table 6). Nonetheless, more-educated immigrants tended to feel more connected to other Latinos than did less-educated ones. Thus, I found that at least one indicator of social class, i.e., education, had a positive impact on the feeling of connectedness to other Latinos in the country

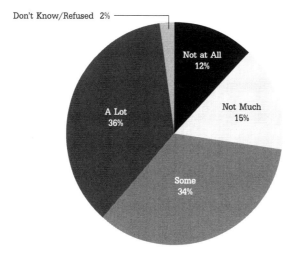

Figure 8. Feeling of Connectedness with Latinos in Other Parts of the Country: Sample of 260 Interviewees in Central Illinois

(Algan, Bisin, and Verdier 2012; Portes and Böröcz 1989; Schleef and Cavalcanti 2009). It may be that bonding social capital and ethnic solidarity can also have a positive effect on incorporation. It is also possible that a higer level of education increases the awareness of interconnectedness with co-ethnics. The length of stay in the country had no significant association with linked fates with other Latinos.

Attitudes toward other individuals can strengthen the sense of commonality with other members of the community. For example, if individuals see other members of society as competitors, they are less likely to have a sense of commonality with them (Sánchez 2008). Feelings of competition were not common among this study's respondents. Further, a set of interviewees emphasized feeling empathy and caring about what happened to other Latinos in the rest of the country. Luis stated, "If something bad happens to them you put yourself in their shoes."[20] Or, in the words of Carlos, "they are your countrymen; one is affected by what happens to one's own people."[21] Moreover, Hugo believed that being linked to other Latinos should help incorporation because "otherwise we only think about our own personal benefit."[22] As these comments show, immigrants cared about what happened to their fellow Latinos and believed the feeling of unity with other Latinos could help the process of incorporation.

Some interviewees believed the sense of linked fates with other Latinos was important for influencing the political system. Concurrently, the literature shows that ethnic solidarity is important for mobilization (Barretto et al. 2009; DeSipio 2011).

Group solidarity requires both the formulation of specific goals defined by the group, and ideological and organizational mobilization for the implementation of these goals (Barretto et al. 2009). Martín, for example, thought that unity gives strength, especially when it comes to politicians paying attention to Latino demands.[23] In a similar vein, Isabel stated that union creates strength.[24] These interviewees believed that unity among Latinos was important for swaying the political system and maybe society as well.

The interviews identified a number of obstacles in the process of incorporation that made Latinos have a stronger sense of commonality among them. Several comments referred to how state legislation passed in Arizona and other states, allowing law enforcement officials to request identification from likely undocumented immigrants, affected them. Immigrants seemed concerned about the direct and indirect consequences of this legislation. Floriberto, for instance, said, "These new laws they are enacting like the one in Arizona hurt all of us because we all have friends and family in other states."[25] Ignacio in turn stated, "The new laws they are enacting in places like Arizona look at all immigrants like illegals and hurt us all."[26] Thus, immigrants believed state bills negatively targeting immigrants affected them all. Clearly, empathy for other Latinos' experiences increased the sense of commonality with them (Sánchez 2008).

Common experiences with discrimination also increase the sense of commonality with other Latinos (Masuoka 2006; Sánchez 2008). Latinos who feel that discrimination against their group is a problem may feel a stronger sense of commonality with it. Some interviewees felt connected to other Latinos because of negative generalizations about them. For example, Alejandra stated, "People generalize; one Latino does something wrong and people think we are all bad."[27] Similarly, Irma commented, "When one Latino does something wrong, people generalize, but if he does something good, he gets no recognition."[28] Or, in the words of Teresa, "Unfortunately, they blame everyone for the mistakes of a few; many people generalize and forget that each person is different."[29] These comments show that the sense of commonality with other Latinos can originate in common experiences with prejudice (Masuoka 2006; Sánchez 2008).

The sense of connectedness with members of other groups is another factor that can shape the process of cultural incorporation. For this reason, my research considered the sense of linked fates with Anglos. To measure linked fates with Anglos, a question asked respondents, "To what extent does what happens to Anglos in your community have to do with your life?," and the possible answers were "not at all (1), not much (2), some (3), and a lot (4)." Close to 57 percent of respondents said they felt that what happens to Anglos in their community had some or a lot to do with their lives (figure 9). This number is much lower than the 71 percent of Latinos

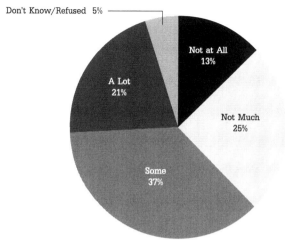

Don't Know/Refused 5%

Not at All 13%

A Lot 21%

Not Much 25%

Some 37%

Figure 9. Feeling of Connectedness with Anglos in the Community: Sample of 260 Interviewees in Central Illinois

having a sense of connectedness with other Latinos in the country. The regression analysis showed an association between social class and linked fates with Anglos (Algan, Bisin, and Verdier 2012; Portes and Böröcz 1989; Schleef and Cavalcanti 2009) (table 6). Specifically, those who felt that the lives of Anglos had some or a lot to do with their lives had higher incomes than those who felt they had not much or nothing to do with their lives.

The length of stay in the country had no significant association with linked fates with Anglos. Thus, the extent to which immigrants felt connected to Anglos may be independent of the length of stay in the country. With regard to the acculturation strategies immigrants were using, correlation analyses showed a positive association between linked fates with other Latinos in the country and linked fates with Anglos (r = 0.33, p = 0.00). More specifically, respondents who had allegiance to their original ethnic group also tended to feel linked to Anglos. It may be that some respondents may be following an integration strategy, which entails a strong sense of identification with both the original and host cultures. At the other end of the spectrum, however, some respondents may be following a path of marginalization, which implies a weak link with both the original culture and the host one.

Finally, the interviews provided insights into how attitudes and beliefs about others shaped immigrants' feelings of connectedness with Anglos (Sánchez 2008). Irma, for instance, said, "It affects me a lot; we are in this country and whatever happens affects everyone."[30] Hilda stated, "I'm a human being and if they [Anglos] are not OK, it hurts."[31] In a similar vein, Carlos remarked, "When seeing abandoned children, one doesn't feel well; we are all human beings."[32] Hilda and Carlos thought that we should feel connected to all human beings and have feelings of empathy toward Anglos.[33] As these comments show, empathetic attitudes toward Anglos shaped the extent to which immigrants felt connected to them.

Another set of comments showed how a negative attitude diminished the feeling of connectedness with Anglos (Barretto et al. 2009). Isabel, for example, said she had little sense of linked fates with Anglos because Anglos accuse immigrants of coming to take something away from them.[34] Isabel's comments reflect immigrants' perception of the common prejudices that blame immigrants for taking away jobs from locals, using government services, and causing other social ills in the host society (Espenshade 1995). Other comments made by immigrants revealed a certain level of indifference. For example, Luis believed that "what happens to them [Anglos] doesn't affect me,"[35] and Teresa stated that "if they don't mess with me, I don't mess with them."[36] As these comments show, some immigrants had a sense of indifference toward Anglos. Maybe these immigrants will never develop feelings of connectedness with them.

In contrast, other interviewees felt that the important roles Anglos play in society made them dependent on Anglos (Barretto et al. 2009). Some of them even felt grateful. Jesús, for example, stated, "If it weren't because of them [Anglos] we wouldn't be here; they are the ones who create the jobs."[37] Or, in the words of Hugo, "they [Anglos] are the owners of the big things, like the economy and politics."[38] As these comments show, some immigrants felt linked to Anglos because the latter control resources in society that affect everyone.

Interaction with Neighbors and Contact with Anglos

The networks of trust and support built by individuals can have an impact on their incorporation into the host society. Research on migration and settlement has usually focused on the role of family members and the ethnic community in helping newcomers find employment and housing (Gidengil and Stolle 2009). These ties, however, may be less helpful for long-term incorporation because immigrants' friends may share the same limited resources and problems (Gidengil and Stolle 2009; Putnam 2000). Thus, more emphasis is placed now on ties that extend outside immigrants' ethnoracial or nationality group. These ties can serve as bridges to social circles beyond one's own, and can bring people in contact with ideas and information they may not otherwise encounter (Gidengil and Stolle 2009).

Moreover, the contact hypothesis predicts that more diversity implies more

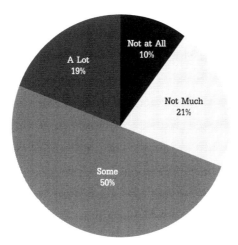

Figure 10. Trust in Neighbors: Sample of 260 Interviewees in Central Illinois

interethnic tolerance and social solidarity (Goto, Gee, and Takeuchi 2002). The reasoning behind this prediction is that if people have more contact with people unlike themselves (in the right context), they can overcome initial barriers of ignorance and hesitation, coming to trust others more. Not everyone agrees that contact with people different from one's own group can have a positive impact. Some, for example, suggest that ethnic diversity might reduce both in-group and out-group trust (Putnam 2007). Despite this debate, these connections remain major indicators of immigrants' incorporation into the host society.

The first variable reflected trust in neighbors. The question asked, "How much do you trust your neighbors to do what is right?," and the possible answers were "not at all (1), not much (2), some (3), and a lot (4)." As figure 10 shows, immigrants in Central Illinois seemed to trust their neighbors to a reasonable degree, with almost 70 percent of them trusting their neighbors some or a lot. Regression analyses did not find an association between the level of trust in neighbors and social class (table 6). Also, trust in neighbors was independent of the length of stay in the country. Gender, however, showed a significant correlation with trust in neighbors; women tended to trust their neighbors less than men. It may be that women's interactions with neighbors are more limited.

The interviews provided additional information about the cultural variables under analysis. For starters, immigrants believed having good neighbors had advantages. For example, Hugo stated, "I have a good relationship with my neighbors and we have a peaceful interaction which allows me to ask for help as I need it."[39] Hilda, in turn, said that having good neighbors could be useful when one needs help watching one's house.[40] As the comments show, some interviewees were positive about their relationship with their neighbors and aware of the importance of having a good relationship with them because of neighborly norms of reciprocity (Putnam 2000).

Not everyone had positive attitudes and beliefs about their neighbors. Alberto, for instance, believed his Anglo neighbors were racist because they never said hello to him.[41] In turn, Rita said that her Anglo neighbors were complaining to her landlord but pretended to be fine when interacting with her.[42] Finally, Floriberto explained that his neighbors reported him to the city government on several occasions for issues that the city considered of no importance.[43] Thus, the interaction between Latinos and Anglos was not without problems.

Residential patterns are important for incorporation. Incorporation usually takes place when immigrants and their descendants live in neighborhoods not limited to their own ethnoracial or nationality group. However, it is common for immigrants to settle in places with a high concentration of co-nationals. Immigrants are drawn to these places because they know someone and hope they can rely on their help and support. Previous research suggests that immigrants in new destinations may be more segregated than those in traditional ones (Jiménez 2011), but this study did not find evidence of Latino housing segregation in Beardstown and Monmouth. Beardstown and Monmouth are new to immigration, and this newness may be beneficial to the residential patterns this research found. Further, many interviewees reported getting along with their Anglo neighbors, being comfortable asking them for favors, and occasionally socializing with them.

Another variable captured respondents' attendance at social functions with Anglo-Americans. This question asked respondents, "How much do you agree with the following statement: I attend social functions with Anglo Americans," and the possible answers were "strongly disagree (1), somewhat disagree (2), somewhat agree (3), and strongly agree (4)." Nearly 50 percent of the interviewees somewhat agreed or strongly agreed with the statement (figure 11). Regression analyses showed that the level of interaction with Anglos was associated with social class (table 6). Those who attended social functions with Anglos tended to have higher levels of education, full-time jobs versus part-time or no jobs, and higher incomes than those who did not attend social functions with Anglo-Americans (Algan, Bisin, and Verdier 2012; Portes and Böröcz 1989; Schleef and Cavalcanti 2009). Clearly, SES is tied to the level of incorporation (Gidengil and Stolle 2009). The length of stay in the country had no significant association with attending social functions with Anglo-Americans.

Several immigrants were positive about socializing with Anglos. Hilda, for instance, stated, "I feel comfortable with Anglos; I've never had problems. Some Anglos are very nice and they even try to speak Spanish."[44] Hilda probably had good

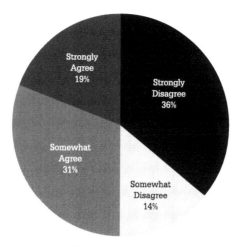

Figure 11. Agreement with Statement "I Attend Social Functions with Anglos": Sample of 260 Interviewees in Central Illinois

experiences with her Anglo friends and this made her enthusiastic about socializing with them. Other respondents emphasized how an interaction with Anglos was beneficial to their incorporation into the United States. For example, Floriberto said, "We have to socialize because we all live in the same town; it helps integration."[45] In turn, Gabriel remarked, "Interaction [with Anglos] is important to learn to live with the local people."[46] In a similar vein, Hilda thought that "interacting with Anglos helps integration because it helps you not to be fearful."[47] As these observations show, some immigrants were optimistic that making Anglo friends could help their incorporation into the United States (Gidengil and Stolle 2009).

Not all attitudes and beliefs helped the interaction with Anglo-Americans. For instance, several immigrants felt that ethnic or cultural barriers precluded their interaction with Anglos. Floriberto, for example, explained, "Interaction with Anglos is complicated because their way of life is so different; it seems there's a lack of trust, there's always like a limit."[48] Florencia stated, "I don't socialize with Anglos because they are from a different race."[49] In turn, Sandro agreed that he did not socialize with Anglos because they were very different.[50] Thus, immigrants' perception of cultural and other barriers was an obstacle to their socialization with Anglos (Putnam 2007).

Some Hispanics were even more skeptical about socializing with Anglos. Leo said, "When a Hispanic friend calls you, he doesn't call you because he needs something; when an American calls you, he calls you because he needs something.

If your car breaks down, the Hispanic person stops but the American doesn't. It's the same with directions."[51] As this comment shows, Leo had negative beliefs about Anglos. He thought Americans only call you when they need something but do not help you when you need them. If we think of social capital as reciprocal relationships of trust and support (Putnam 2000), then the type of friend that Leo describes does not qualify as such.

Finally, the interviews also provided insights on the opportunities immigrants found to socialize with Anglo-Americans. Immigrants met Anglos in different circumstances, including work, church, and their children's schools, or through friends or their children's friends. In turn, immigrants interacted with Anglos through different activities, like eating during work lunch breaks, at barbecues and restaurants, and when attending their children's sports events. Hence, immigrants in Central Illinois found a number of opportunities to interact with Anglo-Americans.

What Can We Learn about the Cultural Incorporation of Immigrants in Central Illinois?

This chapter investigated the level of cultural incorporation among Mexican immigrants in Beardstown and Monmouth and the connection between this level of incorporation and social class. Language use among the respondents showed a reasonable level of incorporation. Further, it was associated with several indicators of social class and the interviewees who used more English or had better language skills were also more likely to have a higher social status (Algan, Bisin, and Verdier 2012; Portes and Böröcz 1989; Schleef and Cavalcanti 2009).

Although English language skills among some respondents were not optimal, immigrants in Central Illinois seemed positive about learning the language, and some managed to find ways to do so both inside and outside classroom settings. Several interviewees considered learning English essential for finding better jobs and communicating with teachers, health professionals, their own children, and society in general. Both towns offer free English classes, and several of the interviewees had attended them in the past or were attending them at the time of the interviews. Others, however, faced obstacles to attending these classes. Lastly, some interviewees reported learning English outside the classroom in different ways. Overall, new immigrants in Beardstown and Monmouth are likely to acquire the necessary language skills for their full incorporation in the not-so-distant future.

The sense of connectedness with other Latinos was notably high among immigrants in Beardstown and Monmouth. Further, this feeling of connectedness was positively associated with education and showed no negative association with the other indicators of social class (Algan, Bisin, and Verdier 2012; Portes and Böröcz 1989; Schleef and Cavalcanti 2009). Thus, bonding social capital may be beneficial for the incorporation of immigrants (Putnam 2000). Interviewees believed a sense of connectedness to other Latinos could help incorporation by giving the Latino community unity and strength (Barretto et al. 2009). Common experiences of exclusion, such as anti-immigration state laws, provided opportunities for an increased sense of connectedness (Sánchez 2008). Moreover, discrimination and social prejudice made immigrants feel closer to other Latinos (Sánchez 2008). In sum, immigrants' sense of connectedness with other Latinos placed them in the full incorporation stage.

The feeling of connectedness with Anglos among immigrants in Beardstown and Monmouth was lower than that with other Latinos. It was also positively associated with social class (Algan, Bisin, and Verdier 2012; Portes and Böröcz 1989; Schleef and Cavalcanti 2009). Further, the feeling of connectedness with Anglos was associated with the same feeling for other Latinos. Immigrants may be following different acculturation strategies. In this sense, whereas some immigrants may have a strong sense of allegiance to both their original culture and the local one, others may have a low sense of allegiance to both. Interviewees with positive attitudes and beliefs about Anglos felt more connected to them, while immigrants who exhibited a sense of distance or indifference toward Anglos not unexpectedly felt less connected to them. Overall, immigrants in Beardstown and Monmouth revealed mixed attitudes and beliefs about Anglos, placing them in the conflict/negotiation stage of incorporation.

The level of trust in neighbors was high among immigrants in Beardstown and Monmouth. It was also independent from social class and the length of stay in the country. Women trusted their neighbors less than men. Although this finding requires further research, it may be that women interact with neighbors less than men. This research showed that for the most part, immigrants lived in integrated neighborhoods, generally had good relationships with their neighbors, and felt having good relationships with their neighbors was important. Overall, the attitudes, beliefs, and opportunities for trusting neighbors placed most immigrants in the incorporation stage. However, integrated neighborhoods also seemed to create some problems between Latinos and Anglos.

Less than half of the immigrants in Beardstown and Monmouth socialized with Anglo-Americans. Socialization with Anglos was positively associated with all the indicators of social class (Algan, Bisin, and Verdier 2012; Portes and Böröcz 1989; Schleef and Cavalcanti 2009); immigrants with higher education, full-time jobs, and higher income socialized with Anglos more. The attitudes and beliefs about socializing with Anglos were mixed, leaning negative. In this sense, whereas some immigrants thought interacting with Anglos helped incorporation (Putnam 2007), others felt this interaction was constrained by ethnic and cultural barriers. Immigrants found different opportunities for meeting Anglos and socializing with them, including through work, church, children's schools or friends, and neighborhoods. Overall, immigrants' interactions with Anglos placed them at the conflict/negotiation stage of incorporation.

CHAPTER 4

The Context of Reception
Discrimination and Acceptance

The police stop immigrants to ask for IDs, even if we are walking.

—Isidro, interview with the author, September 15, 2013, Monmouth, Illinois

IMMIGRATION BRINGS "STRANGERS" INTO A HOMELAND (CITRIN AND SIDES 2008).
The populations on both sides of the Atlantic worry about the economic and cultural
consequences of immigration. Discrimination, an unequal or negative treatment of
people of a certain group (Quillian 2006), can result from racism or fears about the
consequences of immigration. In this chapter, I explore the feelings of acceptance,
perceptions of discrimination, and experiences with discrimination of immigrants
in Beardstown and Monmouth. The life stories reviewed below highlight some
discrimination experiences.

Floriberto lives in Beardstown with his wife and two children. He came to the
United States in 1986 and successfully walked through Tijuana-San Ysidro (San
Diego) with the help of a *coyote* after two previous attempts. He was later able to
apply for the "amnesty" granted by the Immigration Reform and Control Act (IRCA)
of 1986 (Massey and Capoferro 2008). Floriberto spent part of the year in Mexico

and part of the year in the United States until 2000. For several years, he worked picking strawberries and oranges in California. He continued to go back to Mexico during the off-season until his family joined him in 2000 (Valentine 2005).

"The good thing about the United States is that you can live comfortably with one job whereas in Mexico you need several jobs,"[1] Floriberto explained. Like many immigrants, he could not make a living in Mexico. Floriberto and his family had a hog farm in Mexico, but it was not economically viable. Thus, for several years he worked in the United States while his wife took care of the farm. Later, Floriberto and his family moved to Marshall, Missouri. When the Excel plant in Marshall closed, he was offered a job at the Excel plant in Beardstown.

Despite being relatively happy in the United States, Floriberto has had several bad experiences with discrimination. For example, he believes that his supervisors at work discriminate against Latinos by demanding more work from them than from Anglos (Green 2003). In addition, if the plant falls behind, they blame Latinos for it but never Anglos. Floriberto also has had bad experiences with the police (Varsanyi et al. 2012). However, he thinks things in Beardstown are getting better for immigrants.

Relations between Anglos and Hispanics in Beardstown were tense for many years after a Latino allegedly killed an Anglo and a Latino bar was burned down. Floriberto believes the locals treat immigrants better now thanks to the actions of Puerto Rican immigrants who have recently arrived in the town. According to Floriberto, Puerto Ricans defend themselves when attacked. "If the police stop them, they defend themselves; this is the reason why the police have changed, because Puerto Ricans defend their rights."[2] Because Puerto Ricans are American citizens, they can afford to have a more prominent role in improving living conditions in Beardstown.

Isidro lives in Monmouth with his partner. He came to the United States in 2003, arriving in California by plane on a tourist visa. He first stayed in California for four years because he had family there, where he also had several jobs, mostly in the janitorial, construction, and service industries. After that experience, Isidro went to Beardstown because he had family there also. He worked at Excel for a year, but the manager discovered he was working with somebody else's Social Security number and fired him. Several other interviewees also mentioned how immigration controls at the local meatpacking plants in Beardstown and Monmouth have become stricter.

Isidro then moved to Monmouth, where he got a job at Farmland, the local meatpacking plant. He worked there for four years, but he left for California when he started having trouble with his ex-wife. After a year and a half he came back to Monmouth with his new partner, whom he had met in Mexico during his visits. Apparently, Isidro was able to visit Mexico and come back to the United States on a tourist visa. He now works at a cleaning company, but he is unhappy because he feels discriminated against.

His bosses treat him poorly, like a "slave," according to Isidro.[3] "They don't want to treat you like a human being but like something else," he said.[4] He believes his bosses mistreat him because they know he lacks papers to work in the United States, and people without documents have few resources to defend themselves against abusive bosses. As did several other interviewees, Isidro also reported that the police are harsh on immigrants (Varsanyi et al. 2012). He stated that the police stop immigrants to ask for IDs, even when the latter are merely walking around town. He also asserted that "Americans" treat immigrants like they do not belong here.

Isidro speaks English reasonably well, "75% well,"[5] as he puts it. He believes that to become integrated in society, one needs to follow the rules to avoid problems. Isidro also thinks that having papers to work in the United States will help him find a better job and live peacefully in the community he has chosen. "I sometimes feel happy and other times I feel sad for not being able to do things the way I would like to."[6] As was true of many other interviewees, he is hoping to regularize his immigration status sometime soon.

As these life stories show, immigrants' life experiences are full of instances of discrimination by the police, bosses, and other native-born residents.

Discrimination, Prejudice, and Racism

The United States defines itself as a country of immigrants, but its immigration laws have a long history of drawing a line between "desirable" and "undesirable" immigrants (Boswell 2003; Johnson 1998; Joppke 2001; Kilty and Vidal de Haymes 2000). The attitudes of the members of the host society also influence immigrants' lives. These attitudes interact with immigrants' own acculturation patterns to determine the extent to which immigrants feel welcome (Schwartz et al. 2010). Sociologists and anthropologists refer to this dynamic as the context of reception (Portes and Böröcz 1989; Schwartz et al. 2010). To be sure, the context of reception also includes the stance of the host government, employers, and the characteristics of the preexisting ethnic communities (Portes and Böröcz 1989). Nonetheless, discrimination by the host population is also crucial because it influences immigrants' chances for a better life, and perceptions of discrimination are a major source of stress in the lives of immigrants (Potochnic, Pereira, and Fuligni 2012; Schwartz et al. 2010). Unfortunately, social attitudes regarding immigration have deteriorated in most societies from assistance and hospitality to rejection and hostility (Fekete 2001).

Discriminatory practices occur in different contexts, including labor markets (Blau 1980; Brettell 2011; Butcher and DiNardo 2002; Cornelius 1981; Hersch 2011; Mason 2004; Rivera-Batiz 1999; Sánchez and Brock 1996; Valdivia and Flores 2012), retail and services (Evett et al. 2013; Kennedy 2001; Williams, Henderson, and Harris 2001), education (Goodwin 2002; Oxman-Martínez et al. 2012; Portes and MacLeod 1999), and housing markets (Brettell 2011; Dion 2002; Ondrich, Ross, and Yinger 2000; Ondrich, Sticker, and Yinger 1999; Williams 2006; Yinger 1998). Immigrants are also victims of racial profiling (Arnold 2007; Romero 2006) and face discrimination in the criminal justice system (Dovidio et al. 2010; Stowell, Martínez, and Cancino 2012). At the same time, immigrants face discrimination in health care (Williams 2006). Discrimination in general can have lasting consequences on health (Mossakowski 2003; Rumbaut 1994; Stein, González, and Huq 2012; Viruell-Fuentes, Miranda, and Abdulrahim 2012) and life satisfaction in general (Safi 2010).

Prejudice and discrimination are two distinct but interrelated concepts. Prejudice is an "antipathy based on a faulty or inflexible generalization" (Allport 1954 quoted in Quillian 2006, 200). This definition implies both a negative affective feeling toward the target group and a poorly founded belief, or stereotype, held about the members of the target group. Discrimination happens when an exterior manifestation of prejudice materializes and produces an unequal treatment of the target group (Quillian 2006). Discrimination can take place at both the individual and institutional level. Whereas ethnic prejudice is universal, discrimination is not (Berry 2001). Different methods are used to measure discrimination, including income and other outcomes (Williams 2006), imprisonment rates (Dovidio et al. 2010; Stowell, Martínez, and Cancino 2012), and discrimination as perceived by immigrants (Goto, Gee, and Takeuchi 2002; Phinney, Madden, and Santos 1998; Rakosi Rosenbloom and Way 2004; Shorey, Cowan, and Sullivan 2002; Waters 1994). This study uses the last method.

Racism and discrimination usually go hand in hand (Plous 2003). Racism can be defined as a diverse assortment of racist practices, including the unjustly gained economic and political power of Whites, the continuing resource inequalities, and the White-racist ideologies, attitudes, and institutions created to preserve White advantages and power (Feagin 2014). Modern, subtle, or symbolic racism is characterized by three components: denial of continued discrimination, antagonism toward minority group demands, and resentment about special policies for minority groups or groups subordinated to a dominant group (Akrami, Ekehammar, and Araya 2000; Plous 2003). One characteristic of modern or subtle racism is that its existence tends to be denied (Plous 2003). Old-fashioned racism is also the manifestation of three components: defense of traditional values, exaggeration of cultural differences, and denial of positive emotions (Akrami, Ekehammar, and Araya 2000). Although old-fashioned racism has been decreasing over the last century, modern racism is still common.

Americans view recent waves of immigration with skepticism if not outright hostility. Moreover, American attitudes toward immigration have long been conflictive.

After the immigration boom that began in the 1880s, immigrants were accused of taking away jobs from native-born Americans, lowering the wages of native workers, adding to the population living in poverty, and competing for education, health, and other social services (Espenshade 1995). These same accusations are still common among the host population in the United States (Espenshade 1995). Different theories account for the reasons why a society discriminates against newcomers. For instance, both realistic and symbolic threats can be used to justify discrimination (Pereira, Vala, and Costa-Lopes 2010; Stephan, Ybarra, and Bachman 1999).

Realistic threats are threats to the existence, the (economic or political) power, and the (physical or material) well-being of the native population (Pereira, Vala, and Costa-Lopes 2010; Stephan, Ybarra, and Bachman 1999). In other words, social groups compete for resources, and the dominant group perceives an increased number of immigrants as a threat (Zick, Pettigrew, and Wagner 2008). Symbolic threats are related to differences between groups in terms of values or morals, and to how these differences challenge the host population's worldview (Pereira, Vala, and Costa-Lopes 2010; Stephan, Ybarra, and Bachman 1999). Thus, the population fearing symbolic threats believes that the increased numbers of immigrants may change its worldview, or the beliefs held by the general population. Obviously, this change is expected to be for the worse. The recent work by Samuel Huntington (2004) exemplifies both of these perceived threats.

When people move across national borders, they enter a new system of social stratification by class, race, ethnicity, and gender (Bashi and McDaniel 1997; Duany 1998). In particular, the practice of using race as a justification for discrimination among individuals has a long history in the United States (McClain and Stewart 2006). A divide between Blacks and Whites has characterized the United States for centuries. Latino immigrants, who display a wide range of racial phenotypes, complicate the Black/White dynamic of America (Frank, Redstone Akresh, and Lu 2010). Usually, darker skinned Latinos experience skin-color-based discrimination (Frank, Redstone Akresh, and Lu 2010). In addition, not only are most Latino immigrants of different "color," but they also speak Spanish and profess a different religion than the majority of the dominant population in the country (Massey 1995). Thus, discrimination against this group can be based on these factors, as well.

Discrimination in Beardstown and Monmouth

Beardstown and Monmouth are similar in many respects. They both have meatpacking plants and a growing Latino population. However, they differ in two major respects. Beardstown's proportion of Latinos is almost twice that of Monmouth.

In addition, Beardstown has a long history of racial tension, but Monmouth does not. Because these two distinct characteristics are likely to influence the extent of existing discrimination, it is important to analyze separately the results of the surveys in each town.

Beardstown, a blue-collar town, calls itself "redneck" with pride (Longworth 2009). Until the 1980s, Beardstown remained all White (Miraftab 2012). Historically, Faranak Miraftab (2012) categorizes it as a "sundown town," a place where Black people were not allowed on the streets after sunset. Latino immigrants started arriving in the town in the 1990s. In 1996, a Mexican immigrant allegedly killed a White resident over a romantic dispute at the predominantly Latino El Flamingo tavern.[7] A day after the shooting, a cross was left burning outside the tavern. A week later, the tavern was burned to the ground. Even though some community leaders organized an alliance to promote racial harmony, the tensions between Anglos and Hispanics remained high for several years.

The Anglo and Hispanic communities in Monmouth lack such a rocky history. For the most part, the relationship between the communities has been harmonious. However, Monmouth also had a historical presence of the Ku Klux Klan, and racial relations between Blacks and Whites were tense for many years.[8] Despite this, Monmouth hired its first Black police officer in 1950, a decade before the civil rights movement. This is not to say that discrimination is not an issue in Monmouth. Discrimination in Monmouth also seems significant.

In what follows, I explore the perceptions of acceptance and discrimination by immigrants in Beardstown and Monmouth (Goto, Gee, and Takeuchi 2002; Phinney, Madden, and Santos 1998; Rakosi Rosenbloom and Way 2004; Shorey, Cowan, and Sullivan 2002; Waters 1994). More specifically, I examine three issues: the extent to which immigrants feel accepted by Anglos, the extent to which immigrants believe discrimination against Latinos is a major problem, and the direct experience of discrimination in the previous five years. The first question asked was "How much do you agree with the following statement: I feel accepted by Anglo-Americans?" The possible answers were "strongly disagree (1), somewhat disagree (2), somewhat agree (3), and strongly agree (4)." The second question was "In general, do you believe discrimination against Latinos is not a problem (1), is a minor problem (2), or is a major problem (3) in preventing Latinos in general from succeeding in America? In the last five years, have you or a family member experienced discrimination?" The possible answers were no or yes.

Consistent with my expectations, Mexican immigrants in Monmouth felt more accepted by Anglo-Americans than those in Beardstown (figure 12). More specifically, a significantly higher percentage of immigrants in Monmouth strongly agreed with the statement "I feel accepted by Anglo-Americans" than in Beardstown (27 percent

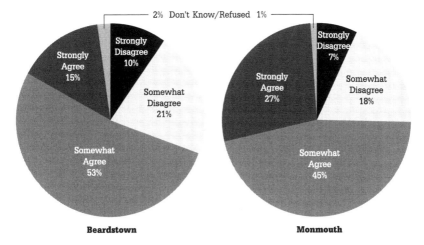

Figure 12. Feeling of Acceptance by Anglos: Beardstown vs. Monmouth, IL

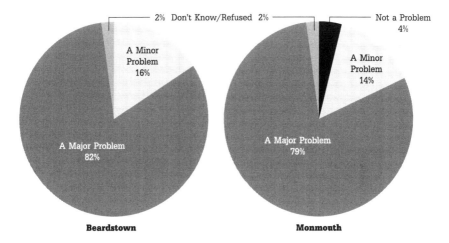

Figure 13. Perception of Discrimination as a Problem: Beardstown vs. Monmouth, IL

versus 15 percent). The numbers reflecting the extent of the discrimination problem in the United States were similar (figure 13). In particular, almost 99 percent of respondents in Beardstown thought discrimination was a minor or major problem preventing Latinos from succeeding in the United States, and no respondent said discrimination was not a problem. The numbers for respondents in Monmouth were 82 percent and 4 percent, respectively. Thus, the perception of the pervasiveness of discrimination in the United States was higher among immigrants in Beardstown than those in Monmouth.

Authors speculate on whether discrimination levels differ between traditional and new destinations of immigration (Fennelly 2008; Hirschman and Massey 2008). It was therefore important to compare my results with those of a national sample of foreign-born Latinos. Largely, the perception of discrimination among my respondents was higher than among the respondents surveyed by the Pew Hispanic Center (2007). Specifically, 78 percent of the respondents in the national sample thought discrimination was a minor or major problem preventing Hispanics from succeeding in America, while the results for the towns under analysis here, as reported above, were 99 percent (Beardstown) and 82 percent (Monmouth). Thus, the perceived discrimination in the United States may be higher in new immigrant destinations.

Immigrants in Beardstown were also slightly more likely to declare that they or a family member had experienced discrimination than those in Monmouth. Whereas 49 percent of respondents in Beardstown had a personal or close experience with discrimination in the previous five years, the rate for Monmouth was 44 percent (figure 14). It was also interesting to explore whether differences existed between Beardstown and Monmouth and the national sample in the number of respondents who had a personal or close experience with discrimination. Results showed that the number of respondents in the national sample of Latinos who declared that they or a family member had experienced discrimination in the previous five years was 42 percent (Pew Hispanic Center 2007). Thus, the evidence suggests that discrimination may be more pronounced in areas new to immigration than in the average immigrant destination.

In conducting this study, I also set out to determine the factors shaping levels of perceived acceptance and discrimination for Mexican immigrants in Beardstown and Monmouth. Research shows that a lower-status group member may be more likely to perceive/experience discrimination than someone of a higher-status group (Portes, Nash Parker, and Cobas 1980; Shorey, Cowan, and Sullivan 2002). Immigrants with higher income (appendix, no. 14) and education (appendix, no. 15) are expected to report lower levels of perceived discrimination and lack of acceptance by the dominant group. Discrimination can also present a threat to group identity, making people increasingly turn toward their own racial group (Goto, Gee, and Takeuchi 2002; Verkuyten 2008; Waters 1994). Thus, the expectation was that immigrants with a strong sense of connectedness to Latinos in their community (appendix, no. 42), namely, immigrants who believed the lives of other Latinos in the community had implications for their own lives, would exhibit higher perceptions of discrimination.

In addition, the ability to get along with members of other ethnic groups can also influence perceptions of discrimination (Goto, Gee, and Takeuchi 2002; Phinney,

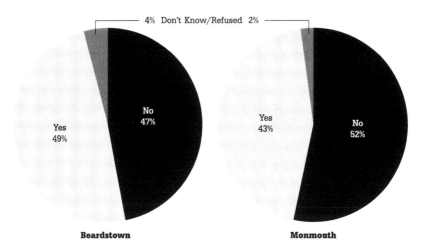

4% Don't Know/Refused 2%

No
47%

Yes
49%

Yes
43%

No
52%

Beardstown

Monmouth

Figure 14. Experience with Discrimination by Immigrants or Family Members: Beardstown vs. Monmouth, IL

Madden, and Santos 1998; Rakosi Rosenbloom and Way 2004). Consequently, it was predicted that those who socialized with Anglos (appendix, no. 44) would show lower perceived discrimination levels. In turn, discrimination is not necessarily based on racial/ethnic categories (Alba 2005; Foner and Alba 2008; Rakosi Rosenbloom and Way 2004); poor language skills, for instance, can be a source of discrimination (Rakosi Rosenbloom and Way 2004). Thus, it was expected that immigrants who were less comfortable speaking English (appendix, no. 19) could show higher perceived discrimination levels. Finally, assimilation can also influence perceptions of discrimination, and people who are more assimilated to the host society may exhibit lower levels of perceived discrimination (Portes, Nash Parker, and Cobas 1980). For this reason, the study used the length of stay in the country (appendix, no. 4) as a proxy for assimilation.

Education and attendance of functions with Anglo-Americans were significant in the regression model predicting perception of acceptance by Anglos (table 7). Specifically, those with lower levels of education (Portes, Nash Parker, and Cobas 1980; Shorey, Cowan, and Sullivan 2002) and who attended social functions with Anglos (Goto, Gee, and Takeuchi 2002; Phinney, Madden, and Santos 1998; Rakosi Rosenbloom and Way 2004) were more likely to feel more accepted by Anglos. Although the second finding makes sense because socialization with members of other groups can decrease prejudice and increase tolerance, the first finding is less straightforward. It was predicted that those with higher levels of education would

Table 7. Linear Regression and Logistic Models Predicting Perceived Acceptance by Anglos, Perception of Discrimination as a Problem, and Experience with Discrimination (Standard Errors in Parentheses): Sample of 260 Interviewees in Central Illinois

Variable	Standardized Beta		Exp(B)
	Acceptance by Anglos (Linear Regression)	Discrimination as a Problem (Linear Regression)	Experience Discrimination (Logistic)
Income	.11 (.15)	.03 (.08)	.81 (.36)
Education	−.13 (.14)*	−.05 (.07)	.85 (.34)
Feels Linked to Latinos	.04 (.08)	.12 (.04)	1.38 (.21)
Attends Social Functions with Anglos	.25 (.06)‡	.13 (.03)	.99 (.16)
Comfortable Speaking English	−.04 (.07)	−.08 (.03)	1.14 (.16)
Length of Stay in United States	−.08 (.01)	.12 (.01)	1.04 (.02)
R Square	.81	.05	.04

$* p < 0.1$ $† p < 0.05$ $‡ p < 0.01$

feel more accepted by Anglos and not less. It may be that people with lower education levels may also have lower expectations about how they expect to be treated by members of other groups. It may also be that the more educated are more aware of the various forms that discrimination takes against them.

None of the other independent variables—namely, income, sense of connectedness with Latinos, language skills, and length of stay in the country—were significant in predicting feelings of acceptance by Anglos (table 7). However, income was positively associated with the feeling of acceptance by Anglos in the correlation analysis. That is, those with higher incomes were more likely to feel accepted by Anglos ($r = 0.13$; $p = < 0.10$). Unexpectedly, the sense of connectedness with other Latinos was positively associated with the feeling of acceptance by Anglos in the model. However, the correlation analysis showed that those who felt accepted by Anglo-Americans also felt less connected with other Latinos ($r = 0.07$; $p = < 0.10$). Also, surprisingly, language skills and length of stay showed a weak but negative association with feeling of acceptance by Anglos. Still, the binary correlations showed that those with better language skills ($r = 0.11$; $p = < 0.10$) who had been in the country longer ($r = 0.00$; $p = < 0 .10$) felt more accepted than those with better language skills who had been in the country for a shorter time.

The model for the factors affecting the perception of discrimination as a problem showed no significant results (table 7). However, several of the associations between the perception of discrimination as a problem and the independent variables leaned in the direction predicted. For instance, those with lower levels of education and poorer language skills also perceived discrimination against Latinos as a larger problem. This finding makes sense because those with lower education levels and poorer language skills are usually more likely to experience discrimination. Also, these persons are likely to pose a greater threat to the lower-status Anglo-Americans who are in contact with them (Fennelly 2008).

In addition, those who perceived discrimination as a bigger problem also felt more connected to other Latinos in the community, partly confirming the prediction that when people feel discriminated against they may turn to their in-group more (Goto, Gee, and Takeuchi 2002; Verkuyten 2008; Waters 1994). Income showed a weak but positive association with perceptions of discrimination, indicating that those with higher income also felt discrimination was a bigger problem. The length of stay in the country also had a positive association with perceptions of discrimination, and those who had been in the country longer were also more likely to believe discrimination in the United States was a major problem preventing Latinos from succeeding in the United States. Finally, the logistic model predicting experiences with discrimination by the immigrant or a member of his or her family showed no significant results (table 7).

Experiences of Discrimination

Almost half of the 260 interviewees reported that they or a member of their family had experienced discrimination. These discrimination experiences occurred in different settings (Cohen and Chavez 2013). The forty-seven in-depth interviews showed that discrimination in Beardstown and Monmouth occurred in all areas of everyday life, including at workplaces (23 percent), restaurants and other businesses or stores (21 percent), and schools (10 percent) (figure 15). Discrimination also occurred in interactions with the local police (36 percent), health care providers (5 percent), and the general population (13 percent).

Twenty-three percent of the interviewees reported instances of discrimination at work.[9] Previous research also shows that 58 percent of foreign-born Latinos thought discrimination in the workplace was a major or a minor problem in 2007 (Pew Research Center 2007). Racial discrimination in the workplace takes place when a member of a certain ethnic or racial group is treated unequally or unfairly because of his or her membership in the group. Title VII of the Civil Rights Act was enacted to combat discrimination in employment (Green 2003). However, discrimination in the workplace is still widespread, although we are said to have moved beyond overt racism and segregation toward more subtle forms of discrimination (Green 2003).

Most of the interviewees in this study have jobs in the meatpacking plants in Beardstown and Monmouth, namely, Cargill and Farmland. Formerly, meatpacking

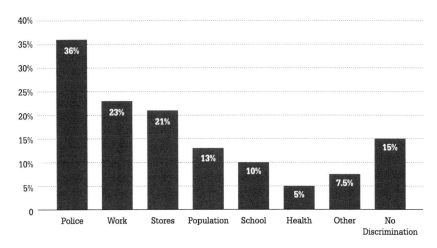

Figure 15. Reported Instances of Discrimination: Sample of 47 Interviewees in Central Illinois

plants were located in urban centers and used unionized labor (Dalla, Ellis, and Cramer 2005). Because of changes in the meat industry and pressures for global production, the beef industry moved to rural areas and opened highly mechanized plants of production (Haverluk and Trautman 2008). This allowed producers to hire cheaper, nonskilled labor; avoid places with a history of labor activism; and achieve lower transportation costs.

Now meatpacking plants recruit laborers from Mexico to Asia (Dalla, Ellis, and Cramer 2005). The foreign-born proportion of Hispanics in this industry increased from 37 to 83 percent between the years 1980 and 2000 (Parrado and Kandel 2008). Meatpacking employees' wages ranged from $7 to $10 an hour in the early 2000s (Dalla, Ellis, and Cramer 2005). The extensive use of knives, manual lifting of heavy meat, continuous refrigeration, and slippery floors contribute to high injury rates, sometimes reaching 36 percent annually (Dalla, Ellis, and Cramer 2005). Research demonstrates that the meatpacking industry also shows evidence of wage suppression, worsening conditions, and segregation (Saucedo 2004).

As mentioned before, immigrants are discriminated against in labor markets (Blau 1980; Brettell 2011; Butcher and DiNardo 2002; Cornelius 1981; Hersch 2011; Mason 2004; Rivera-Batiz 1999; Sánchez and Brock 1996; Valdivia and Flores 2012). The main types of discrimination are usually related to the types of jobs immigrants find and the wages they receive. Some interviewees perceived the lack of opportunities to obtain better jobs as discrimination. However, despite the fact that Latinos in non-metro areas are mostly in low-skill jobs, earn low wages, and have not been able to move upward in recent years (Valdivia and Flores 2012), interviewees in this study did not complain about unfair wages. It may be that even though the immigrants' position in the host society is less than ideal, it is still better than that in their countries of origin (Maxwell 2010a).

Most work environments in the United States, particularly those in emerging immigrant communities in the Midwest, reflect the dominant U.S. culture (Valdivia and Flores 2012). However, no complaints related to "only English" rules at work or cultural norms not friendly to Latino culture were reported in this study. Instances of discrimination commonly found in this research referred to unequal treatment at work. These instances of discrimination usually came from supervisors, but sometimes also from coworkers.

Several immigrants reported discrimination coming from supervisors at the meatpacking plants in Beardstown and Monmouth. For instance, Rosa works at the meatpacking plant in Beardstown with two Hispanics and two "Americans."[10] Her job consists of removing the guts from the animals. According to Rosa, supervisors expect more from Hispanics than from Anglo-Americans. She believes Anglos waste time at work by, for example, using the bathroom a lot or walking around. If Anglos feel they are "working too much," they complain to the supervisors, and the latter usually let them work less consistently. Overall, Rosa's perception is that Hispanics work much harder than "Americans" and supervisors are fine with this difference.

Floriberto agrees with Rosa that treatment between different ethnic groups at the meatpacking plant in Beardstown is unequal.[11] According to him, supervisors defend "Americans" more than they defend the other groups and treat Americans better. He believes that Latino supervisors also favor "Americans" over Hispanics. Overall, Floriberto feels supervisors make Hispanics work more than the other groups. If a delay in production occurs, supervisors blame Hispanics but leave "Americans" alone. Floriberto also believes that supervisors are very careful in their treatment of African Americans. Apparently, he thinks supervisors are "afraid" of African Americans.

Jorge also believes that the supervisors at the plant in Beardstown support Anglos more.[12] He said that supervisors listen to Anglos more and favor them over other groups. Finally, one respondent complained about the treatment by supervisors at the meatpacking plant in Monmouth. Walter thought that supervisors blame immigrants when a problem at work arises.[13] He also stated that supervisors punish Latinos instead of punishing the ones who are to blame for the problem. As these comments by immigrants show, unequal treatment at the meatpacking plants in Beardstown and Monmouth seemed to be common.

Hugo has a college degree and also works as a supervisor at the meatpacking plant in Beardstown.[14] His perspective on discrimination at the plant is important because none of the other interviewees were supervisors. Hugo agreed with Rosa and Floriberto that discrimination in the plant exists. He explained, for example, that "Americans" are preferred for certain activities, but he believes that these preferences may have to do with their command of the English language. According to Floriberto, it would be risky for immigrants to perform certain tasks if they fail to fully understand the security norms involved. However, he also thought favoritism is common at work. Some of this favoritism, according to Hugo, is based on friendship, giving credence to the old saying "It's not what you know but who you know that is important."

Isidro works in cleaning and is unhappy with his job because he believes discrimination at his workplace is a big problem.[15] He stated that supervisors treat him as a slave and not as a human being. According to Isidro, supervisors discriminate against him because he lacks papers to work in the United States. Finally, other immigrants complained about discrimination coming from coworkers. For instance, Jorge explained that at work, Anglos tell him he should go back to his country and he responds, "You wouldn't be able to do the job I'm doing."[16] As these comments show, discrimination at the workplace is widespread in both Beardstown and Monmouth.

The interviewees in this study reported instances of consumer discrimination at restaurants and other businesses (21 percent). Previous research shows that in 2007, about 53 percent of Latinos surveyed received poor treatment at restaurants and stores (Pew Hispanic Center 2007). Up until the post–civil rights era, Blacks were commonly denied service and the opportunity to try on merchandise before buying (Kennedy 2001). Thus, until the civil rights movement, consumption and racial hierarchies were inextricably intertwined (Kennedy 2001). In fact, the civil rights movement challenged the differential treatment of ethnic minorities in public places like restaurants, stores, public transportation, and other settings. Consumer discrimination is still widespread today, but perceiving it is more difficult because it is rarely overt (Evett et al. 2013).

Consumer discrimination occurs when sales clerks and other store employees treat customers differently because of their race or ethnicity (Evett et al. 2013). Examples of this type of behavior include ignoring customers, making them wait a long time for service, treating them rudely, waiting on non-minority customers first, discouragement, mistaken identity, rejection, verbal and/or physical attacks, undue use of force, and requiring additional identification for credit or check purchases, among others (Williams, Henderson, and Harris 2001). Marketplace discrimination covers service experiences that occur in establishments like hotels, restaurants, and gas stations, as well as retail establishments including grocery stores, clothing stores, department stores, home improvement stores, and office equipment stores (Williams, Henderson, and Harris 2001). Consumer racial profiling (CRP) is an extreme case of consumer discrimination in which the customer is suspected of committing a crime.

Most of the discrimination cases noted during this research involved rude treatment and not explicit denial of service. However, an instance described by Jorge came close to denial of service. He explained that he was discriminated against when shopping for faucets at Menards in Springfield, Illinois.[17] When Jorge and his partner were trying to pay for the faucets, the cashier told them, "I couldn't care less if you buy this or not."[18] The cashier took their payment, and Jorge, who seems like an outspoken person, complained to a supervisor at the store about the poor treatment received. However, the supervisor was dismissive and said the employee did nothing wrong. María Isabel also explained that she was treated very poorly by employees in Menards and Home Depot, both located in Springfield.[19]

Discrimination based on race is widespread in restaurants (Brewster 2012). According to Zachary Brewster (2012), the source of this problem is related to social-psychological processes involving the diffusion and reinforcement of racial stereotypes that servers use to inform their interaction with customers. Two immigrants in this study reported being mistreated at restaurants in the area. For example, Gustavo explained that he had a bad experience at a restaurant when trying to order food.[20] According to him, the waiter continued to speak to him in "fast English" even after realizing Gustavo was not fluent. He felt unwelcome because he thought the waiter made no effort to communicate with him.

Crisleiry also experienced discrimination at a restaurant.[21] On one occasion, Crisleiry and her family went to an "American restaurant" to have dinner. When they arrived, the employees gave them a "What are you doing here?" look. Although the employees refrained from making discriminatory or rude remarks, Crisleiry felt unwelcome. Finally, other immigrants reported being mistreated at stores, without specifying which stores. For example, Ignacio[22] and Nancy[23] stated that they faced discrimination in several different stores. Thus, these interviews show that discrimination at restaurants and retail stores was common for Latino immigrants in both Beardstown and Monmouth.

Ten percent of the interviewees reported that their children experienced discrimination in the schools they were attending. At the national level, however, the reported numbers for discrimination in education are much higher. For example, 64 percent of foreign-born Latinos (Pew Hispanic Center 2007) thought discrimination in schools was a major problem for Latinos living in the United States. Racial discrimination in education arises from actions of institutions or in-dividual state actors, their attitudes and ideologies, or processes that systematically treat students from different racial/ethnic backgrounds disparately or inequitably (Mickelson 2003).

Legal segregation has been outlawed since the Civil Rights Act of 1964, although de facto resegregation is on the rise. To be sure, multicultural curricula are used widely, and overtly racist material has been eliminated, but racial disparities in education continue. For instance, the National Assessment of Education Progress (NAEP) results show that White students score higher in reading, mathematics, and science than do Blacks and Latinos. SAT results show similar patterns (Mickelson 2003). Further, a study conducted in an inner-city high school in Houston showed that Mexican-descent students feel uncared for by teachers and other personnel (Salinas 2005). Thus, disparities in education remain, and immigrant-descent students do not feel comfortable in American public schools (Williams 2006).

Schools in Beardstown and Monmouth have high proportions of Latino children. For example, the school district in Beardstown had almost 50 percent Latino students in 2015. For Monmouth, this number was close to 30 percent. School districts in both towns have made efforts to respond to their changing populations. Beardstown established a dual language program in the mid-2000s. This is an encouraging decision because research shows that dual language programs hold the most promise for Latino students (Salinas 2005). Within this program, students take classes both in English and Spanish, switching languages throughout the day. The program is optional and available for native and non-native Spanish speakers alike. In turn, Monmouth set up a bilingual kindergarten program and has recently hired a bilingual teacher to teach first graders.[24] In addition, both districts offer ESL—English as a Second Language—classes. Thus, both towns have attempted to respond to the needs of growing bilingual populations, although Beardstown has made additional efforts to accommodate students whose first language is not English.[25]

One of the instances of discrimination in schools reported in this research was extremely worrisome. A teacher in Monmouth told a Mexican American child that Mexicans should go back to Mexico because they do not work and Americans pay taxes for them.[26] According to Florencia, her children are humiliated at school, "just because they are Mexican." This is an example of realistic threats in which the prejudice results from actual or perceived threats to the well-being of the host population (Pereira, Vala, and Costa-Lopes 2010; Quillian 2006; Stephan, Ybarra, and Bachman 1999). Apparently, Florencia's child's teacher erroneously believes immigrants do not work and do not pay taxes.[27]

Florencia was particularly upset when she told this story. However, she was also proud of her son because he stood up to his teacher. The child told the teacher that she should support President Obama's plan to give papers to undocumented immigrants so that they can then work and pay taxes. The courage of this child is truly remarkable. Florencia believes discrimination in Monmouth is a serious problem. "Discrimination affects us a great deal; they [Americans] shouldn't discriminate against us in this way," Florencia stated.[28] She also believes that the worse one is treated, the more one should stand up for one's rights. Consequently, the day she can vote, Florencia will vote to support the cause of immigrants living in the United States.

Two other instances of perceived discrimination reported in this research were based on teachers' actions. Juana, for example, reported that her children are not fairly treated at school.[29] On one occasion, her children were playing with some Anglo classmates and the teacher admonished her kids but not the Anglos. Walter also complained about unfair treatment of his nephew at school.[30] Walter's nephew is in a wheelchair and his teacher reprimands him when he is late for school. These two instances of reported discrimination are not as clear-cut as the one described in the previous paragraph. Is Juana's children's teacher seemingly unfair just because she did not notice the Anglo children were also playing? Is she always arbitrary, admonishing some children and not others? Is Walter's nephew's teacher just insensitive to the needs of students with disabilities? It is difficult to know for sure if these are instances of racial or ethnic discrimination.

Finally, one of Karen's classmates openly discriminated against her. He called her a "Wetback-Beaner." "Wetback" is a derogatory term used to refer to immigrants who cross the border through the Rio Grande. It was originally used by the government when through Operation Wetback it deported hundreds of thousands of immigrants back to Mexico in 1954 (Calavita 1994). "Beaner" is another pejorative term used to refer to people of Mexican ancestry or Latinos in general. It is supposed to denote the presence of beans in the traditional Mexican diet. Because of the use of ethnic/racial slurs, this is a case of traditional racism (Akrami, Ekehammar, and Araya 2000). Karen was unable to defend herself from the attack by this student. She just asked him to leave her alone, but he continued to yell at her for a while. One wonders what kind of response Karen would have received from the school had she decided to report this incident to her teachers or school authorities.

Importantly, all the cases of discrimination in schools documented during this research came from the immigrants living in Monmouth. As mentioned, the schools in Beardstown have established a dual language program, but the schools in Monmouth have not. It is possible that the establishment of a dual language program brought a number of professionals to Beardstown who are well-equipped to deal with children of Mexican ancestry and have a good disposition to work with them, thus creating a friendlier environment for immigrant children (Salinas 2005).

One interviewee in the sample felt discriminated against at Saint Alexius Church in Beardstown. Catholic churches in both Beardstown and Monmouth offer services in Spanish. Father Weitzel, now retired, decided to establish a Mass in Spanish when, in the 1990s, he noticed the arrival of Mexican families in the town (Longworth

2009). According to Richard C. Longworth (2009), several people in Beardstown resent Father Weitzel because he welcomed the Hispanic community. More than 350 Hispanics attended Mass in Spanish at Saint Alexius in 2009, compared to only 160 Anglos (Longworth 2009).

Alejandra told me that on one occasion Father Weitzel was saying Mass both in English and Spanish.[31] When praying about different issues, he was reading them aloud in both languages. However, when he prayed for the Hispanic families in the community, he did not translate the prayer into English. Alejandra was unable to understand why, if the priest was praying for "good people," he did not translate it into English. Father Weitzel was an advocate for the Hispanic community and it is not clear if his omission was intentional or not.

The owner of an apartment discriminated against one interviewee in the sample. Discrimination in housing occurs when equally qualified people are treated differently because of their membership in a particular group (Ondrich, Stricker, and Yinger 1999). Although housing discrimination has diminished since the pre–civil rights era, it is still pervasive (Dion 2002; Ondrich, Ross, and Yinger 2000; Ondrich, Stricker, and Yinger 1999). More specifically, discrimination in housing is still a common experience for Blacks and Hispanics (Yinger 1998). In addition, the cost of discrimination is high and constrains the opportunities of Blacks and Hispanics to attend good schools, to find jobs, and to accumulate home equity (Yinger 1998).

Apparently, housing discrimination in Beardstown is now less pervasive than in the past. Eduardo and Sonia arrived in Beardstown in 1992.[32] They were among the first Latino families to arrive in town. They recall meeting only one other Latino in the town. This man was married to an American woman. Upon arrival, Sonia and Eduardo looked for housing. However, when they tried to rent an apartment, the owner told them he did not rent to Mexicans. A family from Texas finally offered them a small apartment on the square, next door to a barbershop. They lived in this apartment for a while until they found another place.

The highest number of instances of discrimination involved the police in both Beardstown and Monmouth. Discrimination by the police occurs when members of a certain group are unfairly treated compared to other groups. A trend toward devolution of responsibilities to local levels has characterized immigration policy in recent years. Between 2005 and 2011, there were 370 local governments that proposed or implemented policies designed to address issues related to undocumented immigration in their local communities (Walker and Leitner 2011). Some scholars are concerned that devolution and the rise of grassroots immigration policies have opened the door to discrimination against foreign citizens (Varsanyi et al. 2012).

State and local authorities can check a person's immigration status, report him or her to Immigration and Customs Enforcement (ICE), or both, when a person is arrested for a violent crime or when he or she is involved in a traffic violation (Varsanyi et al. 2012). To be sure, few local governments check a person's immigration status because of a mere traffic violation (Varsanyi et al. 2012). An announcement by President Obama on November 20, 2014, called for an end to a program called Secure Communities, which allowed local authorities to detain and deport immigrants stopped for minor offenses like traffic violations. Under the new rules, local police will no longer be asked routinely to detain immigrants without papers when they are stopped for such violations.

The local police in Beardstown and Monmouth seem to check immigration statuses for mere traffic violations. Some interviewees complained that in many cases the alleged traffic violations were not real. In addition, in some cases the police checked identifications when there were no alleged traffic violations, although the police are not allowed to ask for identification unless there is suspicion that the person was involved in an illegal activity. For instance, the police stopped Manuel for driving over the white line on the side of the road.[33] According to Manuel, the police frequently stop him for "nothing." María Luisa's husband was pulled over by the police for allegedly not wearing a seat belt.[34] María Luisa believes her husband was wearing a seat belt. As a consequence, María Luisa's husband had to appear before a court in Chicago and was given a year to find an immigration lawyer. After this, María Luisa's husband will be deported if he fails to obtain a visa to work in the United States. The police also stopped Zacarias's wife.[35] When they found out she lacked a driver's license, they reported her to ICE. According to Zacarias, the "Migra" treated his wife much better than the local police did. Further, ICE finally let her go.

Floriberto once had a flat tire when driving with a friend.[36] The police stopped, and instead of offering Floriberto and his friend help, they asked to see their driver's licenses without even asking who was driving the car. This was a case in which no traffic violation took place but the police still asked for identification. On another occasion, Floriberto and his wife were working the night shift at the meat-processing plant and a woman was babysitting for them. When they went to pick up their children after their shift ended, a police car followed them from the babysitter's house to their own. When they arrived at their home, a policeman asked Floriberto if he had been drinking beer. Floriberto replied that he had not. The policeman then said he had followed them because their car's taillight was not working. However, Floriberto said his car's taillight was fine.

"The police are very racist," Alberta stated.[37] She reported that the police stop Hispanics all the time and they treat them poorly. Martín also believed the police are discriminatory and harass immigrants.[38] Helena, the owner of one of the Mexican stores in Monmouth also considers the police to be harsh with immigrants, stopping them frequently.[39] Finally, Isidro said the police stop immigrants all the time, even when they are walking.[40] The police in Beardstown and Monmouth seem to have taken the responsibility of checking immigrants' immigration status "seriously." Further, they check immigrants' identifications even when no traffic violations have been committed.

Discrimination in health care was also a problem in Beardstown and Monmouth, and was reported in 5 percent of the cases. Racial discrimination in health care occurs when membership in a certain racial or ethnic group predicts variations in the health services the members of this group receive (Williams 2006). In addition, ethnic minorities are less likely to be insured and have less access to health services than the White population. Further, discrimination and the stress produced by immigration also impact the psychological health of immigrants (Mossakowski 2003; Rumbaut 1994; Safi 2010; Stein, González, and Huq 2012).

This research showed that immigrants in Beardstown had better access to health care than those in Monmouth. The Cass County Health Department in Beardstown offers a full-service primary care clinic, as well as discounted rates on all of its services for uninsured patients. The Warren County Health Department in Monmouth offers only immunizations, smoking-cessation programs, breast-cancer awareness outreach, and cardiovascular-health awareness outreach. In sum, whereas immigrants in Beardstown can access primary care physicians in town at discounted rates, immigrants in Monmouth need to drive fifteen miles to the nearby town of Galesburg, Illinois, to have access to comparable health services.

Alejandro felt discriminated against when he took his child to the health clinic in Beardstown.[41] On this occasion, the nurse was talking to his child in English, but the child was not answering. "Where was this kid born?" the nurse inquired. Alejandro and his wife replied that their child was born in the United States. "How come he doesn't speak English?" the nurse asked in a rude tone. Alejandro and his wife explained to the nurse that Spanish was the language spoken at home and that their child had little exposure to English. Alejandro felt the nurse was judgmental and that she disapproved of Alejandro's family's language choice.

Ursula also had bad experiences with her health providers, in Monmouth.[42] She explained that she was commonly denied doctor's appointments when pregnant. It is unclear what she meant by "denied" doctor's appointments. One possibility is that Ursula's doctors waited a long time to meet with her. Another, somewhat unlikely, possibility is that she could not get appointments at all throughout her pregnancy. Ursula also stated that somebody searched her purse when she visited her doctor's. Apparently, somebody in her doctor's office believed Ursula had stolen something of value. As these statements show, interactions between immigrants and health professionals in Beardstown and Monmouth were far from ideal.

Finally, 12.5 percent of the interviewees in this research felt discriminated against by the local population. This finding mirrors previous research showing that even though America considers itself to be a country of immigrants, it still discriminates against certain immigrant groups. This discrimination occurs because Americans have conflicting views about immigrants and immigration (Stephan, Ybarra, and Bachman 1999). In this sense, the idea of being a country of immigrants is at odds with assumptions that immigrants take jobs away from Americans, lower the wages of the native population, add to the population living in poverty, and compete for public services (Espenshade 1995).

Several factors have contributed to the rise of public opinion against immigration, including fear associated with economic insecurity and concerns with immigrants' undesirable cultural traits (Espenshade 1995; Stephan, Ybarra, and Bachman 1999; Zick, Pettigrew, and Wagner 2008). In addition, public views about immigration have been related to the allegedly rising numbers of undocumented immigrants (Dovidio et al. 2010; Espenshade 1995).

Some authors argue that expressions of racial/ethnic prejudice have become subtler over time (Akrami, Ekehammar, and Araya 2000). Maybe this is the type of discrimination Isidro was referring to when he stated, "Americans treat me like I shouldn't be here."[43] Apparently, Americans in Monmouth have not told him anything offensive, but he still feels unwelcome. However, instances of open discrimination still exist. Karen[44] came to live in Monmouth when she was twelve and she still feels like a stranger. On one occasion, she was just walking around town and somebody told her "go back to your country." When she heard this offensive remark, she just kept walking.

Floriberto[45] and Eduardo[46] believe discrimination in Beardstown is less pronounced now than it was in the past. After the incident in which a Latino allegedly killed an Anglo-American and the Latino bar on the square was burned, relations between Latinos and Anglos were very tense for a period of time. On that occasion, the city government gathered some community leaders to defuse the ethnic tensions between Anglos and Hispanics. Over time, the relationship between the two groups seemed to improve. For example, Eduardo used to be afraid of going to the park because Anglos would damage Latinos' car tires and windshields; however, Eduardo can be around town without fear now. Floriberto also agrees that the town seems to have become increasingly used to the idea of immigration.

Discrimination in Beardstown and Monmouth

Discrimination has a powerful impact on the lives of immigrants, affecting their chances for getting jobs, succeeding in school, and having a good quality of life. This research suggests that discrimination in Beardstown and Monmouth is pervasive and constitutes a barrier to the incorporation of immigrants. Further, immigrants in these two towns feel discrimination is a problem and are more likely to have had a close experience with discrimination than Latino immigrants in a national sample. Thus, it is possible that discrimination in new destinations of immigration may be more pronounced than in other areas more accustomed to the idea of immigration.

The results also revealed differences between Beardstown and Monmouth. Immigrants in Beardstown feel less accepted by Anglos, believe discrimination is a bigger problem, and are more likely to have had a close experience with discrimination than immigrants in Monmouth. Possibly, the history of Beardstown as a sundown town, coupled with the racial tensions originating from violence and arson, explain this difference. Moreover, discrimination in schools was reported in Beardstown but not in Monmouth. However, Beardstown also offers better education and health services for the Latino population.

In this investigation of the factors shaping the feelings of acceptance, perceptions of discrimination, and experiences with discrimination among immigrants in Beardstown and Monmouth, different indicators of social class were associated with the different variables under analysis (Portes, Nash Parker, and Cobas 1980; Shorey, Cowan, and Sullivan 2002). For instance, those with higher incomes tended to feel more accepted by Anglos. The effect of income and education on perceptions of discrimination as a major problem and on direct experience with discrimination requires further research because the models showed no significant results for these variables.

I also found evidence that discrimination can present a threat to group identity, making people increasingly turn toward their own ethnic group (Goto, Gee, and Takeuchi 2002; Verkuyten 2008; Waters 1994). For instance, immigrants who felt accepted by Anglos also felt less connected to other Latinos in the country. In turn, although these findings may require further research, respondents who believed discrimination was a larger problem and those with a close experience with discrimination were more likely to feel more connected to other Latinos. Thus, it may be that discrimination can have bonding results by turning people toward their own ethnic group.

The findings showed that those who attended social functions with Anglos were also more likely to feel accepted by Anglos. This finding is consistent with the research that shows that contact among different ethnic groups can increase understanding and tolerance among them (Goto, Gee, and Takeuchi 2002; Phinney, Madden, and Santos 1998; Rakosi Rosenbloom and Way 2004). It also offers hope for a continued improvement in relationships between Anglos and Hispanics based on continued interactions between the two groups.

Discrimination is not necessarily based on racial/ethnic categories (Alba 2005; Foner and Alba 2008; Rakosi Rosenbloom and Way 2004). Poor language skills, for instance, were also a source of discrimination (Rakosi Rosenbloom and Way 2004). This study found that those with better language skills were more likely to feel accepted by Anglos. When immigrants arrive in a country, they need to learn the local language, and the ability to communicate effectively in the local language is crucial for incorporation (Ager and Strang 2008; Gerstle 2010; Padilla 2006; Padilla and Perez 2003; Schleef and Cavalcanti 2009).

Finally, assimilation can also influence perceptions of discrimination, and people who are more assimilated into the host society may exhibit lower levels of perceived discrimination (Portes, Nash Parker, and Cobas 1980). For this reason, the length of stay in the country could be associated with increased feelings of acceptance by Anglo-Americans, and with the perceptions and experiences of discrimination. As expected, people who had been in the country longer felt more accepted by Anglo-Americans.

Interviewees indicated that they or a member of their family experienced discrimination at workplaces, restaurants and stores, schools, church, and housing complexes. Interviewees also reported instances of discrimination in their interactions with police, health care providers, and members of the community. Although discrimination experiences in these two towns were comparable, discrimination in schools was more pervasive in Monmouth than in Beardstown. It is possible that the lack of a dual language program in the former town explains the poorer experience students have (Salinas 2005). Moreover, the case of discrimination in Monmouth by classmates involved the use of racial slurs to discriminate against a Latino student, hinting that some traditional racist ideas may be present in this community (Akrami, Ekehammar, and Araya 2000).

Finally, the racist history of Beardstown, along with the ethnic tensions resulting from the violent death of a White resident probably made discrimination by the general population in this town more pervasive than in Monmouth for several years. However, relations between Anglos and Latinos in Beardstown seem to be improving. The community leaders addressed this problem in the past, and some religious communities seem to be working toward the incorporation of the different groups that live there. Hopefully, relationships among the different ethnic groups will continue to improve in Beardstown.

CHAPTER 5

The Politics of Incorporation

Participation

The more one is mistreated, the more one should vote.

—Florencia, interview with the author, July 30, 2011, Monmouth, Illinois

POLITICAL PARTICIPATION AND CIVIC ENGAGEMENT ARE IMPORTANT INDICATORS of the political incorporation of immigrants (Black 2011; DeSipio 2011; Hochschild and Mollenkopf 2009; Jones-Correa 2004; Schleef and Cavalcanti 2009). Through participation, people can have input into the political system (Hochschild and Mollenkopf 2009). As the following life stories show, immigrants in Beardstown and Monmouth participated in a variety of social and political activities.

Gustavo lives in Beardstown.[1] He first came to the United States in 1991, after crossing the border through Tijuana-San Ysidro with the help of a *coyote*. Gustavo believes *coyotes* were sexually abusing women while they were crossing, when they were taking them behind the hills. "I couldn't do anything; we all take care of ourselves," Gustavo recounted.[2] He believes women should not cross the border alone.

Gustavo spent many years traveling back and forth between Mexico and the

United States (Massey and Capoferro 2008). During that time, he worked collecting strawberries in Santa Maria, California, between the months of May and October. In 2000, he moved to Missouri and later to Beardstown. "Once you buy the house, have the kid, fix the house, you get motivated to stay," Gustavo explained. His hope is to be able to put his children through college.

Gustavo has a green card he obtained through his father, who became a legal resident through the 1986 IRCA programs. Gustavo has nine siblings and most of them immigrated to the United States. Their mother, however, stayed in Mexico until 1994. Nowadays, Gustavo's parents live part of the time in Mexico and part of the time in the United States. They like Mexico a lot, but Gustavo's father periodically travels to the United States for his doctor's visits.

Gustavo had bad experiences with discrimination. On one occasion, he was driving to Springfield, Illinois, with his friend Jorge and they got a flat tire. The police stopped, but instead of offering to help, they asked to see IDs, without even asking who had been driving the car. Gustavo and Jorge were able to avoid deportation because they have papers. Others have not been this lucky.

Gustavo is active in the community. For example, he volunteers time to help the teacher at his children's school. He also participates in a local organization called Amigos Unidos (United Friends). This organization is led by Julio Flores, a local resident from El Salvador who works at the local school as a liaison with the Latino community. Amigos Unidos helps organize the celebrations for Cinco de Mayo and Mexican Independence Day. The organization collects money from local businesses to hire mariachis, dance groups, and other entertainment. At the same time, it nominates candidates for a pageant that takes place during the Mexican Independence Day celebrations.

Helena lives in Monmouth, and her life story is different from those of most immigrants interviewed for this study. Helena arrived in Galesburg, Illinois, in 1989 to work on her master's degree at a local university. Soon after, she met her current husband while attending a Mass at the Catholic Church in Monmouth. Because Helena's husband is American, she was able to obtain permanent residency with no problem after she got married.

While in the United States, Helena missed the food from Mexico, and so did the twenty other Hispanic families that lived in Monmouth by 1989. Helena then decided to order different food products from Mexico and sell them to the growing Latino community. "I would deliver the food to people's houses because I knew all the addresses of the local Latino residents,"[3] Helena explained. As this business grew bigger, Helena and her husband decided to open a Mexican store in town. Although the store no longer has a restaurant, it is still a popular stop for immigrants who want to buy groceries and other Mexican products, cash checks, send money to Mexico, and buy calling cards.

At first, Helena cooked at the store. The business hours were very demanding and Helena worked between 8:00 a.m. and 10:00 p.m. for several years. After she had children and got too busy with them to work such long hours, she rented the restaurant space to independent cooks. Helena now has a couple of employees and visits the store several times a day to supervise them.

Not only was Helena busy with the business, but she also became involved with community activities. For several years, she and her husband organized the local celebrations for Cinco de Mayo and Mexican Independence. These celebrations featured Mexican food, dance groups, various invited speakers, and a pageant. Although these celebrations were well attended and warmly received by the local Mexican community, Helena got discouraged over the years and stopped organizing them. According to her, the organization of these events was very time consuming and people did not want to contribute money to share the cost.

Helena is very concerned with the situation of immigrants in Monmouth. She explained that the police harass immigrants all the time. According to Helena, this harassment, such as with traffic tickets, may be a way for the local government to raise more money. Helena believes people looking for better lives in the United States deserve a chance, and therefore she participates in marches to support immigration reform. "Being an immigrant is hard; you have to give up a lot of things," Helena explained.[4]

As these stories show, both Jorge and Helena are active members in the societies in which they live. Jorge participated in the organization called Amigos Unidos, and Helena helped organize different festivities for several years. Immigrants of recent arrival are not able to vote because it takes a minimum of seven years to become a citizen. What, then, is the political role of close to 40 million foreign-born people who live in the United States? This research argues that participation in different social and political activities other than voting can turn immigrants into engaged and productive members of society.

It is possible to assess the degree of political incorporation of immigrants by exploring their contribution to different social and political activities, including participating in a church or religious group; volunteering time to a school, neighborhood, or community group; being part of a group representing Mexicans or Latinos; contacting a public official; volunteering time or making a contribution to a political campaign; attending a public meeting or demonstration; registering to vote; and voting in a U.S. election.

Social and Political Participation

Latinos represent a key voting bloc (Djupe and Neiheisel 2012). Besides voting and holding office, immigrants can participate in different social and political activities. This participation can predispose citizens to voting (Verba, Schlozman, and Brady 1995). Further, active and engaged members of society foster effective governments (Putnam 1993). The involvement of immigrants in the political arena can also make the political system responsive to their needs. In this sense, political incorporation can be defined as "the extent to which group interests are effectively represented in policy making" (Hochschild and Mollenkopf 2009, 15).

Social Participation

Upon arrival in a country, immigrants are presented with a number of opportunities to participate in different social activities. Churches, for example, offer various advantages to newly arrived immigrants, in that they provide spiritual support and social networks immigrants can rely on for their incorporation into the host society. Importantly, participation in political activities can increase with the frequency of attendance at religious services (Djupe and Neiheisel 2012; Kam, Zechmeister, and Wilking 2008; Stoll and Wong 2007). Although not everyone is religious, only 4 percent of the survey respondents reported having no religion; 83 percent of them were Catholic, 6 percent were Protestant, and another 7 percent professed other religions.

Saint Alexius Catholic Church and Immaculate Conception Catholic Church, in Beardstown and Monmouth respectively, offer Masses in Spanish, thus providing an important space for immigrants who lack English language skills. Other churches also serve the Latino communities in Beardstown and Monmouth. For example, the churches Nazarene, De Restauración Cristo te Ama, Ebenezer Encuentro con Dios, and Nueva Vida offer services for Spanish speakers in Beardstown. The Solid Rock Apostolic Church offered Spanish services in Monmouth. Unfortunately, the community in Monmouth has fewer religious services that target the Latino population.

Because many immigrants have school-age children, schools are also one of the first institutions within which immigrants come into contact. In addition, schools encourage parents' involvement in school life through their participation in Parent Teacher Associations (PTAs) or Parent Teacher Organizations (PTOs) and other volunteer opportunities. Decades of research suggest that parent involvement is linked to student retention and achievement (Kuperminc, Darnell, and Álvarez-Jiménez 2008; Shah 2009). However, researchers have found that parents of racially, ethnically, and linguistically diverse students often fail to participate in school activities (Shah 2009). Further, the high rates of academic failure and dropout rates among Latino students should be a cause of concern for academics and practitioners alike (Hill and Torres 2010; Kuperminc, Darnell, and Álvarez-Jiménez 2008).

The networks of trust and support built by individuals can have an impact on their incorporation into the host society (Jackson 2009; Lim 2008; Ramakrishnan and Viramontes 2010; Rocha and Espino 2010; Staton, Jackson, and Canache 2007). The role of family members and the ethnic community in helping newcomers to find employment and housing, as well as other opportunities for their incorporation into society, is well documented (Gidengil and Stolle 2009). Different groups gather immigrants for different purposes. For example, Amigos Unidos in Beardstown is a group that organizes the celebration of Cinco de Mayo and Mexican Independence Day. In addition, it invites speakers to address different topics of interest to the community. The Hispanic community in Monmouth seems less organized. The store La Pequeñita organized the celebrations for Cinco de Mayo and Mexican Independence Day for some years, but Helena, profiled earlier in this chapter, gave up on this task. At one point, Monmouth had an AmeriCorps volunteer who offered a variety of community services for the Hispanic community, but after he left, nobody seems to have taken on this task.

Three variables in this study reflected volunteer participation in churches

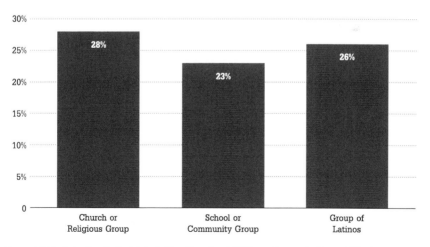

Figure 16. Participation in Social Activities: Sample of 260 Interviewees in Central Illinois

Table 8. Logistic Regression Models for Social Participation: Sample of 260 Interviewees in Central Illinois (Standard Errors in Parentheses)

Variable	Exp(B)					
	Length of Stay	Gender	Education	Employment Status	Income	Nagelkerke R Square
Church or Religious Group	1.05 (.02)†	.76 (.35)	2.35 (.33)*	.74 (.39)	1.60 (.35)	.10
School or Neighborhood Group	1.03 (.02)	.95 (.36)	1.35 (.35)	1.26 (.43)	1.63 (.36)	.04
Organization Nationality or Ethnic Group	1.00 (.02)	1.10 (.36)	1.63 (.34)	2.22 (.43)*	1.51 (.37)	.05

$* p < 0.1$ $† p < 0.05$ $‡ p < 0.01$

or religious groups, schools, neighborhood or community groups, and groups representing Mexicans or Latinos. These questions asked, "In the past year have you volunteered your time to any church or religious group?"; "In the past year have you volunteered your time to any school, or neighborhood or community group?"; and "In the past year have you volunteered your time to any organization representing your own particular nationality or ethnic or racial group?" The possible answers were no or yes. As figure 16 shows, immigrants participated in these activities in significant numbers. Some 28 percent of respondents volunteered time to a church or religious group, 23 percent to a school or neighborhood or community group, and 26 percent to a group representing Mexicans or Latinos.

A purpose of this research was to determine if social class affected the political incorporation of immigrants in Central Illinois, and if a connection exists between political incorporation and gender or length of stay in the country.[5] The logistic regressions showed that certain indicators of social class were associated with social participation (table 8). Specifically, more-educated immigrants were more likely to participate in a church or religious group, and those who worked full-time were more likely to participate in a group representing Mexicans or Latinos. In turn, length of stay in the country significantly predicted participation in a church or religious group, with those who had been in the country longer being more likely to participate in them.

Political Participation

Political participation can be defined as an activity that has the intent or effect of influencing government action. This definition includes forms of participation that are voluntary and not for pay (Verba, Schlozman, and Brady 1995). Citizens and non-citizens alike can have input into the political system in different ways. For instance, people can contact a public official. A public official, broadly defined, is a person holding public office, and may be either elected or appointed. People can contact a public official for a variety of reasons, including filing a report, expressing concerns, or supporting or opposing a potential government decision or bill. Contacting a public official can be an important way to have input into the political process.

Some persons with clear political preferences may participate in political campaigns, either by volunteering time or contributing money. Political campaigns are central in the political process, and in recent decades they have become more expensive than at any other time in history (Open Secrets 2012). Politicians at the federal, state, and local levels see campaigns as important means for mobilizing support behind them and their causes. Although anyone can volunteer time to help during a campaign, immigrants need to at least be lawful permanent residents to be able to contribute money to a candidate running for office at the federal level (Federal Election Commission n.d.).

Regardless of their citizenship, people can also participate in a public meeting. Several states have open public meetings acts requiring that all meetings of governing bodies be open and accessible to the public. A meeting can include any situation in which a majority of a city council, board of county commissioners, or other governing body meets and discusses the business of that body (MRSC 2014). In order to be valid, ordinances, resolutions, rules, regulations, orders, and directives must be adopted at public meetings. The Illinois Open Meetings Act requires public bodies to hold open meetings, provide the public with adequate notice of meeting times, and keep records of public meetings. Thus, people have opportunities to offer input into the political process at public meetings.

Another avenue of expression open to noncitizens is participation in demonstrations. Demonstrations or protests are important for democratic countries because they offer a space for public expression of concerns to groups that otherwise are excluded from the political process. The history of Latino protest movements in the United States is rich. In the 1960s and 1970s, for instance, many Latinos organized and protested against police brutality and limited educational opportunities, and for higher wages and greater political rights, building a movement that continues to have an impact in the present (Shaw 2008). In 2006, thousands of Latinos participated in protests in cities across the country against U.S. House Bill 4437. This bill would have allowed the government to aggressively track undocumented immigrants and impose penalties on people who assisted them. After this first wave of protests, immigration reform rallies became common. Since then, Latino participation in protests has reached areas that previously were not politically mobilized (Barreto et al. 2009; Benjamin-Alvarado, DeSipio, and Montoya 2009).

Unfortunately, far too few people participate in electoral politics, and those who participate are not representative of the overall population (Callahan 2007).

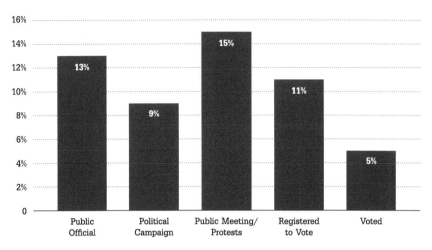

Figure 17. Participation in Political Activities: Sample of 260 Interviewees in Central Illinois

For instance, racial and ethnic minority populations vote at lower numbers than the general population (Martínez 2008). Given their numbers, Mexican Americans have the potential to be an important political force in the United States (Kam, Zechmesiter, and Wilking 2008). Fortunately, the rates of registration and voting are growing among Latinos (DeSipio 2011). Moreover, a few small cities allow noncitizens to vote in local elections, including Cambridge and Amherst, Massachusetts, and Takoma Park, Maryland. In most cases, however, immigrants need to naturalize before they are able to vote.

This chapter analyzes the five forms of political participation described above, namely, contacting a public official, volunteering time or contributing to a political campaign, participating in a public meeting or demonstration, registering to vote, and voting in an election. The questions on political participation asked were: "In the United States, in the past year have you contacted an elected official?"; "In the United States, in the past year have you volunteered time for a political candidate or made a contribution to a political campaign?"; "In the past year have you participated in a public meeting or demonstration?"; "Are you registered to vote?"; "Have you ever voted in an election in the United States?"; and the possible responses were no or yes. As figure 17 shows, 13 percent of respondents contacted an elected official, 9 percent volunteered time to a political candidate or made a contribution to a political campaign, 15 percent attended a public meeting or demonstration, 11 percent were registered to vote, and 5 percent had voted in an election in the United States.

A purpose of this study is to investigate whether the level of incorporation of

Table 9. Logistic Regression Models for Political Participation: Sample of 260 Interviewees in Central Illinois (Standard Errors in Parentheses)

Variable	Length of Stay	Gender	Education	Employment Status	Income	Nagelkerke R Square
	Exp(B)					
Contacted a Public Official	1.05 (.03)*	1.38 (.46)	1.10 (.45)	.76 (.50)	1.00 (.47)	.04
Contributed Campaign	1.02 (.03)	1.37 (.52)	2.34 (.48)*	2.71 (.69)	1.04 (.53)	.06
Public Meeting or Protest	.98 (.03)	.52 (.46)	1.28 (.40)	1.25 (.51)	.63 (.49)	.05
Registered to Vote	1.02 (.03)	.73 (.53)	1.59 (.48)	3.28 (.79)	1.52 (.50)	.07
Voted	1.03 (.04)	1.08 (.68)	1.81 (.65)	3.21 (1.11)	3.45 (.68)*	.06

$* p < 0.1$ $\dagger p < 0.05$ $\ddagger p < 0.01$

immigrants is linked to social class, length of stay in the country, and/or gender. The logistic regression analysis showed that more-educated participants were more likely to volunteer time or make a contribution to a political campaign, and that those with higher incomes were more likely to vote (table 9). Thus, this evidence suggests that some forms of political incorporation may be associated with social class. At the same time, those who had been in the country longer were also more likely to have contacted a public official.

Other Factors Explaining Social and Political Participation

Studies attempting to understand the factors that make people more likely to participate have shaped the political-science literature for decades. For instance, most scholars agree that individuals with higher income and higher education levels (Socio-Economic Status Model) are more likely to participate in social and political activities (Barreto and Muñoz 2003; Downs 1957; Jang 2009; Junn 1999; Leighley and Nagler 1992; Leighley and Vedlitz 1999; Tam Cho 1999; Verba and Nie 1972; Verba, Schlozman, and Brady 1995; Wolfinger and Rosenstone 1980). For this reason, the analyses described in this section included income and education as independent variables.[6] (For coding of variables, see appendix.)

However, the effect of income can be outweighed by other individual factors. For instance, certain individual attitudes can influence both social and political behavior (Abrahamson and Aldrich 1982; Albarracín and Valeva 2011; Bevelander and Pendakor 2009; Brehm and Rahn 1997; Cook and Gronke 2005; Espinal, Hartlyn, and Kelly 2006; Guterbock and London 1983; Hetherington 1999; Verba, Schlozman, and Brady 1995). For example, the degree to which people believe the government cannot be trusted to do what is right can affect their participation. Although the influence of trust in government on participation is sometimes mixed (for instance, see Guterbock and London 1983; Leal 2002; Marshall 2001), declining levels of trust in government can contribute to lower levels of participation (Hetherington 1998). Thus, the analyses presented here included a classical political-science variable on trust in the federal government as an independent variable. (For details about this variable, see appendix.)

The extent to which people pay attention to politics and government affairs also influences their level of participation. "Citizens who are interested in politics—who follow politics, who care about what happens, who are concerned with who wins and who loses—are more politically active" (Verba, Schlozman, and Brady 1995, 345). Thus, being politically interested or knowledgeable enhances the chances that an individual will be active in political activities (Albarracín, Wang, and Albarracín 2012; Leighley and Vedlitz 1999; Verba, Schlozman, and Brady 1995). The effect of interest in politics and government can also extend its influence to social participation. An indicator of interest in politics was included in this study's analyses. This indicator captures the attention paid by respondents to politics and government. (For details about this variable, see appendix.)

In turn, other attitudes like party identification and ideology can influence a person's likelihood to participate (Albarracín and Valeva 2011; Beck 2002; Weisberg 2002). Ideology and party identification can serve as reference groups, providing clear and discernible cues guiding citizens' orientations (Jacoby 2003). Overall, those who have a partisan affiliation may be more interested in participating than those who lack a party identification (Albarracín and Valeva 2011). Consequently, this study included an indicator of partisanship (non-partisans versus partisans) in the analyses.

People's awareness of their disadvantaged group status can influence participation as well (Verba and Nie 1972). Defined as the "identification with a group and a political awareness or ideology regarding the group's relative position in society" (Lien 1994, 243), this sense of group consciousness can derive from pressures exerted on group members by outsiders (Marshall 2001), or from interactions with formal and informal ethnic networks (Dawson 2001). In an effort to compensate for their inability to acquire skills and resources, ethnic minorities exaggerate certain behaviors such as participation in the political process (Marshall 2001). Discrimination can increase the sense of group consciousness. For this reason, the study included a variable reflecting whether the respondent or a member of his family had experienced discrimination as proxy for group consciousness.

Social capital can bring about more democratic and effective political institutions (Brehm and Rahn 1997; Halpern 2005; Putnam 1993, 2000). Robert Putnam defined social capital as the "features of social organization, such as trust, norms and networks that can improve efficiency of society by facilitating coordinated actions" (1993, 167). The literature has discussed whether all types of social capital are beneficial for social cooperation (Portes 1998; Putnam 2000; Woolcock and Narayan 2000). Putnam distinguished between bridging and bonding social capital. Bridging social capital consists of norms/networks "that are outward looking and encompass people across diverse cleavages" and bonding social capital of norms/ networks that are "inward looking [and] tend to enforce exclusive identities and homogenous groups" (Putnam 2000, 22). Hypothetically, bridging social capital is more likely to foster engagement and participation than bonding social capital (Putnam 2000).

Thus, I used this study to explore the role of the two forms of social capital in increasing participation. To represent bridging social capital, it included variables reflecting the extent to which Latinos felt their life has to do with the lives of Anglos or African Americans (norms) and attended social functions with Anglos (networks). For bonding social capital, the study included indicators assessing the degree to which people felt their life has some or a lot to do with the lives of Hispanics or Latinos in the rest of the country (Sánchez and Morin 2011). (For details about this variable, please see appendix.)

The logistic regression analysis used to examine the factors shaping social and political participation showed interesting results. To begin with, the inclusion of individual characteristics beyond income and education seemed to outweigh the effects of some of the latter variables. More specifically, when the additional variables reflecting attitudes, party identification, experience with discrimination, and social capital were added in the analyses, the influence of education and income on social participation disappeared (table 10). Thus, political variables seem to outweigh the effect of education. As for political participation, even though the effect of income on voting disappeared, education continued to predict voter registration. Those with higher education levels were more likely to be registered to vote (table 11).

Paying attention to politics and government affairs was a major factor in predicting both social and political participation. For instance, those who paid more attention to politics and government were more likely to volunteer time to a church or religious group, and to a school or neighborhood group (table 10). In addition, these persons were more likely to contact a public official (table 11). Thus, paying attention to politics and government affairs predisposed people to participating in both social and political activities (Leighley and Vedlitz 1999; Verba, Schlozman, and Brady 1995).

Several indicators of social capital predicted participation in social and political activities. Those who felt connected to African Americans were more likely to volunteer time to a school or neighborhood organization (table 10), and those who

Table 10. Logistic Regression Models for Social Participation with Political Variables: Sample of 260 Interviewees in Central Illinois (Standard Errors in Parentheses)

Variable	Exp(B)		
	Church or Religious Group	School or Neighborhood Group	Organization, Nationality, or Ethnic Group
Education	2.07 (.56)	1.02 (.52)	1.18 (.51)
Income	1.84 (.60)	1.76 (.58)	2.26 (.56)
Trust in Government	1.54 (.35)	.90 (.35)	.96 (.33)
Attention to Politics	2.30 (.40)†	1.87 (.38)*	2.09 (.40)
Party Affiliation	.62 (.45)	1.21 (.43)	1.10 (.43)
Discrimination	1.08 (.52)	1.20 (.50)	1.81 (.48)
Linked Fates with Anglos	1.58 (.33)	.61 (.32)	1.12 (.32)
Linked Fates with Afros	1.20 (.30)	1.76 (.31)*	1.07 (.29)
Social Functions	2.18 (.26)‡	1.61 (.24)†	1.28 (.24)
Linked Fates with Latinos	.63 (.32)	.91 (.29)	.97 (.30)
Nagelkerke R Square	.39	.21	.17

* $p < 0.1$ † $p < 0.05$ ‡ $p < 0.01$

Table 11. Logistic Regression Models for Political Participation with Political Variables: Sample of 260 Interviewees in Central Illinois (Standard Errors in Parentheses)

Variable	Exp(B)				
	Contacted a Public Official	Contributed Campaign	Public Meeting or Demonstration	Registered to Vote	Voted
Education	.56 (.73)	1.94 (.78)	.63 (.63)	4.36 (.81)*	.51 (1.15)
Income	.99 (.78)	.43 (1.00)	.32 (.80)	2.10 (.89)	4.29 (1.21)
Trust in Government	.88 (.49)	2.04 (.55)	.95 (.38)	1.68 (.51)	1.26 (.62)
Attention to Politics	3.71 (.59)†	1.55 (.56)	.94 (.44)	.98 (.63)	.62 (.80)
Party Affiliation	.73 (.60)	1.66 (.69)	.64 (.55)	1.56 (.73)	.51 (1.01)
Discrimination	2.82 (.70)	.45 (.82)	1.54 (.58)	1.66 (.80)	.68 (1.00)
Linked Fates with Anglos	2.30 (.48)*	1.58 (.59)	1.89 (.42)	2.97 (.56)†	2.74 (.78)
Linked Fates with Afros	.61 (.48)	1.61 (.46)	.61 (.39)	.59 (.49)	.81 (71)
Social Functions	2.51 (.36)‡	1.86 (.40)	2.11 (.30)‡	1.19 (.40)	.97 (.62)
Linked Fates with Latinos	1.03 (.43)	1.24 (.57)	1.30 (.36)	.62 (.52)	1.63 (.76)
Nagelkerke R Square	.36	.28	.19	.23	.26

* $p < 0.1$ † $p < 0.05$ ‡ $p < 0.01$

felt connected to Anglo-Americans were more likely to contact a public official and to be registered to vote (table 11). Thus, a sense of connectedness with people outside the respondent's ethnic group disposed people to participating in selected social and political activities (Putnam 2000).

Moreover, the networks built by immigrants with people outside their own ethnic group (Putnam 2000) were more likely to influence their participation than any other variable. In this sense, those who attended social functions with Anglo-Americans were more likely to volunteer time to a church or religious group and to a school or neighborhood organization, and to contact a public official and participate in a public meeting or demonstration (tables 10 and 11). In sum, both perceptions of connectedness and actual connections with members of other ethnic groups enhanced participation.

Differences in Participation between Beardstown and Monmouth

The existence of dissimilar levels of political incorporation between immigrants in these two towns became apparent during the analysis of the data. Specifically, immigrants in Beardstown participated at higher rates than immigrants in Monmouth in most activities. For example, when it came to social activities, 35 percent of immigrants in Beardstown volunteered time to a religious group, while this number for Monmouth was 22 percent. The differences between Beardstown and Monmouth were less pronounced in terms of those who volunteered time to a school or neighborhood organization (26 percent versus 21 percent) and a group representing Mexicans or Latinos (30 percent versus 25 percent).

The rates for participation in political activities also differed between the two towns. For example, whereas 24 percent of immigrants in Beardstown had contacted a public official, this number for Monmouth was 4 percent. Differences in participation rates between Beardstown and Monmouth also occurred for participation in a political campaign (14 percent versus 5 percent) and in a public meeting or demonstration (20 percent versus 10 percent). Conversely, the number of people who were registered to vote and had voted in an election in the United States was slightly higher for Monmouth (12 percent and 6 percent) than for Beardstown (10 percent and 4 percent).

The logistic regression analyses (tables 8 and 9) showed that those who had been in the country longer were also more likely to volunteer time to a church or religious group or to contact a public official. One possible explanation for the higher participation rates for most activities in Beardstown may be that the community in Monmouth is of more recent settlement than the one in Beardstown. Whereas the average length of stay in the country among the respondents in Beardstown was 11.04 years, this number for Monmouth was 10.50. However, the difference in the average length of stay between the two towns is not statistically significant.

Education and income were also positively associated with several forms of participation (tables 8 and 9), and the education and income levels were higher among immigrants in Beardstown than in Monmouth. For example, whereas 64 percent of immigrants in Beardstown had only a middle school education or less, in Monmouth it was 68 percent. In turn, 29 percent of immigrants in Beardstown had an income of $30,000 or less, while in Monmouth 34 percent were in that income category. However, these differences were minor and may not explain the different levels of participation among the two towns.

A number of other factors were also significant in predicting social and political participation (tables 10 and 11). For instance, those who paid more attention to politics and government affairs were more likely to participate in a number of social and political activities. According to the survey with 260 participants, immigrants in Beardstown paid more attention to politics and government affairs than those in Monmouth. Specifically, whereas only 5 percent of immigrants in Beardstown reported paying no attention to politics and government, this number for Monmouth was 15 percent. Thus, the level of attention to politics and government affairs may explain the higher rates of participation for most activities in Beardstown.

Immigrants who felt connected to Anglos or African Americans were also likely to participate in a number of activities. Thus, it was interesting to explore if differences in the sense of connectedness with Anglos and African Americans were apparent between the two towns. Overall, analyses showed that immigrants in Beardstown had a stronger sense of connectedness with both Anglos and African Americans. For example, 65 percent of immigrants in Beardstown thought what happens to Anglos had some or a lot to do with their lives, but just 49 percent in Monmouth felt the same. In turn, whereas 41 percent of immigrants in Beardstown thought what happens to African Americans had some or a lot to do with their lives, this number for Monmouth was 32 percent. However, the degree to which immigrants attended social functions with Anglo-Americans was similar in both towns. More specifically, almost half of respondents in both towns somewhat or completely agreed with the statement "I attend social functions with Anglos."

Other Attitudes and Beliefs

This study argues that the attitudes and beliefs about the different outcomes considered as part of the incorporation process will influence immigrant behavior

(Albarracín, Johnson, and Zanna 2005; Alba and Nee 2003; De Souza Briggs 2013; Waters and Jimenez 2005). In general, the attitudes toward participating in different social and political activities were positive, and several interviewees expressed an interest in participating more. However, a handful of respondents seemed to lack the disposition for participation. Gabriela, for instance, explained that she failed to participate because the thought did not cross her mind.[7] Walter stated, "I don't participate because I don't give [participation] the attention it deserves."[8] Or in the words of Hilda, "I get conformist but I should fight more."[9] As these statements show, a few respondents acknowledged paying little attention to participation, although two of them clearly thought participating was important. As Martín put it, "We [Latinos] only get interested in things when there's an emergency; otherwise, we don't participate."[10]

Nonetheless, several interviewees lamented not having more time or better language skills to be able to participate more. Further, interviewees showed positive attitudes toward voting even though only 9 percent of them were citizens and therefore able to vote. For example, Leo, referring to voting, stated, "The day I can vote I will vote for one of the two political parties because voting is very important; they need to know one is here [in the United States]."[11] This comment makes clear that Leo thought voting is an important way in which Mexican immigrants in the United States can be "noted" and eventually heard in the political system.

People's belief in the degree to which the government can be trusted can have an impact on participation (Guterbock and London 1983; Hetherington 1999; Verba, Schlozman, and Brady 1995). Particularly, people who trust the government more may also be more likely to participate in the political system. However, the effect of trust in government can sometimes be mixed (for instance, see Guterbock and London 1983; Leal 2002; Marshall 2001). For example, those who feel the government fails to represent them may be compelled to participate more in the political system. Although the indicator of trust in government was not significant in the logistic regression analyses, it is interesting to explore the direction of the relationship between trust and participation. As tables 10 and 11 show, the effect of trust on participation was mixed. Whereas trust in government had a positive impact on participation in half of the activities considered, it had a negative one on the rest of them. More specifically, trust in government increased participation in a church or religious group and in a political campaign, and boosted the chances that a person would be registered to vote or have voted in an election.

The connection between trust in government and participation also became apparent during the interviews. Several people believed that a sense of trust in government is a necessary condition for voting. For example, Zacarías stated, "The less I trust the government, the less I will vote."[12] In the words of Teodoro, "The lack of trust in the government wouldn't help me to vote; I would vote if I believed the government would do something."[13] Gabriel held the same view. "If I trusted the government more I would be more likely to vote because maybe my vote would help elect somebody who would do things differently."[14] People's commitment to participation was not unconditional, but dependent on the degree to which they felt they could trust the government in Washington, D.C., to do what is right.

Opportunities for Participation

This study contends that the availability of opportunities and resources to immigrants or the lack thereof can shape their process of incorporation into society (De Souza Briggs 2013; Portes and Böröcz 1989; Portes and Rumbaut 2001; Portes and Zhou 1993, 1994). Consequently, the availability of opportunities for participation in social and political activities can shape the process of political incorporation. Immigrants in this study found plenty of opportunities for participation in activities that do not require citizenship or permanent residency: volunteering time to a church or religious group, a school or neighborhood organization, or a group representing Latinos or Mexicans; contacting a public official; and attending a public meeting or demonstration.

For example, immigrants participated in numerous church activities. Catholic churches rely on a number of volunteers to help during Mass: at least two people to read, two to help with the offering plate (a plate passed around for people to donate money), and from two to four to help with Communion. In addition, a group of people may be in charge of playing music and/or participating in the church choir. Some of the respondents in this study seemed to be volunteering time to fulfill these roles. Irma, for example, acts as a lay Eucharistic minister and assists the priest in administering Communion during Mass.[15] Several interviewees were probably referring to this type of participation in church volunteer activities.

Churches are also responding to the needs of other growing immigrant communities. In addition to the Latino community, the meatpacking plants in Beardstown and Monmouth are also attracting an increasing number of immigrants from Africa. About eight hundred West Africans from countries like Togo, Senegal, Cameroon, the Democratic Republic of Congo, and Benin live mainly in Beardstown and Rushville, Illinois, but also in Springfield and Jacksonville.[16] In response to this fact, the former priest at the Catholic Church in Beardstown, Chris Brade, was working to integrate the three Catholic communities present in the town, namely, Francophone Africans, Anglos, and Latinos. For this purpose, he said the Mass simultaneously in French, English, and Spanish. In addition, he organized different potlucks and festivities to which all three communities were invited. Some of our interviewees celebrated these efforts and attended these events, and three reported volunteering time to help with them.

A Central Illinois not-for-profit organization called Faith Coalition for the Common Good (FCCG) has a presence in Beardstown. "Faith Coalition for the Common Good is an organization whose purpose is to unite congregations with other faith-based and community organizations to identify common issues of concern in Central Illinois; to educate themselves and others about these issues and to work together for systemic change that will advance their shared values."[17] This group consists of an alliance of more than twenty organizations working together for common purposes. FCCG has a branch in the Rushville-Beardstown area. Alejandro has volunteered time to this branch of the organization. However, according to Alejandro, this effort has had limited success because of the lack of unity among members.[18]

Another faith-based organization immigrants participated in was Mom to Mom (Mamá a Mamá). "Mom to Mom is a Biblically-based parenting program designed around the Titus 2:4 concept of older women teaching and encouraging younger women in their relationships with their husbands and children."[19] Activities of the group include instruction in parenting, small group discussion, and the interaction of more experienced mothers with younger moms. In addition, the group distributes bags with diapers, soap, and different products new mothers may need. Teresa, for instance, was involved with this group and volunteered time to help distribute food and diapers, and to teach classes on different topics, including health issues.[20]

Several immigrants reported being involved or having been involved in their children's schools. For example, Floriberto explained, "I was involved with a parents' committee in my kids' school because I wanted to learn how things are handled inside and outside the school, as well as to learn the culture of the town."[21] Floriberto added that being a member of this committee gave him the opportunity to attend conferences in Chicago at which parents were instructed on children's rights. Some immigrants talked about volunteering time to help take care of the children at school. Florencia stated, "When my kids were in kindergarten, I volunteered to help in the classroom once a week."[22] In a similar vein, Isabel and Rosa reported that they used to volunteer time at their children's school when their children were younger.[23] Moreover, María Isabel remarked that she felt accepted in the school system and felt her contributions were valued there.[24]

More than a quarter of the respondents in this study reported having participated in a group representing Mexicans or Latinos. It was especially encouraging to see that the Hispanic community in Beardstown, older than the one in Monmouth, seemed to be fairly well organized. For example, Martín participated in a group called CAR, in charge of organizing activities for children that develop their imagination.[25] He explained that he acted as a coach for this organization.

Jorge participates in Amigos Unidos, a group that is devoted to organizing Cinco de Mayo and Mexican Independence Day festivities, and to bringing a variety of speakers to town.[26] He explained, "Amigos Unidos raises funds for the festivities and hires mariachis and dance groups; it puts up flags, and selects the candidates for the pageant that names the local queen. To raise funds, the group sends letters to different businesses."[27] Amigos Unidos has been sponsoring these celebrations for seventeen years. Gustavo was also a member of Amigos Unidos.[28] He stopped participating, however, because he disagreed with the group's leadership. Floriberto was also a member of Amigos Unidos.[29] "It was a good experience," he said, "because one gets to find out what's going on in the school."[30] Apparently, some of Amigos Unidos's activities are related to the schools.

The group Convivencia, Amistad, Sericio y Accion (CASA), backed by a group of Latino university students, including Ricardo Montoya and Paola Gil, also assists the Latino community in Beardstown. The aim of this group is to "promote higher education amongst our Latino youth who will or have graduated from a senior high school. Assist those in need among our Hispanic community by any form possible and to maintain a prominent Latino presence/awareness."[31] Floriberto mentioned that this group helped him with the financial planning to cover his children's college education.[32] María Isabel also participated in this group.[33] Her partner, however, prefers the group Amigos Unidos.[34] Nonetheless, the two groups seem to collaborate on many activities.

Immigrants in the sample also engaged in a number of political activities. For example, several of them reported having contacted a public official. Alejandra went to see Aaron Schock (R-IL), U.S. Representative for the 18th District, with a group of churches and families.[35] Further, Alejandra explained that sometimes the church invites him to come to Beardstown to answer questions and meet with immigrant families. Alejandro met with public officials twice.[36] On one occasion, he requested an interview with Representative Schock to speed up his wife's immigration paperwork. Alejandro explained that when he became a citizen he applied for his wife's permanent residency because she lacked "papers." The process was long and entailed being separated from his wife and child for years. According to Alejandro, the interview with the representative was unsuccessful. "He [Aaron Schock] doesn't support anything related to immigration; they have no idea of how much harm they cause by separating families," Alejandro declared.[37]

On another occasion Alejandro participated in a vigil in support of immigration reform. During the visit, a congressperson answered questions drawn from a basket. "The congressperson listened to concerns but failed to provide clear answers. He was talking about how the immigration system is broken but thought change should start with a tighter control of the border." Alejandro's experience with U.S. Senator Dick Durbin, who is a well-known supporter of immigration reform, was remarkably different. On this occasion, an African and a Mexican immigrant met with the senator. "He supports immigration reform and understands the needs of immigrants," Alejandro stated. Alejandro thought meeting in person was important because "you can't explain the suffering of a child on a piece of paper."[38] Alejandro was referring to the period when his child and wife had to wait in Mexico for the approval of their immigration paperwork.

Several interviewees participated in demonstrations. Almost half of these protests (49 percent) were related to immigration reform. As mentioned above, participation in protests by Latinos became common after 2006. For instance, Latinos all over the country often show their support for immigration reform on May 1. Walter, for one, participated in a rally for immigration reform. "It was a good experience, feeling that we all support each other; everyone was there."[39] Helena also participates in immigration reform rallies to stop deportations.[40]

Immigrants requested meetings with different legislators and congresspersons to lobby for immigration reform. On one occasion, however, a group of immigrants went to see recently resigned representative Aaron Schock in Springfield, but he refused to meet with them. Because people remained at the door and were not seen by the congressman, this instance was classified as a protest and not as contacting a public official. María Isabel attended this protest.[41] According to her, the goal of the visit to the congressman's office was to "make him understand the needs of Latinos who lack their papers."[42] Jorge also participated in this protest and reported that some 150 people attended.[43] As these instances show, immigration reform was a major motivation for participation in protests. Some immigrants, however, also participated in protests unrelated to immigration reform (20 percent). For example, Gabriel participated in a protest at his workplace.[44] The reason for the protest was that his workplace was trying to change some rules, but Gabriel disagreed with the change.

Networks

"Often political activity arises more or less spontaneously from individuals when they become excited about issues, connect politics to their basic interest, or get involved out of a sense of civic duty." More generally, however, somebody requests their participation. Personal connections can account for a large share of the requests to participate (Verba, Schlozman, and Brady 1995, 133). Several respondents in this sample reported having found out about opportunities for participation in political activities through friends. For example, Gabriel participated in a protest at work because a man brought the protest to his attention.[45] In turn, Leo stated that when someone invited him to a political party meeting, he attended.[46]

Alejandra participated in a protest because her friend Martín told her about it. Martín was also one of my interviewees from Beardstown; he is a very intelligent man who is an active member of the community and participates in a number of groups, including Mom to Mom, Amigos Unidos, and CAR. In addition, he attends the Catholic Church regularly and used to work at the local meatpacking plant. Martín is a key community organizer and often coordinates calls for mobilization among the members of the community. People like Martín have great potential for mobilizing the community and can constitute a vital engine of social movements.

Different institutions in society can also provide a context in which recruitment takes place (Verba, Schlozman, and Brady 1995). Often, institutions that get involved in politics are more likely to recruit participants for political activities. The data in this study show that religious organizations play an important role in recruiting immigrants to participate in different activities. Several interviewees, for instance, found out about opportunities for participation through the local Catholic Church in Beardstown. María Isabel found out at church about the trip to visit a congressperson.[47] Alejandra explained that the priest tells them it is important to participate in different social and political activities.[48]

Further, on a few occasions, the local Catholic Church brought United States representatives to town with the purpose of meeting with immigrants and thus becoming acquainted with the problems facing immigrant families. As this evidence shows, the Catholic Church constituted an important place for the recruitment of immigrants for different social and political activities. One possible explanation of this may be that the particular priest who was in charge of the Catholic parish in Beardstown, Chris Brade, was more politically inclined than most priests in the Catholic Church and discussed political issues with the community (Verba, Schlozman, and Brady 1995). However, other religious organizations also seemed to have a role in mobilizing the community around participation opportunities. For example, Alejandro found out about a protest in Springfield through the Faith Coalition for the Common Good.[49]

Obstacles and Barriers to Participation

Immigrants in Beardstown and Monmouth encountered various obstacles that precluded their participation. Several of these obstacles related to the amount of time available for participation. The availability of time is a crucial resource for participation and can be calculated as the residual time after accounting for the time spent during necessary household tasks including childcare, working for pay (including commuting), and sleeping (Verba, Schlozman, and Brady 1995). The lack of time as a limitation for participation because of housework and time spent with young children became apparent during my interviews (13 percent).

Moreover, one third of respondents lacked the time for participation because they had time-demanding jobs. Most interviewees had blue-collar jobs in the meatpacking industry, cleaning, and construction. Even though the job level is not necessarily associated with the number of hours spent working, the number of days and hours spent working seemed to limit participation for these interviewees. For example, Romulo, Floriberto, and José Guadalupe indicated that they had only one day off a week.[50] Diana and José Luis, in turn, reported lacking the time to participate because they commute for work.[51] Luis stated he was too busy to participate because he had two jobs.[52] Finally, María Luisa said she works at night and sleeps during the day.[53] As these comments show, job responsibilities limited participation.

About 23 percent of the immigrants interviewed declared their language skills were not good enough for participation (Albarracín and Valeva 2011). Martín, for example, explained that lacking the necessary language skills limited his ability to participate.[54] Florencia stated, "I'm not very comfortable participating because I don't speak English."[55] Luis, in turn, said, "[The main obstacle for participation] is the language, being understood. If I knew the language better I could communicate with society more."[56] Carlos also noted that he does not understand the language well enough to participate. Finally, Alejandra remarked that she would participate in more activities if these activities required only Spanish.[57] Thus, these statements show that not knowing the language was a major obstacle for the participation of immigrants in Beardstown and Monmouth.

As mentioned before, some forms of participation require permanent residency (contributions to campaigns) or citizenship (registering to vote or voting). Thus, opportunities for participation in these political activities were restricted by the nature of immigration and related rules. For example, becoming documented was highly difficult for some interviewees until the recent action by the Obama administration to allow temporary work permits to immigrants who have been in the country for at least five years and who have children who are U.S. citizens. Thus far, though, this program does not include a path to residency or citizenship. Moreover, naturalization is a demanding process, requiring five years of permanent residency, and knowledge of English and of the United States Constitution. For these reasons, strict immigration rules constituted obstacles to certain forms of participation.

What Can We Learn about the Political Incorporation of Immigrants in Central Illinois?

Participation is an essential part of the incorporation process (Black 2011; DeSipio 2011; Hochschild and Mollenkopf 2009; Jones-Correa 2004; Schleef and Cavalcanti 2009). The level of political incorporation among Mexican immigrants in Central Illinois seems to be related to participation in social and political activities. The rates of participation in social activities were relatively high, indicating a reasonable level of political incorporation. The rates for participation in political activities were somewhat lower, indicating that immigrants may be at the conflict/negotiation level of incorporation where these activities are considered. Different reasons may explain the lower levels of political participation. First, residency and citizenship requirements limit campaign contributions, voter registration, and voting. Second, many interviewees were undocumented, and typically, undocumented immigrants live in fear of authorities. They are therefore not likely to contact a public official or attend a public meeting.

Social class, length of stay in the country, and gender influence participation. Results of this study showed that social participation was associated with education, and political participation with education and income. Thus, the process of political incorporation may be influential on social class and/or social class may influence the process of incorporation (Algan, Bisin, and Verdier 2012; Portes and Böröcz 1989; Schleef and Cavalcanti 2009; Verba, Schlozman, and Brady 1995). In addition, the length of stay in the country was associated with participating in church or religious groups and contacting a public official (Cabassa 2003). Although the relationship between length of stay in the country and incorporation is not a necessary one, it seems the length of stay in the country is related to incorporation in some respects.

Results of the study also showed that a number of factors, including attention paid to politics and government affairs, are also associated with social and political participation. The same was true of a number of indicators of social capital. Likely, the benefits of social capital also help the process of political incorporation of immigrants. Further, the relationship between participation and social capital may be a reinforcing one.

Immigrants in Central Illinois had positive attitudes toward participation and found different opportunities to participate in church or religious groups, schools and neighborhood organizations, and groups representing Mexicans or Latinos. Overall, the level of opportunities to participate in social activities was considerably high. However, immigrants faced a number of obstacles that precluded participation, including lack of time due to family obligations or work, and lack of the necessary language skills.

In general, immigrants had positive attitudes about participating in political activities, as well. However, the opportunities for participation in political activities seemed dependent upon contact with a person or institution that requested participation. In addition, the obstacles shaping social participation, including lack of time and limited language skills, also influenced political participation. Other obstacles to participation came from the immigration and citizenship requirements for making contributions to political campaigns, registering to vote, and voting.

CHAPTER 6

More on Political Incorporation
Trust in Government Institutions

Supposedly, the government wants to grant amnesty and I trust that one day Obama may help.

— Florencia, interview with the author, July 30, 2011, Monmouth, Illinois

TRUST IN GOVERNMENT INSTITUTIONS IS AN IMPORTANT INDICATOR OF THE level of immigrants' political incorporation in society (Doerschler and Irving Jackson 2012; Maxwell 2010b). Trust is important for democracy because it influences participation (Guterbock and London 1983; Leal 2002; Marshall 2001) and legitimacy (Mishler and Rose 2001). This chapter explores trust in government institutions among immigrants in Beardstown and Monmouth. The life stories below show some of the ideas immigrants had about the government.

Jorge lives in Beardstown with his partner.[1] He came to the United States in 1984 through Tijuana-San Ysidro (San Diego). Jorge and a group of people made several attempts to cross the border in the two weeks before they finally succeeded. Like most immigrants who move to new destinations, Jorge did not go straight to

Beardstown. Instead, he first went to Los Angeles, where he stayed for seventeen years (Leach and Bean 2008).

In Los Angeles, Jorge worked at a clothing factory making dresses and overalls. He did not like his job much because he had to work extremely hard. Besides, Jorge explained, the cost of living in California was high. He then decided to move to Beardstown, where he had a cousin. Jorge found a job at the local meatpacking plant, Cargill (now Excel). At first, he could work only thirty-six hours a week. For this reason, he left for Kansas for a few years. In 2000, Jorge decided to go back to Beardstown and has been working at the meatpacking plant since then.

"We live in an environment where there's discrimination, both for Latinos and African Americans."[2] As explained in chapter 4, Jorge was stopped by the police, but was able to avoid deportation because he had obtained a green card through 1986 IRCA. Jorge believes that he would better integrate into society if he could study. His dream is to become a lawyer and help the community of Hispanics in Beardstown. He explained that immigrants in Beardstown are "on their own" and need a lawyer. He would feel more connected to society if he could help the community. "The more united Latinos are, the easier is going to be their integration into society," Jorge believes.[3]

Jorge does not have many Anglo friends, even though his department at the plant is 40 percent Anglo. "I only have brief interactions at work; for example I ask, 'Did you have a good Thanksgiving? What did you eat?'" he stated.[4] Jorge does not attend social functions with Anglos because he believes he is discriminated against. He feels Hispanics' opinions are usually not taken into account. Further, some coworkers sometimes tell him he should go back to his country.

Jorge is active in the community where he lives and participates in an organization called Amigos Unidos. However, he does not trust the government in Washington, D.C., to do what is right. "There are many conflicts among them [politicians]; this is the reason they can't reach any agreements."[5] As this statement shows, Jorge is critical of politicians in the United States.

Alejandra lives in Beardstown with her husband and two kids. She came to the United States after she got married.[6] She and her husband did not have a home in Mexico and this was a major factor in their decision to move. Her husband came first, after swimming the Rio Grande and walking for two days. He went straight to Beardstown because he had family there. Alejandra was able to join him after two years.

Joining her husband in the United States was not easy for Alejandra. She and a group of Africans and Brazilians crossed the border through El Paso–Ciudad Juarez with the help of a *coyote*. After taking several buses, Alejandra finally arrived in Beardstown.

Alejandra regularly attends gatherings at the Saint Alexius Catholic Church because she feels comfortable there. Both Anglos and Hispanics attend these activities. Further, she would invite Anglos to her house if her English were a little better. Yet, she feels what happens to Anglos in her community does not affect her life very much. According to Alejandra, she cannot feel really connected with people with whom she has not interacted much.

Alejandra thinks her life is only somewhat tied to what happens to other Hispanics in the country. She does, however, feel close to other Hispanics in her community, especially if they belong to her church. Alejandra believes that being surrounded by good people helps integration.

Alejandra participated in a vigil at the door of United States Representative Aaron Schock. She attended the vigil with a group of families and members of different churches, but the state representative refused to meet with them. Alejandra would like to participate in other social activities, but even after twelve years, her English is not good enough. "I would participate in more activities if they were in Spanish."[7]

Alejandra trusts her neighbors considerably, especially the families that seem well established in the community. However, she trusts the government in Washington, D.C., to do what is right only about 50 percent of the time. "Sometimes they get it right, and sometimes they don't," Alejandra explained.

As the stories above illustrate, neither Jorge nor Alejandra trust the government much. Political trust, defined here as a "basic evaluative orientation toward the government founded on how well the government is operating according to people's normative expectations," is essential for democracy (Hetherington 1998, 791). Political trust is important because it links citizens to the institutions that are intended to represent them (Mishler and Rose 2001). It also enhances the legitimacy of democratic governments in that the more people trust the government, the more likely they are to accept the institutions of government and the people occupying them (Mishler and Rose 2001). Trust also determines individual political behavior (Hetherington 1998; Michelson 2007); with some exceptions (for instance, see Guterbock and London, 1983; Leal 2002; Marshall 2001), most authors believe that trust in government increases participation (Hetherington 1998). Finally, trust in government can be an indicator of the health of civil society (Putnam 1993, 2000).

Trust in Government

Trust is essential for democracy (Hetherington 1998; Michelson 2007; Putnam 1993). Feelings of trust are related to the sense of belonging and the acquisition of the host

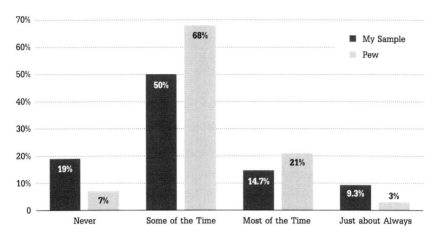

Figure 18. Levels of Trust in Government: Sample of 260 Interviewees in Central Illinois vs. National Sample Pew Research Center's 2004 National Survey of Latinos

culture's beliefs (Maxwell 2010b; Michelson 2007). Unfortunately, political trust has been declining in the United States since the 1960s (André 2014; Levi and Stoker 2000; Michelson 2007). This finding has generated efforts to explain, and ultimately to reverse this trend (Catterberg and Moreno 2006; Citrin 1974; Citrin and Green 1986; Chanley, Rudolph, and Rahn 2000; Hetherington 1998; Levi and Stoker 2000; Miller 1974). Few works, however, have attempted to understand the determinants of trust among Latinos (for example, see Abrajano and Álvarez 2010; Michelson 2003, 2007; Wenzel 2006).

Further, the literature disagrees as to whether Latinos' levels of trust are higher or lower than those of non-Latino Whites. For example, whereas early socialization studies found trust among Latinos to be lower than among Whites (Wenzel 2006), more recent ones have found the opposite (Abrajano and Álvarez 2010; Bonner 2009; Wenzel 2006). Given the cynicism about the government among Whites, one could expect Latinos to become more cynical as they become incorporated into society. However, research has shown that sometimes changes in the level of trust depend on the type of assimilation strategy immigrants pursue (Michelson 2007).

One variable in this study reflected the extent to which people trusted the federal government. Specifically, the question asked: "How much of the time do you trust the government in Washington to do what is right?" The possible answers were "never," "some of the time," "most of the time," and "just about always." This wording corresponds with the most traditional political science question used to assess trust in government. As figure 18 shows, immigrants in Beardstown and

Table 12. Regression Model for Trust in Government: Sample of 260 Interviewees in Central Illinois (Standard Errors in Parentheses)

Variable	Standardized Beta Coefficients
Length of Stay in the Country	0.09 (0.01)
Gender	−0.03 (0.13)
Education	−0.08 (0.13)
Employment Status	0.09 (0.15)
Income	−0.15 (0.14)[†]
R Square	0.04

$^*p < 0.1$ $^†p < 0.05$ $^‡p < 0.01$

Monmouth trusted the government at levels comparable to those from a national sample of Latinos collected by Pew Research in 2004.

Those who never trusted the government or who trusted the government some of the time totaled 69 percent for the Beardstown and Monmouth sample, and 75 percent for the national sample. On the one hand, respondents in my sample were almost three times more likely to state they never trusted the government. On the other hand, they were also three times more likely to state that they trusted the government just about always. Overall, the level of trust in the federal government for Beardstown and Monmouth was comparable to that of the national sample.

A purpose of this research was to determine if social class affected the political incorporation of immigrants in Central Illinois and to determine if a connection existed between political incorporation and gender and length of stay in the country. The logistic regression showed that income was associated with political trust (table 12). That is, immigrants with higher incomes were less likely to trust the government (André 2014; Hetherington 1998; Wilkes 2015). However, none of the other factors, namely, education, employment status, gender, and length of stay in the country, were significant in predicting trust in government.[8]

Other Determinants of Trust in Government

Some studies have analyzed the effect of acculturation on trust in government. They argue that acculturation erodes trust in government (Michelson 2003, 2007; Wenzel 2006). As immigrants acculturate, they may go from the point of view of a newcomer looking forward to being a member of mainstream society to that of a person who has been denied full membership in this society (Michelson 2003; Wenzel 2006).

Thus, those who are more acculturated may be more aware of discrimination and may become more cynical about the government (Michelson 2007). Also, as immigrants assimilate into the host society, they may acquire more cynical views, especially given the current gridlock in Congress. To test whether more acculturated immigrants trusted the government less, the analysis included an indicator of the length of stay in the country.

A number of socio-demographic factors are likely to influence political trust.[9] For example, younger persons tend to trust the government more than older ones (Abrajano and Álvarez 2010; Hetherington 1998; Wilkes 2015). The role of income and education in predicting trust is less understood. On the one hand, higher levels of education may make people trust the government less because the more they know about politicians the less they may trust them (André 2014; Hetherington 1998; Wilkes 2015). On the other hand, a deterioration of the economic circumstances people face can be linked to negative sentiments about the government if they link those economic circumstances to government policies (Citrin and Green 1986). Still, even if immigrants' position in society is not ideal, they may still trust the government in the host society more because they are better off than they were in their country of origin (Maxwell 2010a).

Also, the effect of income and education may vary across different countries. For example, income decreases trust in established democracies but boosts it in Eastern Europe and Latin America (Catterberg and Moreno 2006). However, education decreases trust in government in Latin America. To elucidate the role of income and education in predicting political trust, the model to explain political trust controlled for education and income (for details on the variables, please see appendix).

Most of the research on immigrants' political attitudes and behavior focuses on post-arrival factors (for example, see Abrajano and Álvarez 2010; Albarracín and Valeva 2011; Barreto and Muñoz 2003; Barreto et al. 2009; Benjamin-Alvarado, DeSipio, and Montoya 2009; De La Garza, Falcon, and García 1996; DeSipio 2011). However, it is likely that the political views immigrants hold were acquired before migration. "Immigrants don't enter the United States as political blank slates" (Wals 2011, 2). Instead, pre-migration political experiences may shape or modify the effect of post-migration factors (Wals 2011). In addition, it is likely that trust in institutions originates in long-standing and deep-seated beliefs about people that are rooted in cultural norms and communicated through early-life socialization (Mishler and Rose 2001). To test the weight of pre-migration factors in predicting political trust, this research included a question on trust in the Mexican government, which asked respondents how much they trusted the government in Mexico to do what is right (for details about this variable, please see appendix).

People who pay attention to politics and government affairs are more likely to participate in politics (Verba, Scholzman, and Brady 1995). However, do those persons who pay more attention to politics and government affairs trust the government more or less than those who pay less attention to politics and government affairs? A cynical view of politics would argue that the more people know about politics, the more they tend to distrust those involved in it (Catterberg and Moreno 2006). Conversely, a more psychological view may expect people who like politics to be more politically engaged and to exhibit higher levels of trust in government (Catterberg and Moreno 2006). Thus, I included an indicator of interest in politics and government affairs in my analysis.

Perceptions about the existence/importance of discrimination and personal experiences with discrimination can also shape political trust. More specifically, those who feel discrimination is a major problem and those who have had a close experience with discrimination may be less likely to trust the government (Abrajano and Álvarez 2010; Michelson 2003, 2007; Schildkraut 2005). It is also possible that a personal or close experience with discrimination may be more influential on the level of political trust than the mere perception that discrimination is a problem. The reason behind this is that those who have experienced discrimination may project this experience onto government institutions (Brehm and Rahn 1997). For these reasons, the model on the determinants of political trust included an indicator of discrimination. Specifically, a question asked respondents if they or a member of their family had been discriminated against in the previous five years.

Even though the literature agrees that trust is essential for democracy (Hetherington 1998; Michelson 2007; Putnam 1993), there is less agreement about people's understanding of the questions on trust in government. The debate centers on whether people are evaluating the incumbent authorities (Citrin 1974) or the system of government in general (Miller 1974). David Easton (1965), for instance, drew a distinction between specific and diffuse support. Whereas specific support relates to the evaluation of the authorities in power, diffuse support applies to the assessment of the regime or system of government.

This distinction is important because if distrustful people doubt the entire system of government, this distrust could jeopardize the stability of democracy. For instance, Miller worried that "when dissatisfaction with the existing situation leads . . . to pervasive and enduring distrust of the government," this dissatisfaction can increase the potential for radical change (Miller 1974, 951). Although fears of radical change are uncommon today, if people's discontent is sustained over time, increasing their trust in institutions may be difficult (Miller 1974). Moreover, deciphering what low levels of trust mean can have an impact on how the government functions (Citrin and Green 1986).

To reflect dissatisfaction with the regime or system of government, or more specifically, the degree to which people feel the system of government does not function for them, my analysis included a variable reflecting the extent to which

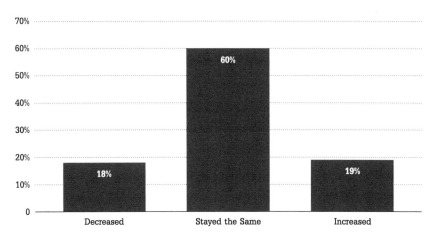

Figure 19. Changes in Levels of Trust in the Government in Washington, DC: Sample of 260 Interviewees in Central Illinois

people feel leaders show concern for the problems affecting Latinos. This variable implies a long-run evaluation of how the system of government works. Dissatisfaction with incumbent authorities can be understood as discontent with recent progress in achieving generally desired objectives (Citrin and Green 1986). To capture dissatisfaction with incumbent authorities (Chanley, Rudolph, and Rahn 2000; Citrin and Green 1986), this research used a variable that reflected the extent to which people thought the economic situation in the United States was good (for details about this variable, please see appendix).

Policy considerations can also reflect trust in incumbent authorities (Citrin 1974; Citrin and Green 1986; Hetherington 1998). If people perceive that the government is pursuing policies with which they agree, they may trust the government more. It would be of interest to know whether people's position on immigration policy had an effect on political trust. Recent administrations have been pursuing policies that limit the number of immigrants (for details about these policies, see chapter 2). The expectation was thus that those who trusted the government more would be more likely to agree with decreasing the number of immigrants. Consequently, the study included a question that asked respondents whether the government should increase the number of immigrants accepted into the United States, leave it the same, or decrease it.

The regression analysis showed that several factors predicted immigrants' levels of trust in government. This study did not find support for the contention that the more acculturated Latinos trust the government less. This finding goes against the literature that shows that as Latinos become more acculturated they adopt the

Table 13. Model for Trust in Government with Political Variables: Sample of 260 Interviewees in Central Illinois (Standard Errors in Parentheses)

Variable	Standardized Beta Coefficients
Length of Stay in United States	0.11 (0.01)
Age	0.07 (0.01)
Education	−0.14 (0.07)*
Income	−0.18 (0.06)
Trust in the Government Country of Origin	0.08 (0.08)
Attention to Politics	0.27 (0.09)[‡]
Experience with Discrimination	−0.02 (0.14)
Leaders' Concern Problems Latinos	0.14 (0.13)*
Economic Situation in the United States	0.14 (0.07)*
Position on Immigration Policy	0.14 (0.13)*
R Square	0.22

*$p < 0.1$ [†]$p < 0.05$ [‡]$p < 0.01$

more cynical views of the American mainstream society (Michelson 2003, 2007; Wenzel 2006).

Further, another question in the survey asked respondents if their trust in the government in Washington had increased, stayed the same, or decreased since their arrival in the United States. Responses to this question showed that the levels of trust in government seem to be somewhat stable over time (figure 19). Almost identical numbers of respondents indicated that their level of trust in government increased or decreased; for most respondents the level of trust in government stayed the same. Thus, the level of trust in government may be partly determined by factors predating people's immigration to the United States.

Even though age was expected to be negatively associated with trust (Abrajano and Álvarez 2010; Hetherington 1998; Wilkes 2015), it was not significant in the model (table 13). Further, the sign of the association between age and trust was positive, implying that older people may trust the government more. Importantly, whereas only income predicted trust in government in the previous model (table 12), both income and education significantly predicted trust in government in the second model, including the political variables (table 13). More specifically, those with higher incomes and education levels tended to trust the government less than those with lower incomes and education levels. This finding is consistent with previous research that shows that as people become wealthier and more informed about government affairs, they also become more distrustful of government institutions (André 2014; Hetherington 1998; Wilkes 2015).

Previous research showed that trust in the United States' government was associated with trust in the government of Mexico (Wals 2011). Even though the variable on trust in the government of the country of origin was not significant in the model (table 13), there was a positive correlation between trust in the government of origin and trust in the government in Washington (r = 0.23, p = < 0.001). That is, those who trusted the government in Mexico more also trusted the government in the United States more. This finding provides support for the contention that people may form their political views before they arrive in the host country (Mishler and Rose 2001; Wals 2011).

This research set out to understand the relationship between attention to politics and government affairs and political trust (Catterberg and Moreno 2006). The attention paid to politics and government affairs significantly predicted trust in government, with those who paid more attention to politics and government also more likely to trust the government more (table 13). One possible explanation for this finding is that those who take an interest in politics and government affairs come to trust the government more as they learn more about it. Another possibility is that those who trust the government more to begin with are more likely to take an interest in politics and government affairs. In contrast, those who pay less attention to politics may end up losing trust in the government, or those who trust the government less may choose to stay less informed about current issues. In any case, this study shows that those who paid more attention to politics and government were also more likely to trust the government more.

Research shows that those who perceive discrimination as a problem or who have had a close experience with discrimination may also trust the government less (Abrajano and Álvarez 2010; Michelson 2003, 2007; Schildkraut 2005). However, having had an experience with discrimination was not significant in the model (table 13). Nonetheless, the sign of the association between having an experience with discrimination and trust in government was negative, indicating that those who had a close experience with discrimination may project that experience onto government institutions (Brehm and Rahn 1997).

The last set of factors attempted were used to determine how people make judgments about their trust in government. The regression analysis showed that those who thought political leaders were interested in the problems of concern for Latinos were also more trusting of the government (Miller 1974) (table 13). Thus, the degree of responsiveness of the political system to the problems facing different groups may be important, independent of who is in power. At the same time, the evaluation of the performance of the incumbent authorities also was significant in the model. Those immigrants who believed the economic situation was better were likely to trust the government more than those who believed the economic situation was worse. Thus, people may also be evaluating the performance of incumbents when evaluating their trust in government (Chanley, Rudolph, and Rahn 2000; Citrin and Green 1986).

Finally, the respondent's policy position on immigration also explained trust in government (Hetherington 1998). More specifically, those who seemed to agree with the strict policies of the recent administrations were also more likely to trust the federal government (table 13). It may be worth mentioning that whereas 50 percent of the respondents thought the government should increase the number of immigrants from Latin America, 40 percent thought the government should reduce this number. Overall, when immigrants assess their degree of trust in the government, they may take into account both their degree of trust/distrust in the system of government (Miller 1974) and their evaluation of the performance of the incumbent authorities (Citrin 1974; Citrin and Green 1986). This question is explored further in the next section, which analyzes the results of the interviews.

Why Do People Say They Trust or Distrust the Government?

As mentioned before, the literature disagrees on what the trust questions actually measure (Citrin 1974; Citrin and Green 1986; Miller 1974; Craig, Niemi, and Silver 1990). Forty-three percent of the respondents described trusting/not trusting the government because of the way the system of government works. Forty-seven percent of the respondents reported trusting/not trusting the government due to its immigration policies or lack of immigration reform. Finally, another 7 percent related their degree of trust in government to their experience with the government in Mexico. It thus may be that people form their views about government before coming to the United States (Wals 2011).

Some people may feel the sort of discontent that leads to a negative orientation toward the political system, a feeling that this system should not be trusted because it does not function for them (Miller 1974). Several interviewees showed a general trust or distrust of the way the system of government works. One interviewee, Teresa 2, was especially positive about how the system works.[10] She explained, "I trust the government most of the time because they (those in positions of power) have a set of rules and regulations they have to follow." As this remark shows, Teresa 2 believes in the system of government and thinks the rules in place guarantee that those in positions of power do the right thing. Other interviewees, however, were less optimistic about the way the government works.

Sandro had a clear understanding that some level of trust is necessary for government institutions to work effectively (Miller 1974). He said, "I trust the government most of the time; [I believe] it tries to do the right thing. When they [politicians] run campaigns, they talk and talk and then don't deliver. But you have to trust them because they are the ones running the country and something good needs to come out of it."[11] Although Sandro acknowledged that politicians make promises during campaigns but fail to keep them, he also thought we should have faith in them because they are the ones ruling the country. He also seemed to imply that trust is necessary for them to rule.

Some interviewees were critical of the political divisions between Democrats and Republicans. To be sure, political parties are "against each other" in other parts of the world as well. However, because of the way the United States' system works, deep divisions between the political parties can lead to a gridlock in Congress, especially in a situation of divided government. This outcome has become more likely since the emergence of the Tea Party in American politics (Williamson, Skocpol, and Coggin 2011). These two interviewees described these current problems to perfection. Benita, for example, stated, "The way in which the parties are against each other is dysfunctional."[12] Jorge also said that there are many conflicts among politicians and that they seem to be unable to reach an agreement.[13] These interviewees showed a good understanding of the United States' political system and of the impact of the divisions between political parties on congressional inaction.

Several interviewees demonstrated a distrust of politicians in general. Diana, for example, stated, "Politicians make promises during campaigns, but then don't deliver when they come to power."[14] In turn, Gabriel remarked, "They [those in government] say many things, like they will help people, but they only do it to get votes."[15] Or, in the words of Juana, "Sometimes they don't do things the way they should; they do things for their own good."[16] Zacarías agreed: "They [politicians] only do things to benefit themselves."[17] As these statements show, these interviewees believed politicians should not be trusted because politicians do not keep their campaign promises, and they work toward their own benefit.

Some immigrants' trust in government was determined by discontent with specific policies (Citrin 1974). President Obama promised to reform immigration law and provide a solution to the problems of undocumented immigrants during his campaigns. The immigration reform proposed by the Obama administration includes continuing to strengthen border security, facilitating legal immigration with special attention to family reunification, providing undocumented immigrants with a legal way to earn citizenship, and cracking down on employers hiring undocumented immigrants.[18] The U.S. Senate passed an immigration reform bill on June 27, 2013, but the U.S. House of Representatives has been unable to reach the consensus necessary to enact it. To be sure, the gridlock in Congress regarding immigration policy can be attributed to the Republican Party's lack of support for comprehensive immigration reform. However, not all immigrants may be able to understand this and therefore blame the Obama administration for the lack of immigration reform. Only recently has the Obama administration adopted an action that would allow immigrants who have been in the country for at least five years and who have children born in the United States to regularize their immigration status. This action, however, applies only to a subset of immigrants and provides only a temporary solution for this group.

Many of the interviewees in this study were undocumented, and at the time of the interviews, it was difficult to obtain a visa to work in the United States without a college degree and support from an employer. For this reason, most of them were waiting for congressional immigration reform to provide them with a legal way to obtain a visa, a green card, and/or citizenship. Thus, several respondents were frustrated with the lack of approval of such immigration reform. Further, most of them blamed President Obama for this lack of approval. Only one respondent acknowledged that the lack of immigration reform was due to Congress's inaction. Ignacio stated, "He [President Obama] has promised many things but he hasn't delivered. He can say something but if Congress doesn't support him . . . the president is not alone; congresspersons need to support him to get things done."[19] Ignacio clearly had a great understanding of the issues surrounding immigration reform and recognized that Congress is the institution that needs to enact it. Most interviewees, however, were frustrated with President Obama and seemed to lack an understanding of the way the system of government works.

María Isabel, for example, explained, "This man demoralized me; there was a Brazilian woman who said that if Obama came to power, he would fix our papers."[20] When stating "he would fix our papers," María Isabel was referring to the promise by President Obama to provide a path to citizenship for undocumented immigrants. Rómulo, in turn, said, "Obama promised to help Hispanics but he's not doing anything . . . many Hispanics may not vote for Obama again."[21] The help Rómulo was referring to was also the promised path to citizenship. In the words of Florencia, "Supposedly, the government wants to grant amnesty and I trust that one day Obama may help. For now, however, he [Obama] hasn't helped much. We are waiting for the amnesty and I don't see anything."[22] Although Florencia had not lost hope, she was also disappointed about the lack of immigration reform at the time and blamed Obama for it.

Immigration law is a federal matter. Its approval and enforcement has been a responsibility of federal government for centuries. However, state and local governments have taken up different immigration responsibilities in recent years. Between 2005 and 2011, there were 370 local governments that proposed or implemented policies designed to address issues related to undocumented immigration in their communities (Walker and Leitner 2011). Section 287(g) of the 1996 Illegal

Immigration Reform and Immigrant Responsibility Act (IIRIRA)[23] authorized the devolution of immigration policy enforcement (Varsanyi et al. 2012). In addition, some local policies regarding immigration are grassroots responses to the presence of immigrants (Walker and Leitner 2011).

Several interviewees distrusted the government because of this tendency toward the devolution of immigration responsibilities. Martín, for example, explained, "I'm bothered by things like the law in Alabama. I'm not going through it personally but it is a person like me, who comes to look for a job and they enact very harsh rules."[24] Here, Martín was referring to legislation passed in Alabama in 2011, known as House Bill 56, which was the strictest state immigration law at the time. This bill made it a crime for businesses to hire undocumented immigrants, required legal immigrants to carry documentation with them at all times, and had a "show me your papers" provision, which allowed police to detain people during traffic stops for the purpose of checking their citizenship status (Immigration Direct 2013). This law was deemed unconstitutional by the U.S. District Court for the Northern District of Alabama on November 26, 2013, because its provisions conflicted with federal immigration law and undermined federal immigration-enforcement efforts.

Even better known is Arizona Senate Bill 1070 from 2010, which has also been challenged in different courts and was partly struck down by the United States Supreme Court on June 25, 2014. This bill had several provisions, including the requirement that state and local law enforcement reasonably attempt to determine the immigration status of a person involved in a lawful stop, detention, or arrest in the enforcement of any other local or state law or ordinance, where suspicion exists that the person is an alien and is unlawfully present (National Conference of State Legislatures 2011). One respondent tied her level of trust in government to this law. Hilda explained, "There are many Latinos battling to get jobs, but there's discrimination like in Arizona."[25] As this statement makes clear, Hilda was concerned about the harm caused to Latinos by SB 1070.

Teresa was concerned about the separation of families. She stated, "This policy of separating Hispanic families is not good, right? They leave the children who are citizens here and they send the parents back to Mexico."[26] Immigrants found to be undocumented can be deported to their home countries, even if their children are American citizens. Teresa was probably referring to a raid in 2007 that led to the arrest of sixty-two people. The raid occurred at Cargill, the meatpacking plant in Beardstown, and targeted the company contracted to clean the plant. On this occasion, several Hispanic families in Beardstown were separated when some of their members were deported.

Some of the comments on immigration showed a general dissatisfaction with the way immigrants are treated in the United States. For example, Irma said, "This country has developed and moved forward thanks to immigration. Americans don't want to take certain types of jobs . . . the government attacks immigration instead of embracing it as part of the solution for this country. They use the excuse that we are illegal, that we come to do bad things, when in reality we only come here to work."[27] As this statement shows, Irma was frustrated that although the United States is a "country of immigrants," immigrants are not welcome in today's society.

Some interviewees made reference to the government in Mexico when asked why they trusted or distrusted the government (Wals 2011). Floriberto, for instance, explained, "I only trust the government sometimes because one couldn't trust the government in Mexico . . . we've been distrusting the government because of the way they treated us there [in Mexico]."[28] Floriberto is aware that his views about government were formed back in Mexico (Wals 2011). In the case of immigrants, it is important to "acknowledge that individuals' perceptions of government and their expectations regarding government outcomes might be colored by the way these immigrants were socialized in their countries of origin" (Wals 2011, 4).

What Have We Learned about Trust in Government among Immigrants in Beardstown and Monmouth?

Upon moving to a country, immigrants tend to acquire the attitudes and beliefs of the host society (Michelson 2007). Immigrants' trust in government is an indication of their level of political incorporation in society (Doerschler and Irving Jackson 2012; Maxwell 2010b). It was interesting to compare the levels of trust of this study's sample with those of the general population (Abrajano and Álvarez 2010; Bonner 2009; Wenzel 2006). The data showed that immigrants in Beardstown and Monmouth exhibited levels of trust in government that were comparable to those of a national sample of the general population.

Social class, length of stay in the country, and gender seem to influence the level of trust in institutions. Mirroring findings for the general population, this study showed that immigrants with higher levels of income trusted the government less than those with lower incomes (André 2014; Hetherington 1998; Wilkes 2015) (table 12). Further, the second model presented in this chapter showed that education also predicted trust in government; those with higher levels of education trusted the government less than those with lower levels of education (table 13). These findings give support to the contention that the process of incorporation is associated with social class (Algan, Bisin, and Verdier 2012; Portes and Böröcz 1989; Schleef and Cavalcanti 2009). Further, they also support the assertion that as immigrants in Beardstown and Monmouth learn more about the government, they may trust it less.

It was also meaningful to discover whether the political factors identified in this study predicted trust among immigrants in Beardstown and Monmouth. Two findings in my sample supported the argument that views about politics and government affairs can be acquired before the process of migration (Mishler and Rose 2001; Wals 2011) (table 13). First, although the variable on trust in the government of Mexico was not significant in the model, it was positively associated with trust in the government in Washington. In other words, those who trusted the government in Mexico also tended to trust the government in the United States. Second, the data also showed that views about the trustworthiness of the government remained somewhat stable after migration (figure 19).

Political-science literature contends that the attention paid to politics and government affairs can influence the levels of trust in government (Verba, Scholzman, and Brady 1995). The data showed that immigrants in Beardstown and Monmouth who paid more attention to politics and government affairs also exhibited higher levels of trust in government. It may be that those who trust the government more tend to keep up with government affairs.

Immigrants who perceive that discrimination against them is a major problem, or those who have had a close experience with discrimination, may trust the government less than those who lack this perception or experience (Abrajano and Álvarez 2010; Michelson 2003, 2007; Schildkraut 2005). As chapter 4 shows, perceptions of the existence of discrimination were high among the interviewees in this study. Specifically, few respondents stated that they thought discrimination was not a problem for the success of Latinos in the United States, and almost 50 percent declared that they or a member of their family had suffered discrimination. The analysis performed here indicates that those who had an experience with discrimination were less likely to trust the government (table 13).

Finally, my research investigated the underpinnings of immigrants' trust in government. To do this, I have explored whether immigrants' lack of trust in government is shaped by their distrust of the political system altogether (Miller 1974) or by their evaluation of the incumbent authorities and their policies (Citrin 1974). The quantitative data showed that both the variable reflecting beliefs about political leaders' concern with the problems affecting Latinos and the one assessing immigrants' agreement with the policies of the incumbent authorities were significant in the model (Citrin 1974; Miller 1974) (table 13). Further, the standardized beta coefficients for all the variables were the same. Thus, it seems that immigrants in Beardstown and Monmouth were evaluating both the way the system of government works (Miller 1974) and the incumbent authorities (Citrin 1974) when answering the question about trust in government.

The qualitative data also shed light on the factors shaping immigrants' trust or distrust in the government. A significant number of immigrants reported trusting/distrusting the government because of the way the system works (Miller 1974). In particular, some respondents distrusted the government because of the way political parties disagree with each other, or because campaign promises are not met. An even larger number of immigrants, however, rejected the immigration policies of the current administration and were frustrated with the lack of immigration reform (Citrin 1974). It seems that even though immigrants' attitudes about the government were comparable to those of the general population and were influenced by some of the same factors, immigration policies may be central in shaping trust in government among immigrants in Beardstown and Monmouth.

Conclusion

ABOUT 16 PERCENT OF THE POPULATION IN THE UNITED STATES ARE OF LATINO or Hispanic origin. People of Mexican origin represent 63 percent of the Latino population and 55 percent of the foreign-born population in the United States (U.S. Census Bureau 2011). Latinos continue to be concentrated in the South and West (Massey and Capoferro 2008; Riosmena and Massey 2012). However, two developments in the geographic distribution of Latinos are notable. First, Hispanics are living in states outside of the West in growing numbers. Between 2000 and 2010, for instance, the largest growth in the proportion of Latinos occurred in regions outside the West. Second, Latinos are also settling in non-metropolitan and rural areas. The recent settlement of immigrants in Beardstown and Monmouth exemplifies these developments. Thus, understanding the process of incorporation among Mexican immigrants in these two towns is important for understanding the process of incorporation of immigrants in new immigrant destinations.

Immigrants in new destinations are transforming small-town America. As mentioned before, in 2010 the proportion of Latinos in Beardstown and Monmouth was 33 percent and 15 percent, respectively (U.S. Census Bureau 2013a, 2013b). Further, the proportion of the Latino population in Beardstown almost doubled and the Latino population in Monmouth more than tripled between the years 2000 and 2010. In 2010, the Mexican population accounted for 78 percent of Latinos in Beardstown and 88 percent of this population group in Monmouth (U.S. Census 2013a). Immigrants in Beardstown and Monmouth find jobs in services, farms, and construction, among others. However, the main drivers of immigration to these two towns are their hog processing plants. Beardstown is home to Excel, the largest hog processing plant in the state, which employs 2,300 workers (Jensen 2006). The major employer of immigrants in Monmouth is Farmland Foods, which employs 1,500 workers (Farmland n.d.).

Incorporation can be defined as gaining a position in society that is secure (Hochschild and Mollenkopf 2009). Gerstle (2010) defines three different dimensions of political incorporation used in this book: legal, cultural, and political or institutional. The legal dimension refers to immigration status and the final attainment of citizenship as an important stage in the incorporation of immigrants (Bean, Brown, and Rumbaut 2006; DeSipio 2011; Gerstle 2010; Hochschild and Mollenkopf 2009; Jones-Correa 2004). The cultural dimension of incorporation refers to the acculturative process through which immigrants come to feel part of the host society (Gerstle 2010; Schleef and Cavalcanti 2009; Setzler and McRee n.d.). Finally, the political or institutional dimension of incorporation refers to the process through which the political system becomes responsive to the needs of immigrants (Hochschild and Mollenkopf 2009). Participation and engagement in the political system are indicators of the political incorporation of immigrants (Black 2011; DeSipio 2011; Hochschild and Mollenkopf 2009; Jones-Correa 2004; Schleef and Cavalcanti 2009). Trust in institutions is also an essential part of the process of political incorporation.

Formerly, immigrants and their offspring were expected to first acculturate and then seek entry and acceptance among the native-born for their social and economic advancement (Portes and Zhou 1993). Nowadays scholars agree that the incorporation of immigrants is a dynamic process that does not require immigrants to acculturate first and then get incorporated into the host society (Black 2011; Bean, Brown, and Rumbaut 2006; DeSipio 2011; Gidengil and Stolle 2009; Gerstle 2010; Hochschild and Mollenkopf 2009; Jones-Correa 2004; Mahler and Siemiatcki 2011; Mollenkopf and Hochschild 2010; Setzler and McRee n.d.).

This study argues that the process of incorporation can follow different stages, including contact, conflict/negotiation, incorporation, and full incorporation. In my findings, these stages vary in the extent to which immigrants command the use of English; believe they are linked to other Latinos and Anglos; interact with Anglos and neighbors, as well as other members of society; participate in social and political activities; and acquire the political attitudes of the host population. In addition, to achieve the higher degrees of incorporation, immigrants need to at least be documented—that is, be in the United States legally.

The progression through different stages also depends on a number of individual and social factors. In this study, I have considered the effect on incorporation of social class, length of stay in the country, immigrants' attitudes and beliefs, and the opportunities and constraints encountered in society through an analysis of 260 surveys and forty-seven in-depth interviews with Mexican immigrants living in Beardstown and Monmouth.

My findings showed that immigrants' levels of incorporation differed across the various dimensions of incorporation considered. The degree of legal incorporation among immigrants in the sample was uneven, placing immigrants at stages of incorporation that ranged from a stage of conflict/negotiation to one of full incorporation. This finding is important because immigrants' legal incorporation determines the level of political inclusion, the kinds of jobs they get, and their quality of life in general. Two facts account for this conclusion. First, the number of immigrants who were undocumented was high (50 percent in the sample of interviewees). As of November 2014, the United States' immigration system poses various obstacles for those who lack a child who is a resident or citizen, have less than five years of residence, have a criminal background, and/or came to the United States after they were sixteen years of age.

Second, immigrants in Beardstown and Monmouth naturalized at lower rates than other Mexican immigrants in the United Sates in 2012 (9.4 percent versus 26 percent) and at much lower rates than other immigrants in the United States (9.4 percent versus 40 percent) (U.S. Census Bureau, 2013b, 2013c). Further, almost 30 percent of this study's interviewees were not planning to ever apply for citizenship. Thus, less than 10 percent of immigrants in Beardstown and Monmouth had acquired full legal incorporation. The rest of them were at the conflict/negotiation stage (undocumented immigrants without chances for legalizing their status) or incorporation stage (undocumented immigrants with chances for legalizing their status/documented immigrants who were not planning to become citizens). The context of reception in the United States is less than ideal when it comes to legal incorporation.

The level of cultural incorporation among immigrants in Beardstown and Monmouth was quite high, placing most immigrants at the level of incorporation. When immigrants arrive in a country, they need to learn the local language, and their ability to communicate effectively is crucial for incorporation (Ager and Strang 2008; Gerstle 2010; Padilla 2006; Padilla and Perez 2003; Schleef and Cavalcanti 2009). Although language skills among immigrants were not optimal, immigrants seemed to be acquiring the necessary language skills to get by in society.

Most authors agree that immigrants need not abandon their ethnic identity and allegiance to their country of origin to successfully incorporate into American society (Black 2011; Bean, Brown, and Rumbaut 2006; Gerstle 2010; Jones-Correa 2004; Portes and Zhou 1993). Thus, this study looked at the sense of connectedness with other Latinos and also with Anglos. The sense of connectedness with other Latinos (which placed immigrants at the full level of incorporation) was higher than the feeling of connectedness with Anglos (which placed immigrants at the conflict/ negotiation level of incorporation). Further, the feeling of connectedness with Anglos was associated with the same feeling for other Latinos. Thus, immigrants may be following different acculturation strategies. In this sense, whereas some immigrants may have a strong sense of allegiance to both their original culture and the local one, others may have a low sense of allegiance to both.

The networks of trust and support built by individuals can have an impact on their incorporation into the host society. These networks can serve as bridges to social circles beyond one's own, and can bring people into contact with ideas and information they may not otherwise encounter (Gidengil and Stolle 2009). Moreover, the contact hypothesis predicts that more diversity implies more interethnic tolerance and social solidarity (Goto, Gee, and Takeuchi 2002). My study investigated two types of networks outside immigrants' own ethnic group: trust in neighbors and socialization with Anglos. The level of trust in neighbors was high among immigrants in Beardstown and Monmouth, placing them at the level of incorporation. However, less than half of the immigrants in Beardstown and Monmouth socialized with Anglo-Americans, placing them at the conflict/negotiation stage of incorporation in this dimension.

Participation is an essential part of the incorporation process (Black 2011; DeSipio 2011; Hochschild and Mollenkopf 2009; Jones-Correa 2004; Schleef and Cavalcanti 2009). My research considered the level of political incorporation among Mexican immigrants in Central Illinois as it related to participation in social and political activities. The participation rates in social activities were relatively high, placing immigrants at the level of incorporation. The rates for participation in political activities were somewhat lower, indicating that immigrants may be at the conflict/negotiation level of incorporation where these activities are considered.

This study also explored immigrants' trust in government as an indication of their level of political incorporation in society (Doerschler and Irving Jackson 2012; Maxwell 2010b). Trust is important for democracy because it influences participation (Guterbock and London 1983; Leal 2002; Marshall 2001) and legitimacy (Mishler and Rose 2001). It was interesting to compare the levels of trust in this study's sample with those of the general population (Abrajano and Álvarez 2010; Bonner 2009; Wenzel 2006). The data showed that immigrants in Beardstown and Monmouth exhibited levels of trust in government that were comparable to those of a national sample of the general population.

I also investigated whether different indicators of social class—namely, education, employment status, and income—were associated with the process of incorporation (Algan, Bisin, and Verdier 2012; Portes and Böröcz 1989; Schleef and Cavalcanti 2009). The evidence showed that the processes of legal, cultural, and political incorporation were associated with social class. Thus, either the process of incorporation shapes social status, or social status influences the opportunities for incorporation. Income was associated with citizenship acquisition, implying either that those with higher incomes had fewer difficulties acquiring their citizenship and/or that the acquisition of citizenship can lead to a better standard of living (Algan, Bisin, and Verdier 2012; Bloemraad 2002, 2006; Gonzalez-Barrera et al. 2013; Portes and Böröcz 1989; Schleef and Cavalcanti 2009).

A number of indicators of social class were associated with cultural incorporation. English language use was associated with several indicators of social class, and the interviewees who used more English or had better language skills were also more likely to have a higher socioeconomic status. Further, the feeling of connectedness with other Latinos was positively associated with education and showed no negative association with the other indicators of social class. The feeling of connectedness with Anglos was also positively associated with social class. Specifically, those who felt that the lives of Anglos had something or a lot to do with their lives had higher incomes than those who felt it had not much or nothing to do with their lives. Those who attended social functions with Anglos tended to have higher levels of education, full-time jobs, and higher incomes than those who did not attend social functions with Anglo-Americans (Algan, Bisin, and Verdier 2012; Portes and Böröcz 1989; Schleef and Cavalcanti 2009).

Results showed that both social participation and political participation were associated with education. Mirroring findings for the general population, immigrants with higher levels of income trusted the government less than did those with lower incomes (André 2014; Hetherington 1998; Wilkes 2015). Further, education also predicted trust in government; those with higher levels of education trusted the government less than did those with lower levels of education (table 13). These findings support the contention that the process of incorporation is associated with social class (Algan, Bisin, and Verdier 2012; Portes and Böröcz 1989; Schleef and Cavalcanti 2009).

This study argues that the attitudes and beliefs among immigrants about the different outcomes considered as part of the incorporation process will influence this process (Alba and Nee 2003; De Souza Briggs 2013; Waters and Jiménez 2005), and presents supporting evidence that attitudes shape the processes of legal, cultural, and political incorporation. Almost half of the immigrants in the interviews were undocumented, and these immigrants had a positive disposition toward becoming documented. Further, all of them were hoping for immigration reform to allow them to regularize their immigration status. Not everyone, however, wanted to become a citizen. Specifically, 28.8 percent of immigrants were not planning to apply for citizenship. Thus, almost one third of immigrants in the sample may never achieve full legal incorporation.

Attitudes and beliefs also shaped the process of cultural incorporation (Alba and Nee 2003; De Souza Briggs 2013; Waters and Jiménez 2005). Although English language skills varied considerably among respondents, immigrants in Central Illinois seemed positively disposed overall toward learning the English language. Further, several interviewees considered learning English to be essential to finding better jobs and communicating with teachers, health professionals, their own children, and society in general. Attitudes and beliefs of the respondents influenced their sense of connectedness with other groups, as well. In this instance, a set of interviewees emphasized feeling empathy and caring about what happened to other Latinos in the rest of the country (Sanchez 2008). Interviewees also believed a sense of connectedness to other Latinos could help incorporation by giving the Latino community unity and strength (Barretto et al. 2009). In addition, interviewees with positive attitudes and beliefs about Anglos felt more connected to them, while immigrants who exhibited a sense of distance or indifference toward Anglos felt less connected to them (Sanchez 2008). Overall, immigrants in Beardstown and Monmouth revealed mixed attitudes and beliefs about Anglos.

My research showed that, for the most part, immigrants had good relationships with their neighbors, and felt that having good relationships with their neighbors was important. These attitudes partly explained the high levels of trust in neighbors found in this study. The attitudes and beliefs about socializing with Anglos were mixed, leaning toward the negative. Whereas some immigrants thought interacting with Anglos helped incorporation (Putnam 2007), others felt that such interaction was constrained by ethnic and cultural barriers. These latter attitudes partly accounted for the somewhat low levels of socializing between immigrants and Anglo-Americans.

Different attitudes shaped the process of political incorporation, including attention paid to politics and government affairs (Albarracín, Wang, and Albarracín 2012; Leighley and Vedlitz 1999; Verba, Schlozman, and Brady 1995). Further, attitudes toward participating were mostly positive among respondents in the interviews. The political-science literature also contends that the attention paid to politics and government affairs can influence levels of trust in government (Verba, Scholzman, and Brady 1995). The data showed that immigrants in Beardstown and Monmouth who paid more attention to politics and government affairs also exhibited higher levels of trust in government. It may be that those who trust the government more tend to keep up with government affairs. It may also be that the more information people acquire about government affairs, the more they trust the government.

This study argues that the opportunities and constraints available in society shape the process of incorporation. It showed that these opportunities and constraints shaped the processes of legal, cultural, and political incorporation. The legal incorporation of immigrants is strongly determined by the policies for admission of foreign citizens (De Souza Briggs 2013; Portes and Böröcz 1989; Portes and Rumbaut 2001; Portes and Zhou 1993, 1994). Almost half of the sample of interviewees were undocumented and all of them were looking forward to acquiring green cards, but as discussed earlier, U.S. immigration law makes it difficult for immigrants who do not meet certain criteria to achieve legal residency. Recent changes in immigration policy may allow some of them to acquire temporary relief from deportation and to work legally in the United States, but many will remain undocumented for the foreseeable future, even though their desire for legal incorporation is strong.

The naturalization process can also be complex. Applicants for naturalization need to have good moral character, knowledge of U.S. history and government and the English language, and an inclination to support and defend the United States and the Constitution (Congressional Budget Office 2006). Because immigration procedures can be cumbersome, immigrants wanting to become permanent residents or citizens need to hire attorneys. Immigration attorneys can be expensive, with their fees ranging from $800 to $15,000, depending on the lawyer and the complexity of the paperwork. The legal fees can thus pose an additional obstacle for immigrants trying to advance in their process of legal incorporation.

The opportunities and constraints present in society shaped the process of cultural incorporation, as well. The availability of free English classes in Beardstown and Monmouth provided an opportunity for immigrants to learn English. Many interviewees reported having attended classes or were doing so at the time of the interviews. Others, however, faced obstacles to attending these classes because of work and family responsibilities. Society itself can provide opportunities for learning English as immigrants are faced with real-life situations that force them to learn the language. In this manner, several respondents reported learning English outside of a classroom setting. Some of these immigrants learned the language reading or watching TV, while others did so through interactions with coworkers and their own children.

Common experiences of exclusion, like anti-immigration state laws, provided opportunities for an increased sense of connectedness or solidarity with other

Latinos. Moreover, discrimination and social prejudice made immigrants feel closer to other Latinos (Sánchez 2008). Residential patterns are important for incorporation. Incorporation usually takes place when immigrants and their descendants live in neighborhoods not limited to their own ethnoracial or nationality group (Jiménez 2011). My research found no evidence of Latino housing segregation in Beardstown and Monmouth. These two towns are new to immigration, and this newness may be beneficial to the residential patterns found in this study. Further, the residential patterns observed provided immigrants with opportunities for meeting neighbors from diverse backgrounds, getting along with them, and occasionally socializing with them.

Finally, the interviews also provided insights on the opportunities immigrants found to socialize with Anglo-Americans. Immigrants met Anglos in different circumstances, including work, church, and their children's schools, or through friends or their children's friends. In turn, immigrants interacted with Anglos through various activities, such as eating during lunch breaks at work, at barbecues and restaurants, and when attending their children's sports activities. Hence, immigrants in Central Illinois found a number of opportunities to interact with Anglo-Americans. However, several immigrants felt that ethnic or cultural barriers inhibited their interaction with them.

Immigrants in Central Illinois found opportunities to participate in church or religious groups, schools and neighborhood organizations, and groups representing Mexicans or Latinos. Overall, the level of opportunities to participate in social activities was considerably high. Immigrants faced a number of obstacles that precluded social participation, including lack of time due to family obligations or work, and lack of the necessary language skills. The opportunities for participation in political activities seemed dependent upon contact with a person or institution that requested participation. In addition, the obstacles affecting social participation, including lack of time and limited language skills, also influenced political participation. Other obstacles to participation came from the immigration and citizenship requirements for making contributions to political campaigns, registering to vote, and voting.

In this study, I tested the hypothesis that the length of stay in the country influenced the process of incorporation (Cabassa 2003). Evidence showed that the length of stay shaped the processes of cultural and political participation. Not surprisingly, length of stay in the country was positively associated with the language of TV and radio use and with English reading skills; people who had been in the country longer were more likely to watch TV or listen to the radio in English only versus Spanish only and had better English reading skills. This finding makes sense considering that a longer stay in the United States would provide immigrants with additional time and opportunities to learn English. The length of stay in the country significantly predicted participation in a church or religious group, with those who had been in the country longer being more likely to participate in them. In addition, the length of stay in the country was associated with one form of political participation, namely, contacting a public official (Cabassa 2003). Although the relationship between length of stay in the country and incorporation is not a necessary one, it seems that length of stay in the country may help incorporation in some respects.

Gender influenced the process of cultural incorporation. For starters, women tended to watch TV and listen to the radio predominantly in Spanish. Coincidentally, women's language skills were poorer than their male counterparts.' A comparison of the education levels of men and women showed that men were more likely to have a high school education (35 percent) than women (31 percent). It may be that the level of education is shaping language skills. It may also be that women are more isolated and have fewer opportunities to learn English because they tend to stay at home more. The data gave partial support to this view, showing that whereas only 1 percent of the men stayed at home, this number for women was 23 percent. Thus, language skills may be related to both education and occupation.

Women also trusted their neighbors less than men. This finding is somewhat puzzling and requires further research. One possibility is that perhaps Mexican women are less trusting than Mexican men in general. However, women trusted the governments in the United States and in Mexico at higher rates. The mean score for trust in the government in Washington for women was 3.29, and for men, 3.13. Those same numbers for trust in the government in Mexico were 3.04 and 2.94. The only information that came up during the interviews related to this topic was that a few men reported interacting with their neighbors while mowing the lawn. It may be that mowing is a male-dominated activity and facilitates interaction with neighbors. However, this fact alone could not account for the differences in trust in neighbors between men and women. It may be that women are more isolated in general.

The Context of Reception

Immigration brings "strangers" into a homeland (Citrin and Sides 2008). Discrimination, an unequal or negative treatment of people of a certain group (Quillian 2006), has a powerful impact on the lives of immigrants, affecting their chances for getting jobs, performing well at school, and having a good quality of life. According to the respondents, discrimination in Beardstown and Monmouth is prevalent and constitutes a barrier for the incorporation of immigrants. Further, immigrants in these two towns feel discrimination is a major problem and are more likely to have had a close experience with discrimination than Latinos in a national sample.

Thus, it is possible that discrimination in some areas where immigration is a recent phenomenon may be more pronounced than in other areas more accustomed to the idea of immigration.

My research investigated the factors shaping the feelings of acceptance, perceptions of discrimination, and experiences with discrimination among Mexican immigrants in Beardstown and Monmouth. Different indicators of social class were associated with the variables under analysis. For instance, the sign of the statistical association was not always the one expected. Specifically, those with lower levels of education were more likely to feel accepted by Anglos. However, correlation analysis showed that those with higher incomes also tended to feel more accepted by Anglos. This latter finding hints that the existence of discrimination can complicate the process of incorporation into the host society, as those with lower income and education levels may be discriminated against more, and this discrimination may in turn marginalize them further in society.

My findings showed that those who attended social functions with Anglos were also more likely to feel accepted by Anglos and less likely to have had a close experience with discrimination. This finding is consistent with the research that shows that contact among different ethnic groups can increase understanding and tolerance among them (Goto, Gee, and Takeuchi 2002; Phinney, Madden, and Santos 1998; Rakosi Rosenbloom and Way 2004). It also offers the possibility for continued improvement in relationships between Anglos and Hispanics based on continued interaction between the two groups.

Mexican immigrants face discrimination in different contexts. The interviewees in this study, or a member of their family, experienced discrimination at workplaces, restaurants and stores, schools, churches, and housing complexes. Interviewees also reported instances of discrimination in their interactions with the police, health care providers, and members of the community. Although discrimination experiences in these two towns were comparable, discrimination in schools was more pervasive in Monmouth than in Beardstown. It is possible that the lack of a dual language program in the former town explains the poorer experiences of students (Salinas 2005). Moreover, the case of discrimination in Monmouth by classmates involved the use of racial slurs to discriminate against a Latino student, indicating that some traditional racist ideas may be present in this community (Akrami, Ekehammar, and Araya 2000).

Finally, the racist history of Beardstown along with the ethnic tensions resulting from the violent death of a White resident probably made discrimination by the general population in this town more pervasive than in Monmouth. However, relations between Anglos and Latinos in Beardstown seem to be improving. The community leaders addressed this problem in the past, and some religious communities are working toward the incorporation of the different groups that live there. Hopefully, relationships among the different ethnic groups will continue to improve in Beardstown.

Differences between Beardstown and Monmouth

The school districts in Beardstown and Monmouth have responded to the population changes in these two towns. Beardstown established a dual language program in the mid-2000s. This is an encouraging decision because research shows that dual language programs hold the most promise for the success of Latino students (Salinas 2005). Within this program, students take classes both in English and Spanish, switching throughout the day. The program is optional and available for native and non-native speakers alike. Monmouth has not gone as far as Beardstown. It did, however, set up a bilingual kindergarten program and hired a bilingual teacher to teach first graders.[1] Thus, both towns have responded to the needs of growing bilingual populations.

Churches offer different forms of support to newly arrived immigrants in that they provide spiritual comfort and social networks that the newcomers can rely on for their incorporation into the host society. Saint Alexius Catholic Church and Immaculate Conception Catholic Church, in Beardstown and Monmouth respectively, offer Masses in Spanish, thus offering support for immigrants who lack English language skills. Other churches serve the Latino communities in Beardstown and Monmouth as well. For example, the churches Nazarene, De Restauración Cristo te Ama, Ebenezer Encuentro con Dios, and Nueva Vida offer services for Spanish speakers in Beardstown. However, only the church Solid Rock offers Protestant Spanish services in Monmouth.[2] Thus, it seems that the community in Beardstown has more religious services targeting the Latino community.

My research showed that immigrants in Beardstown had better access to health care than those in Monmouth. The Cass County Health Department in Beardstown offers a full-service primary care clinic, as well as discounted rates on all of their services for uninsured patients. The Warren County Health Department in Monmouth offers only immunizations, smoking cessation programs, breast-cancer awareness outreach, and cardiovascular-health awareness outreach. In sum, whereas immigrants in Beardstown can access primary care physicians in town at discounted rates, immigrants in Monmouth need to drive fifteen miles to the nearby town of Galesburg, Illinois, to do so.

This study also exposed dissimilar levels of political incorporation between immigrants in these two towns. Overall, the civil society was more vibrant in

Beardstown than in Monmouth. Beardstown had a variety of groups, including Amigos Unidos, CASA, CAR, and Faith Coalition for the Common Good, but Monmouth lacked groups representing Latinos. Additionally, immigrants in Beardstown participated at higher rates than immigrants in Monmouth in most activities. For example, when it came to social activities, 35 percent of immigrants in Beardstown volunteered time to a religious group, while this number for Monmouth was 22 percent. The differences between Beardstown and Monmouth were less striking in terms of those who volunteered time to a school or neighborhood organization (26 percent versus 21 percent) and a group representing Mexicans or Latinos (30 percent versus 25 percent).

The rates for participation in political activities also differed between the two towns. For example, whereas 24 percent of immigrants in Beardstown had contacted a public official, this number for Monmouth was 4 percent. The differences in participation rates between Beardstown and Monmouth were comparable for participation in a political campaign (14 percent versus 5 percent) and in a public meeting or demonstration (20 percent versus 10 percent). Conversely, the number of people who were registered to vote and had voted in an election in the United States was slightly higher for Monmouth (12 percent and 6 percent) than for Beardstown (10 percent and 4 percent).

This study also showed differences between Beardstown and Monmouth in regard to discrimination. In this case, however, Beardstown seemed a less friendly place for them. Immigrants in Beardstown feel less accepted by Anglos, believe discrimination is a bigger problem, and are more likely to have had a close experience with discrimination than immigrants in Monmouth. This town's history as a "sundown town" and conflict among Hispanics and Whites may explain these differences. However, relationships between Hispanics and Whites in this town have improved over the years. This is not to say that discrimination is not an issue in Monmouth.

President Obama's Immigration Executive Order

As mentioned above, the lack of proper documents has important consequences for the lives of immigrants. Almost half of this sample of interviewees were undocumented. The recent changes in immigration policy may allow some of these immigrants to acquire temporary relief from deportation and to work legally in the United States. As of November 2014, this applies to those who have a child who is a resident or citizen, have five years of residence in the United States, or came to the country before they were seventeen years of age. These people may be able to get better jobs, see their families in Mexico, and, overall, have a better quality of life. They may also be able to achieve fuller cultural and political incorporation. The rest of the undocumented immigrants, however, may remain in limbo until comprehensive immigration reform that benefits all undocumented immigrants is passed.

I have argued that legal incorporation is an essential part of the process of immigrant incorporation. Strict immigration policies do not stop immigrants from coming to this country, but curtail immigrants' prospects for finding a good job and having a decent standard of living. The United States will continue to attract immigrants in agriculture, manufacturing, meatpacking, and construction, among other sectors. Most of these immigrants will continue to lack college degrees. As chapter 3 showed, getting a work visa is very difficult for a person who lacks a college degree. Thus, immigration reform needs to provide a pathway to legal residency for immigrants who lack a college education but can find job opportunities in the United States.

Survey Instrument

GENERAL AND DEMOGRAPHIC INFORMATION

Screener (if answers anything other than Mexican, stop interview)

1: Now I want to ask you about you and your family's heritage. Are you Mexican, Puerto Rican, Cuban, Dominican, or Salvadoran, or are you and your ancestors from another country?

1	Mexican	32	Italy
2	Puerto Rican	33	Africa
3	Cuban	34	Spain
4	Dominican	35	Portugal
5	Salvadoran	91	USA
6	Other Central America	97	Other (indicate) _____
7	Other South America	98	Don't know
30	Jamaica	99	Refused
31	Trinidad/Caribbean Islands		

2: Were you born in the United States, the island of Puerto Rico?

1   United States

2   Puerto Rico

3   Another country

8   Don't know

9   Refused

Only the persons born in Mexico were selected for this study.

3: From what region or state are you? _____

4: If you weren't born in the United States, how many years have you been in the country? _____

5: Would you prefer to be interviewed in English or Spanish?

1   English

2   Spanish

6: Gender

1   Male

2   Female

7: What is your age? _____

99   Refused

8: What is your age? (Top Range 65+)

1   18–29

2   30–39

3   40–54

4   55–64

5   65+

9   Refused

9: What race do you consider yourself to be? White, Black or African American, Asian, or some other race?

1   White

2   Black or African American

3   Asian

4   Some other race

5   Hispanic or Latino

9   Refused

10: Are you currently married, living with a partner, widowed, divorced, or separated, or have you never been married?

1   Married

2   Living with a partner

3   Widowed

4   Divorced

5   Separated

6   Never been married

9   Refused

11: Do you have kids?

1   Yes   9   Refused

2   No

12: Including yourself, how many people live in your household? _____

99 Refused

13: What is your employment status? Are you

1   Employed full time   6   Unemployed

2   Employed part time   7   Laid off

3   A homemaker or stay at   8   Disabled

    home parent   98 Don't know

4   Retired   99 Refused

5   A student

*This variable was recoded as full time versus the rest. Students (*n = 1*) and retired persons (*n = 2*) were dropped.*

14: Is your total annual household income from all sources, and before taxes?

1   Between $10,000 and $20,000   5   Between $50,000 and $60,000

2   Between $20,000 and $30,000   6 $60,000 and more

3   Between $30,000 and $40,000   8   Don't know

4   Between $40,000 and $50,000   9   Refused

The income variable used as a control in the analyses divided income levels into less than $30,000 or $30,000 or more.

15: What is the last grade or class that you completed in school?

1   None, or grade 1–8   6   Some college, no 4-year degree

2   Middle school incomplete/   7   College graduate

    complete   8   Post-graduate training/

3   High school incomplete/complete   professional schooling after

4   GED   college

5   Business, technical, or vocational 9   Refused

    school after high school

The education variable used as a control in the analyses divided education levels into incomplete/complete middle school or less and high school incomplete or more.

16: Aside from weddings and funerals, how often do you attend religious services? Would you say more than once a week, once a week, once or twice a month, a few times a year, seldom, or never?

1	More than once a week	5	Seldom
2	Once a week	6	Never
3	Once or twice a month	8	Don't know
4	A few times a year	9	Refused

17: What is your religious preference? Are you Protestant, Catholic, Jewish, some other religion, or no religion?

1	Protestant	4	Some other religion
2	Catholic	5	No religion
3	Jewish	9	Refused

18: Now we would like to ask you about U.S. citizenship. Are you

1	A U.S. citizen	4	Not planning to become a citizen
2	Currently applying for citizenship	8	Don't Know
3	Planning to apply for citizenship	9	Refused

This question was reverse scored so that higher values represented more closeness to the acquisition of citizenship.

LANGUAGE QUESTIONS

19: How much do you agree with the following statement about you?: "I feel comfortable speaking English." Is that strongly agree, somewhat agree, somewhat disagree, or strongly disagree?

1	Strongly agree	4	Strongly disagree
2	Somewhat agree	8	Don't know
3	Somewhat disagree		

This question was reverse scored so that higher values represented increased agreement.

20: Would you say you can read a newspaper or book in English? Very well, pretty well, just a little, or not at all?

1	Very well	4	Not at all
2	Pretty well	8	Don't Know
3	Just a little	9	Refused

This question was reverse scored so that higher values represented better reading skills.

21: In what language are the news programs you usually watch on TV or listen to on the radio? Only Spanish, more Spanish than English, both equally, more English than Spanish, or only English?

1	Only Spanish	6	Do not watch TV or listen to
2	More Spanish than English		Radio
3	Both equally	8	Don't Know
4	More English than Spanish	9	Refused
5	Only English		

POLITICS

22: How much attention would you say you pay to politics and government? A lot, a fair amount, not much, or none at all?

1	A lot	4	None at all
2	A fair amount	8	Don't Know
3	Not much	9	Refused

This question was reverse scored so that higher values represented more attention paid to politics and government.

23: Continuing to think about politics, how much of the time do you trust the government in Washington to do what is right—just about always, most of the time, or only some of the time?

1	Just about always	4	Never
2	Most of the time	8	Don't Know
3	Some of the time	9	Refused

This question was reverse scored so that higher values represented higher levels of trust in government.

24: Since you arrived in this country, has your trust in the government in Washington increased, stayed the same, or decreased?

1	Increased	8	Don't Know
2	Stayed the same	9	Refused
3	Decreased		

25: How much did you trust the government in your country of origin to do what is right?

1   A lot

2   Some

3   Not much

8   Not at all

9   Refused

This question was reverse scored so that higher values represented higher levels of trust in government.

26: People express their opinions about politics and current events in a number of ways. In the United States, in the past year, have you contacted any elected official, or not?

1   Yes

2   No

8   Don't know

9   Refused

This question was reverse scored so that a higher value represented participation in the activity.

27: In the United States, in the past year have you worked as a volunteer for or made a contribution to a political candidate, or not?

1   Yes

2   No

8   Don't know

9   Refused

This question was reverse scored so that a higher value represented participation in the activity.

28: In the United States, in the past year have you attended a public meeting or demonstration in the community where you live, or not?

1   Yes

2   No

8   Don't know

9   Refused

This question was reverse scored so that a higher value represented participation in the activity.

29: Was the public meeting or demonstration specific to Latino concerns, or not?

1   Specific to Latino concerns

2   Not specific to Latino concerns

8   Don't know

9   Refused

30: Next I would like to talk with you about volunteer (spending time helping without being paid for it) activity. In the past year have you volunteered your time to any church or religious group?

1	Yes, volunteered	8	Don't know
2	No, did not volunteer	9	Refused

This question was reverse scored so that a higher value represented participation in the activity.

31: In the past year have you volunteered your time to any school, or neighborhood or community group?

1	Yes, volunteered	8	Don't know
2	No, did not volunteer	9	Refused

This question was reverse scored so that a higher value represented participation in the activity.

32: In the past year have you volunteered your time to any organization representing your own particular nationality or ethnic or racial group?

1	Yes, volunteered	8	Don't know
2	No, did not volunteer	9	Refused

This question was reverse scored so that a higher value represented participation in the activity.

33: Are you registered to vote?

1	Yes	8	Don't Know
2	No	9	Refused

This question was reverse scored so that a higher value represented yes.

34: Have you ever voted in an election in the United States, or not?

1	Yes	8	Don't Know
2	No	9	Refused

This question was reverse scored so that a higher value represented yes.

35: In politics today, do you consider yourself a Republican, a Democrat, an Independent, or something else?

1	Republican	7	Something else
2	Democrat	8	Don't Know
3	Independent	9	Refused

36: Based on your experience, do you think political leaders are interested in the problems of particular concern to Hispanics/Latinos living here or not?

1   Yes   8   Don't know
2   No   9   Refused

This question was reverse scored so that a higher value represented yes.

37: Now I'm going to ask you about the economic situation of the United States. Do you think the economy is doing very well, well, not so well, or not at all well?

1   Very well   4   Not at all well
2   Just well   8   Don't know
3   Not so well   9   Refused

This question was reverse scored so that higher values reflected a better perceived economic situation.

38: Do you think the United States should increase the number of Latin Americans allowed to come and work in this country legally, reduce the number, or allow the same number as it does now?

1   Increase the number of Latin   3   Allow the same number of Latin
    Americans   Americans
2   Reduce the number of Latin   8   Don't know
    Americans   9   Refused

This variable was recoded as follows: increase (1), allow the same (2), decrease (3).

CONNECTEDNESS AND SOCIALIZATION

39: How much do you trust your neighbor to do what is right—a lot, some, not much, or not at all?

1   A lot   4   Not at all
2   Some   8   Don't Know
3   Not much   9   Refused

This question was reverse scored so that higher values represented more trust in neighbors.

40: How much do you think what happens generally to the Anglo (non-Hispanic White) people in the city or town you are living in has to do with what happens in your life?

1	A lot	4	Not at all
2	Some	8	Don't Know
3	Not much	9	Refused

This question was reverse scored so that higher values represented an increased sense of connectedness.

41: How much do you think what happens generally to the African American people in the city or town you are living in has to do with what happens in your life?

1	A lot	4	Not at all
2	Some	8	Don't Know
3	Not much	9	Refused

This question was reverse scored so that higher values represented an increased sense of connectedness.

42: How much do you think what happens generally to the Hispanic/Latino people in the city or town you are living in has to do with what happens in your life?

1	A lot	4	Not at all
2	Some	8	Don't Know
3	Not much	9	Refused

This question was reverse scored so that higher values represented an increased sense of connectedness.

43: How much do you think what happens generally to the Hispanic/Latino people living in other parts of the country has to do with what happens in your life?

1	A lot	4	Not at all
2	Some	8	Don't Know
3	Not much	9	Refused

This question was reverse scored so that higher values represented an increased sense of connectedness.

44: How much do you agree with the following statement about you? "I attend social functions with Anglo Americans." Is that strongly agree, somewhat agree, somewhat disagree, or strongly disagree?

1	Strongly agree	4	Strongly disagree
2	Somewhat agree	8	Don't know
3	Somewhat disagree	9	Refused

This question was reverse scored so that higher values represented an increased agreement with the statement.

DISCRIMINATION AND ACCEPTANCE

45: How much do you agree with the following statement about you?: "I feel accepted by Anglo Americans." Is that strongly agree, somewhat agree, somewhat disagree, or strongly disagree?

1	Strongly agree	4	Strongly disagree
2	Somewhat agree	8	Don't know
3	Somewhat disagree		

This question was reverse scored so that higher values represented an increased agreement with the statement.

46: In general, do you think discrimination against Latinos is a major problem, minor problem, or not a problem in preventing Latinos in general from succeeding in America?

1	Major problem	8	Don't Know
2	Minor problem	9	Refused
3	Not a problem		

This question was reverse scored so that higher values represented a larger problem.

47: In the past five years, have you or a family member experienced discrimination?

1	Yes	8	Don't know
2	No	9	Refused

This question was reverse scored so that a higher value represented a yes answer.

Comparison of Selected Demographic Characteristics of Mexican Immigrants

THIS TABLE SHOWS SELECTED DEMOGRAPHIC CHARACTERISTICS OF THIS STUDY'S sample of 260 interviewees in Central Illinois compared with those of a sample collected by the Pew Hispanic Center's 2004 National Survey of Latinos. The table presents percentages and absolute numbers in parentheses.

| | Percentages (Absolute Numbers in Parentheses) | |
	Central Illinois	Pew Sample
Sample Size	260	614
Beardstown	50 (131)	
Monmouth	50 (129)	
State in Mexico		
Mexico (includes Federal District)	22 (58)	———
Michoacán	14 (35)	———
Durango	9 (23)	———
Guanajuato	7 (19)	———
Guerrero	5 (12)	———
Veracruz	3 (8)	———

	Percentages (Absolute Numbers in Parentheses)	
	Central Illinois	Pew Sample
Chihuahua	3 (7)	————
Other	22 (57)	————
Missing	16 (41)	————
Years in the United States		
Mean	10.76	16.11
Standard Deviation	7.01	11.82
Language of the Interview		
English	2 (5)	14 (86)
Spanish	98 (255)	86 (528)
Gender		
Males	56 (146)	51 (310)
Females	44 (114)	49 (304)
Age		
Mean	32.20	36.46
Standard Deviation	10.20	12.95
Race		
White	5 (12)	43 (262)
Hispanic	95 (239)	38 (231)
Black	0	3 (17)
Other	0 (1)	15 (95)
Relationship Status		
Married	64 (130)	53 (325)
Living with Partner	28 (57)	13 (79)
Widowed	1 (2)	3 (19)
Divorced	3 (6)	5 (32)
Separated	4 (8)	7 (40)
Never Married	20 (51)	19 (116)
Children		
No	33 (84)	————
Yes	67 (173)	————
No. of People Living in Household		
Mean	4.30	————
Standard Deviation	1.67	————
Employment Status		
Full-time	68 (174)	52 (320)
Part-time	11 (27)	16 (97)
Stay Home	11 (28)	17 (103)

	Percentages (Absolute Numbers in Parentheses)	
	Central Illinois	Pew Sample
Retired	1 (2)	2 (15)
Student	0 (1)	2 (15)
Unemployed/Laid Off	9 (23)	4 (26)
Disabled	0 (1)	3 (19)
Income		
Less than $30,000	71 (156)	53 (326)
$30,000 or More	29 (65)	47 (288)
Education		
Middle School or Less	66 (170)	———
Some High School or More	34 (86)	———
Religion		
Catholic	83 (210)	79 (485)
Protestant	6 (16)	4 (27)
No Religion	4 (9)	4 (25)
Other	7 (17)	11 (65)

Notes

**CHAPTER 1. CASE STUDIES: THE CASES OF BEARDSTOWN
AND MONMOUTH, ILLINOIS**

1. North and South Dakota were excluded because none of their counties had a proportion of Latinos of at least 5 percent.
2. Romulo, interview with the author, July 31, 2011, Monmouth, IL.
3. Helena, interview with the author, September 27, 2013, Monmouth, IL.
4. Rita, interview with the author, July 31, 2011, Monmouth, IL.
5. Alejandra, interview with the author, November 26, 2011, Beardstown, IL.
6. Annie Zak, "Sunday Focus: Hispanic Population Blooms in Monmouth," *(Galesburg, IL) Register-Mail*, August 23, 2010.
7. José Guadalupe, interview with the author, December 3, 2011, Beardstown, IL.
8. Martín, interview with the author, August 5, 2009, Macomb, IL.
9. Jeff K. Lowenstein, "More Diverse Latino, African Communities in Beardstown Five Years after the Raid," *Vívelo Hoy*, April 11, 2012, http://www.vivelohoy.com.
10. Stephen Spearie, "Beardstown's Latest Wave of Immigrants Celebrate Heritage," *(Springfield, IL) State Journal-Register*, August 24, 2014.
11. Floriberto and Jorge, interviews with the author, December 3, 2011, Beardstown, IL.
12. Rosa, interview with the author, December 3, 2011, Beardstown, IL.

13. Molly Beck, "Some Beardstown Students Receive Bilingual Experience," *(Springfield, IL) State Journal-Register*, September 3, 2011.
14. Zak, "Sunday Focus."
15. Ibid.
16. Beardstown also has an increasing number of French speakers.
17. Irma, interview with the author, November 26, 2011, Beardstown, IL.
18. Martín, interview with the author, August 5, 2009, Macomb, IL.
19. Jorge, interview with the author, November 26, 2011, Beardstown, IL.
20. Because of the way education was measured, the samples cannot be compared.

CHAPTER 2. LEGAL INCORPORATION: IMMIGRATION STATUS AND CITIZENSHIP

1. Helena, interview with the author, September 27, 2013, Monmouth, IL.
2. Gabriela, interview with the author, September 15, 2013, Monmouth, IL.
3. María Isabel, interview with the author, September 7, 2013, Beardstown, IL.
4. Ibid.
5. María Isabel, interview with the author, September 17, 2013, Beardstown, IL.
6. Ibid.
7. Some devolutionary powers derive from the 1996 Personal Responsibility and Work Opportunity Reform Act.
8. María Isabel, interview with the author, September 17, 2013, Beardstown, IL.
9. Gustavo, interview with the author, September 15, 2013, Beardstown, IL.
10. Ibid.
11. Ibid.
12. Floriberto, interview with the author, September 7, 2013, Beardstown, IL.
13. Jorge, interview with the author, September 7, 2013, Beardstown, IL.
14. Isabel, interview with the author, September 15, 2013, Beardstown, IL.
15. Karen, interview with the author, September 15, 2013, Monmouth, IL.
16. Gustavo, interview with the author, September 15, 2013, Beardstown, IL.
17. Ibid.
18. I did not estimate percentages because some immigrants held several jobs before coming to the towns under study.
19. Because of the sensitive nature of the information discussed, I prefer not to reveal the name of my interviewee.
20. Floriberto, interview with the author, September 7, 2013, Beardstown, IL.
21. Gustavo, interview with the author, September 15, 2013, Beardstown, IL.
22. Rosa, interview with the author, September 21, 2013, Beardstown, IL.
23. Ibid.
24. Alejandro, interview with the author, September 21, 2013, Beardstown, IL.

25. Ibid.

26. Alejandra, interview with the author, September 21, 2013, Beardstown, IL.

CHAPTER 3. THE CULTURE OF INCORPORATION:
LANGUAGE USE, IDENTITY, AND SOCIAL CONNECTEDNESS

1. Martín, interview with the author, November 26, 2011, Beardstown, IL.

2. María Luisa, interview with the author, September 27, 2013, Monmouth, IL.

3. Ibid.

4. Ibid.

5. For details about these variables, please see appendix: length of stay in the country (appendix, no. 4), gender (appendix, no. 6), education (appendix, no. 15), employment status (appendix, no. 13), and income (appendix, no. 14).

6. Benita, interview with the author, July 30, 2011, Monmouth, Il; Úrsula, interview with the author, July 31, 2011, Monmouth, IL.

7. Walter, interview with the author, July 31, 2011, Monmouth, IL.

8. Luis, interview with the author, November 26, 2011, Beardstown, IL.

9. Estela, interview with the author, July 30, 2011, Monmouth, IL.

10. Gabriel, interview with the author, July 30, 2011, Monmouth, IL; Zacarias, interview with the author, July 31, 2011, Monmouth, IL.

11. Florencia, interview with the author, July 30, 2011, Monmouth, IL; Alberta, interview with the author, July 31, 2011, Monmouth, IL.

12. Hilda, interview with the author, July 30, 2011, Monmouth, IL.

13. Estela, interview with the author, July 30, 2011, Monmouth, IL.

14. Hugo, interview with the author, December 3, 2011, Beardstown, IL.

15. Benita, interview with the author, July 30, 2011, Monmouth, IL.

16. Hilda, interview with the author, July 30, 2011, Monmouth, IL; Sandro, interview with the author, July 31, 2011, Monmouth, IL.

17. Luis, interview with the author, November 26, 2011, Beardstown, IL.

18. Martín, interview with the author, November 26, 2011, Beardstown, IL.

19. Hilda and Florencia, interviews with the author, July 30, 2011, Monmouth, IL.

20. Luis, interview with the author, November 26, 2011, Beardstown, IL.

21. Carlos, interview with the author, July 30, 2011, Monmouth, IL.

22. Hugo, interview with the author, December 3, 2011, Beardstown, IL.

23. Martín, interview with the author, November 26, 2011, Beardstown, IL.

24. Isabel, interview with the author, November 26, 2011, Beardstown, IL.

25. Floriberto, interview with the author, November 26, 2011, Beardstown, IL.

26. Ignacio, interview with the author, July 30, 2011, Monmouth, IL.

27. Alejandra, interview with the author, November 26, 2011, Beardstown, IL.

28. Irma, interview with the author, November 26, 2011, Beardstown, IL.

29. Teresa, interview with the author, December 3, 2011, Beardstown, IL.

30. Irma, interview with the author, November 26, 2011, Beardstown, IL.

31. Hilda, interview with the author, July 30, 2011, Monmouth, IL.

32. Carlos, interview with the author, July 30, 2011, Monmouth, IL.

33. Hilda, interview with the author, July 30, 2011, Monmouth, IL.

34. Isabel, interview with the author, November 26, 2011, Beardstown, IL.

35. Luis, interview with the author, November 26, 2011, Beardstown, IL.

36. Teresa, interview with the author, December 3, 2011, Beardstown, IL.

37. Jesús, interview with the author, November 26, 2011, Beardstown, IL.

38. Hugo, interview with the author, September 21, 2013, Beardstown, IL.

39. Ibid.

40. Hilda, interview with the author, July 30, 2011, Monmouth, IL.

41. Alberto, interview with the author, July 31, 2011, Monmouth, IL.

42. Rita, interview with the author, July 31, 2011, Monmouth, IL.

43. Floriberto, interview with the author, December 3, 2011, Beardstown, IL.

44. Hilda, interview with the author, July 30, 2011, Monmouth, IL.

45. Floriberto, interview with the author, December 3, 2011, Beardstown, IL.

46. Gabriel, interview with the author, July 30, 2011, Monmouth, IL.

47. Hilda, interview with the author, July 30, 2011, Monmouth, IL.

48. Floriberto, interview with the author, December 3, 2011, Beardstown, IL.

49. Florencia, interview with the author, July 30, 2011, Monmouth, IL.

50. Sandro, interview with the author, July 31, 2011, Monmouth, IL.

51. Leo, interview with the author, July 30, 2011, Monmouth, IL.

**CHAPTER 4. THE CONTEXT OF RECEPTION:
DISCRIMINATION AND ACCEPTANCE**

1. Floriberto, interview with the author, September 7, 2013, Beardstown, IL.

2. Ibid.

3. Isidro, interview with the author, September 15, 2013, Monmouth, IL.

4. Ibid.

5. Ibid.

6. Ibid.

7. Lisa Kernek, "Growing Pains," *Illinois Issues*, September 2001, http://illinoisissues.uis.edu.

8. Annie Pittman, "Kenny Wallace Left His Mark as Monmouth Police Chief," *Daily Review Atlas*, July 19, 2013, http://www.reviewatlas.com.

9. I did not ask respondents to discuss all their experiences with discrimination, but just one example. Therefore, the fact that, for example, 23 percent of respondents reported a case of discrimination at work does not mean these same persons did not also experience discrimination in other settings.

10. Rosa, interview with the author, September 21, 2013, Beardstown, IL.

11. Floriberto, interviews with the author, November 26, 2011, and September 21, 2013, Beardstown, IL.

12. Jorge, interview with the author, September 7, 2013, Beardstown, IL.

13. Walter, interview with the author, July 31, 2011, Monmouth, IL.

14. Hugo, interview with the author, September 21, 2013, Beardstown, IL.

15. Isidro, interview with the author, September 13, 2013, Monmouth, IL.

16. Jorge, interview with the author, December 3, 2011, Beardstown, IL.

17. Ibid.

18. Ibid.

19. María Isabel, interviews with the author, December 3, 2011, and September 7, 2013, Beardstown, IL.

20. Gustavo, interview with the author, September 15, 2013, Beardstown, IL.

21. Crisleiry, interview with the author, September 13, 2013, Monmouth, IL.

22. Ignacio, interview with the author, July 31, 2011, Monmouth, IL.

23. Nancy, interview with the author, September 13, 2013, Monmouth, IL.

24. Annie Zak, "Sunday Focus: Hispanic Population Blooms in Monmouth," *(Galesburg, IL) Register-Mail*, August 23, 2010.

25. Beardstown also has an increasing number of French speakers.

26. Florencia, interview with the author, July 30, 2011, Monmouth, IL.

27. Immigrants, even if they are undocumented, pay sales taxes, property taxes either directly or through their rent, and may pay federal income tax.

28. Florencia, interview with the author, July 30, 2011, Monmouth, IL.

29. Juana, interview with the author, July 30, 2011, Monmouth, IL.

30. Walter, interview with the author, July 31, 2011, Monmouth, IL.

31. Alejandra, interview with the author, September 21, 2013, Beardstown, IL.

32. Eduardo, interview with the author, November 26, 2013, Beardstown, IL.

33. Manuel, interview with the author, July 30, 2011, Monmouth, IL.

34. María Luisa, interview with the author, September 27, 2013, Monmouth, IL.

35. Zacarías, interview with the author, July 31, 2011, Monmouth, IL.

36. Floriberto, interview with the author, September 7, 2013, Beardstown, IL.

37. Alberta, interview with the author, July 31, 2011, Monmouth, IL.

38. Martín, interview with the author, November 26, 2013, Beardstown, IL.

39. Helena, interview with the author, September 27, 2013, Monmouth, IL.

40. Isidro, interview with the author, September 15, 2013, Monmouth, IL.

41. Alejandro, interview with the author, September 21, 2013, Beardstown, IL.

42. Úrsula, interview with the author, July 31, 2011, Monmouth, IL.

43. Isidro, interview with the author, September 15, 2013, Monmouth, IL.

44. Karen, interview with the author, September 15, 2013, Monmouth, IL.

45. Filiberto, interview with the author, November 26, 2013, Beardstown, IL.

46. Eduardo, interview with the author, November 26, 2013, Beardstown, IL.

CHAPTER 5. THE POLITICS OF INCORPORATION: PARTICIPATION

1. Gustavo, interview with the author, September 15, 2013, Beardstown, IL.
2. Ibid.
3. Helena, interview with the author, September 27, 2013, Monmouth, IL.
4. Ibid.
5. For details about these variables, see education (appendix, no. 15), employment status (appendix, no. 13), income (appendix, no. 14), length of stay in the country (appendix, no. 4), and gender (appendix, no. 6).
6. For details about these variables, see: trust in government (appendix, no. 23); attention paid to politics (appendix, no. 22); party identification (appendix, no. 35); experience with discrimination (appendix, no. 47); a sense of connectedness with Anglo-Americans (appendix, no. 40), African Americans (appendix, no. 41), and other Latinos (appendix, no. 42); and interaction with Anglos (appendix, no. 44).
7. Gabriela, interview with the author, September 13, 2013, Monmouth, IL.
8. Walter, interview with the author, July 30, 2011, Monmouth, IL.
9. Hilda, interview with the author, July 30, 2011, Monmouth, IL.
10. Martín, interview with the author, November 26, 2011, Beardstown, IL.
11. Leo, interview with the author, July 30, 2011, Monmouth, IL.
12. Zacarías, interview with the author, July 31, 2011, Monmouth, IL.
13. Teodoro, interview with the author, July 31, 2011, Monmouth, IL.
14. Gabriel, interview with the author, July 30, 2011, Monmouth, IL.
15. Irma, interview with the author, November 26, 2011, Beardstown, IL.
16. Stephen Spearie, "Beardstown's Latest Wave of Immigrants Celebrate Heritage," *(Springfield, IL) State Journal-Register*, August 24, 2014.
17. Additional information about FCCG can be found at http://faithcoalition-il.org.
18. Alejandro, interview with the author, September 15, 2013, Beardstown, IL.
19. From Mom to Mom website, http://www.momtomom.org.
20. Teresa II, interview with the author, November 26, 2011, Beardstown, IL.
21. Floriberto, interview with the author, November 26, 2011, Beardstown, IL.
22. Florencia, interview with the author, July 30, 2012, Monmouth, IL.
23. Isabel, interview with the author, September 15, 2013, Beardstown, IL; Rosa, interview with the author, November 26, 2011, Beardstown, IL.
24. María Isabel, interview with the author, December 3, 2011, Beardstown, IL.
25. Martín, interview with the author, November 26, 2011, Beardstown, IL.
26. Jorge, interview with the author, September 7, 2013, Beardstown, IL.
27. Ibid.
28. Gustavo, interview with the author, September 15, 2013, Beardstown, IL.
29. Floriberto, interview with the author, November 26, 2011, Beardstown, IL.

30. Ibid.
31. CASA's Facebook page, https://www.facebook.com/oficial.casa/info.
32. Floriberto, interview with the author, November 26, 2011, Beardstown, IL.
33. María Isabel, interview with the author, December 3, 2011, Beardstown, IL.
34. Ibid.
35. Alejandra, interview with the author, September 21, 2013, Beardstown, IL.
36. Alejandro, interview with the author, September 21, 2013, Beardstown, IL.
37. Ibid.
38. Ibid.
39. Walter, interview with the author, July 31, 2011, Monmouth, IL.
40. Helena, interview with the author, September 27, 2013, Monmouth, IL.
41. María Isabel, interview with the author, September 7, 2013, Beardstown, IL.
42. Ibid.
43. Jorge, interview with the author, September 7, 2013, Beardstown, IL.
44. Gabriel, interview with the author, July 30, 2011, Monmouth, IL.
45. Ibid.
46. Leo, interview with the author, July 30, 2011, Monmouth, IL.
47. María Isabel, interview with the author, September 7, 2013, Beardstown, IL.
48. Alejandra, interview with the author, September 21, 2013, Beardstown, IL.
49. Alejandro, interview with the author, September 21, 2013, Beardstown, IL.
50. Romulo, interview with the author, July 31, 2011, Monmouth, IL: Floriberto, interview with the author, November 26, 2011, Beardstown, IL; José Guadalupe, interview with the author, November 26, 2011, Beardstown, IL.
51. Diana, interview with the author, July 30, 2011, Monmouth, IL; José Luis, interview with the author, November 26, 2011, Beardstown, IL.
52. Luis, interview with the author, November 26, 2011, Beardstown, IL.
53. María Luisa, interview with the author, September 27, 2013, Beardstown, IL.
54. Martín, interview with the author, November 26, 2011, Beardstown, IL.
55. Florencia, interview with the author, July 30, 2011, Monmouth, IL.
56. Luis, interview with the author, November 26, 2011, Beardstown, IL.
57. Alejandra, interview with the author, September 21, 2013, Beardstown, IL.

**CHAPTER 6. MORE ON POLITICAL INCORPORATION:
TRUST IN GOVERNMENT INSTITUTIONS**

1. Jorge, interviews with the author, December 3, 2011, and September 7, 2013, Beardstown, IL.
2. Ibid.
3. Ibid.
4. Ibid.

5. Ibid.

6. Alejandra, interviews with the author, November 26, 2011, and September 21, 2013, Beardstown, IL.

7. Ibid.

8. For details about these variables, see education (appendix, no. 15), employment status (appendix, no. 13), income (appendix, no. 14), length of stay in the country (appendix, no. 4), and gender (appendix, no. 6).

9. For details about these variables, see trust in the government of the country of origin (appendix, no. 25), attention paid to politics and government affairs (appendix, no. 22), and experience with discrimination (appendix, no. 47).

10. Teresa II, interview with the author, November 26, 2011, Beardstown, IL.

11. Sandro, interview with the author, July 30, 2011, Monmouth, IL.

12. Benita, interview with the author, July 30, 2011, Monmouth, IL.

13. Jorge, interview with the author, December 3, 2011, Beardstown, IL.

14. Diana, interview with the author, July 30, 2011, Monmouth, IL.

15. Gabriel, interview with the author, July 30, 2011, Monmouth, IL.

16. Juana, interview with the author, July 30, 2011, Monmouth, IL.

17. Zacarías, interview with the author, July 31, 2011, Monmouth, IL.

18. More recently, President Obama promised to ease the situation of undocumented immigrants through executive orders, but this study's interviews predate this promise.

19. Ignacio, interview with the author, July 31, 2011, Monmouth, IL.

20. María Isabel, interview with the author, December 3, 2011, Beardstown, IL.

21. Rómulo, interview with the author, July 31, 2011, Monmouth, IL.

22. Florencia, interview with the author, July 30, 2011, Monmouth, IL.

23. Some devolutionary powers derive from the 1996 Personal Responsibility and Work Opportunity Reform Act.

24. Martín, interview with the author, December 3, 2011, Beardstown, IL.

25. Hilda, interview with the author, July 30, 2011, Monmouth, IL.

26. Teresa I, interview with the author, November 26, 2011, Beardstown, IL.

27. Irma, interview with the author, November 26, 2011, Beardstown, IL.

28. Floriberto, interview with the author, November 26, 2011, Beardstown, IL.

CONCLUSION

1. Annie Zak, "Sunday Focus: Hispanic Population Blooms in Monmouth," *(Galesburg, IL) Register-Mail*, August 23, 2010.

2. While completing the final revision of this book, I was unable to contact this church and believe it may have closed.

References

Abrahamson, Paul R., and John H. Aldrich. 1982. "The Decline of Electoral Participation in America." *American Political Science Review* 76, no. 3: 502–20.

Abrajano, Marisa, and Michael Álvarez. 2010. "Assessing the Causes and Effects of Political Trust among U.S. Latinos." *American Politics Research* 38, no. 1: 110–41.

Ackerman, Edwin. 2011. "NAFTA and Gatekeeper: A Theoretical Assessment of Border Enforcement in the Era of the Neoliberal State." *Berkeley Journal of Sociology* 55:40–56.

Ager, Alastair, and Alison Strang. 2008. "Understanding Integration: A Conceptual Framework." *Journal of Refugee Studies* 21, no. 2: 166–91.

Akrami, Nazar, Bo Ekehammar, and Tadesse Araya. 2000. "Classical and Modern Racial Prejudice: A Study of Attitudes toward Immigrants in Sweden." *European Journal of Social Psychology* 30, no. 4: 521–32.

Alba, Richard. 2005. "Bright vs. Blurred Boundaries: Second-Generation Assimilation and Exclusion in France, Germany and the United States." *Ethnic and Racial Studies* 28, no. 1: 20–49.

Alba, Richard, and Victor Nee. 1997. "Rethinking Assimilation Theory for a New Era of Immigration." *International Migration Review* 31, no. 4: 826–74.

———. 2003. *Remaking the American Mainstream.* Cambridge, MA: Harvard University Press.

Albarracín, Dolores, Blair T. Johnson, and Mark P. Zanna. 2005. "Attitudes: Introduction and Scope." In *The Handbook of Attitudes*, ed. Dolores Albarracín, Blair T. Johnson, and Mark

P. Zanna, 3–19. Mahwah, NJ: Lawrence Erlbaum Associates.

Albarracín, Julia. 2004. "Selecting Immigration in Modern Argentina: Economic, Cultural, International and Institutional Factors." PhD diss., University of Florida.

Albarracín, Julia, and Anna Valeva. 2011. "Political Participation and Social Capital among Mexicans and Mexican Americans in Central Illinois." *Hispanic Journal of Behavioral Sciences* 33, no. 4: 507–23.

Albarracín, Julia, Wei Wang, and Dolores Albarracín. 2012. "Do Confident People Behave Differently? The Role of Defensive Confidence in Partisan Defection, Attention to Politics, and Political Participation." In *Improving Public Opinion Surveys: Interdisciplinary Innovation and the American National Election Studies*, ed. John H. Aldrich and Kathleen M. McGraw. Princeton, NJ: Princeton University Press.

Algan, Yann, Alberto Bisin, and Thierry Verdier. 2012. "Perspectives on Cultural Integration of Immigrants: An Introduction." In *Cultural Integration of Immigrants in Europe (Studies of Policy Reform)*, ed. Yann Algan, Alberto Bisin, Alan Manning, and Thierry Verdier. Oxford: Oxford University Press.

André, Stéfanie. 2014. "Does Trust Mean the Same for Migrants and Natives? Testing Measurement Models of Political Trust with Multi-group Confirmatory Factor Analysis." *Social Indicators Research* 115, no. 3: 963–82.

Aponte, Robert. 1999. *Latinos in Indiana: On the Throes of Growth*. East Lansing, MI: Julian Samora Research Institute.

Arceneaux, Kevin, and Stephen P. Nicholson. 2012. "Who Wants to Have a Tea Party? The Who, What, and Why of the Tea Party Movement." *PS: Political Science & Politics* 45, no. 4: 700–710.

Arnold, Carrie L. 2007. "Racial Profiling in Immigration Enforcement: State and Local Agreements to Enforce Federal Immigration Law." *Arizona Law Review* 49:113–42.

Baker, Phyllis, and Douglas R. Hotek. 2003. "Perhaps a Blessing: Skills and Contributions of Recent Mexican Immigrants in the Rural Midwest." *Hispanic Journal of Behavioral Sciences* 25, no. 4: 448–68.

Barreto, Matt A., Betsy L. Cooper, Benjamin González, Christopher S. Parker, and Christopher Towler. 2011. "The Tea Party in the Age of Obama: Mainstream Conservatism or Out-Group Anxiety." *Political Power and Social Theory* 22, no. 1: 105–37.

Barreto, Matt A., Sylvia Manzano, Ricardo Ramírez, and Kathy Rim. 2009. "Mobilization, Participation, and Solidaridad: Latino Participation in the 2006 Immigration Protest Rallies." *Urban Affairs Review* 44, no. 5: 736–64.

Barreto, Matt A., and José A. Muñoz. 2003. "Reexamining the 'Politics of In-Between': Political Participation among Mexican Immigrants in the United States." *Hispanic Journal of Behavioral Sciences* 25, no. 4: 427–47.

Bashi, Vilma, and Antonio McDaniel. 1997. "A Theory of Immigration and Racial Stratification." *Journal of Black Studies* 27, no. 5: 668–82.

Bean, Frank D., Susan Brown, and Rubén G. Rumbaut. 2006. "Mexican Immigrant Political and Economic Incorporation." *Political Science and Politics* 4, no. 2: 309–13.

Beck, Paul A. 2002. "Encouraging Political Defection: The Role of Personal Discussion Networks in Partisan Desertions to the Opposition Party and Perot Votes in 1992." *Political Behavior* 24, no. 4: 309–37.

Benjamin-Alvarado, Jonathan, Louis DeSipio, and Celeste Montoya. 2009. "Latino Mobilization in New Immigrant Destinations: The Anti-H.R. 4437 Protest in Nebraska's Cities." *Urban*

Affairs Review 44, no. 5: 718–35.

Berry, J. W. 2001. "A Psychology of Immigration." *Journal of Social Issues* 57, no. 3: 615–31.

Bevelander, Pieter, and Ravi Pendakur. 2009. "Social Capital and Voting Participation of Immigrants and Minorities in Canada." *Ethnic and Racial Studies* 32, no. 8: 1406–30.

Bickerton, Maria Elena. 2001. "Prospects for Bilateral Immigration Agreement with Mexico: Lessons from the Bracero Program." *Texas Law Review* 79:895–906.

Black, Jerome H. 2011. "Immigrant and Minority Political Incorporation in Canada: A Review with Some Reflections on Canadian-American Comparison Possibilities." *American Behavioral Scientist* 55, no. 9: 1160–88.

Blau, Francine D. 1980. "Immigration and Labor Earnings in Early Twentieth Century America." *Research Population Economics: A Research Annual* 2:21–41.

Blee, Kathleen M., and Elizabeth A. Yates. 2015. "The Place of Race in Conservative and Far-Right Movements." *Sociology of Race and Ethnicity* 1, no. 1: 127–36.

Bloemraad, Irene. 2002. "The North American Naturalization Gap: An Institutional Approach to Citizenship Acquisition in the United States and Canada." *International Migration Review* 36, no. 1: 193–228.

———. 2006. "Becoming a Citizen in the United States and Canada: Structured Mobilization and Immigrant Political Incorporation." *Social Forces* 85, no. 2: 667–95.

Bloemraad, Irene, Anna Korteweg, and Gökçe Yurdakul. 2008. "Citizenship and Immigration: Multiculturalism, Assimilation, and Challenges to the Nation-State." *Annual Review of Sociology* 34, no. 1: 153–79.

Bonner, Dean E. 2009. "A Comprehensive Examination of the Determinants and Consequences of Political Trust among Latinos." PhD diss., University of New Orleans.

Boswell, Richard A. 2003. "Racism and U.S. Immigration Law: Prospects for Reform after 9/11?" *Immigration & Nationality Law Review* 24:65.

Brehm, John, and Wendy Rahn. 1997. "Individual-Level Evidence for the Causes and Consequences of Social Capital." *American Journal of Political Science* 41, no. 3: 999–1023.

Brettell, Caroline B. 2011. "Experiencing Everyday Discrimination: A Comparison across Five Immigrant Populations." *Race and Social Problems* 3, no. 4: 266–79.

Brewster, Zachary W. 2012. "Racially Discriminatory Service in Full-Service Restaurants: The Problem, Cause, and Potential Solution." *Cornell Hospitality Quarterly* 53, no. 4: 274–85.

Butcher, Kristin F., and John DiNardo. 2002. "The Immigrant and Native-Born Wage Distributions: Evidence from United States Censuses." *Industrial and Labor Relations Review* 56, no. 1: 97–121.

Cabassa, Leopoldo J. 2003. "Measuring Acculturation: Where We Are and Where We Need to Go." *Hispanic Journal of Behavioral Sciences* 25, no. 2: 127–46.

Calavita, Kitty. 1994. "U.S. Immigration and Policy Responses: The Limits of Legislation." In *Controlling Immigration: A Global Perspective*, ed. Wayne A. Cornelius, Philip L. Martin, and James F. Hollifield. Stanford, CA: Stanford University Press.

Callahan, Kathe. 2007. "Citizen Participation: Questions of Diversity, Equity and Fairness." *Journal of Public Management & Social Policy* 13, no. 1: 53–68.

Catterberg, Gabriela, and Alejandro Moreno. 2006. "The Individual Bases of Political Trust: Trends in New and Established Democracies." *International Journal of Public Opinion Research* 18, no. 1: 31–48.

Chanley, Virginia A., Thomas J. Rudolph, and Wendy M. Rahn. 2000. "The Origins and Consequences of Public Trust in Government: A Time Series Analysis." *Public Opinion Quarterly* 64, no. 3: 239–56.

Cisneros, David J. 2015. "A Nation of Immigrants and a Nation of Laws: Race, Multiculturalism, and Neoliberal Exception in Barack Obama's Immigration Discourse." *Communication, Culture & Critique*. Http://onlinelibrary.wiley.com/doi/10.1111/cccr.12088/abstract.

Citrin, Jack. 1974. "The Political Relevance of Trust in Government." *American Political Science Review* 68, no. 3: 973–88.

Citrin, Jack, and Donald Philip Green. 1986. Presidential Leadership and the Resurgence of Trust in Government." *British Journal of Political Science* 16, no. 4: 431–53.

Citrin, Jack, and John Sides. 2008. "Immigration and the Imagined Community in Europe and the United States." *Political Studies* 56, no. 1: 33–56.

Cohen, Jeffrey H., and Nidia Merino Chavez. 2013. "Latino Immigrants, Discrimination, and Reception in Columbus, Ohio." *International Migration* 51, no. 2: 24–31.

Congress of the United States, Congressional Budget Office. 2006. "Immigration Policy in the United States." Http://www.cbo.gov.

Cook, Timothy E., and Paul Gronke. 2005. "The Skeptical American: Revisiting the Meanings of Trust in Government and Confidence in Institutions." *Journal of Politics* 67, no. 3: 784–803.

Cook-Martin, David, and David FitzGerald. 2010. "Liberalism and the Limits of Inclusion: Race and Immigration Law in the Americas, 1850–2000." *Journal of Interdisciplinary History* 41, no. 1: 7–25.

Cornelius, Wayne A. 1981. "Migration to the United States." *Proceedings of the Academy of Political Science* 34, no. 1: 67–77.

———. 2001. "Death at the Border: The Efficacy and Unintended Consequences of U.S. Immigration Control Policy, 1993–2000." *Population and Development Review* 27, no. 4: 661–85.

———. 2004. "Controlling 'Unwanted' Immigration: Lessons from the United States, 1993–2004." *Center for Comparative Immigration Studies Working Papers* 92 (December). Http://ccis. ucsd.edu.

Cornelius, Wayne A., and Takeyuki Tsuda. 2004. "Controlling Immigration: The Limits of Government Intervention." In *Controlling Immigration: A Global Perspective*, 2nd edition, ed. Wayne A. Cornelius, Takeyuki Tsuda, Philip L. Martin, and James F. Hollifield. Stanford, CA: Stanford University Press.

Cox, Adam B., and Eric A. Posner. 2007. "The Second Order Structure of Immigration Law." *Stanford Law Review* 59, no. 4: 809–56.

Craig, Stephen C., Richard G. Niemi, and Glenn E. Silver. 1990. "Political Efficacy and Trust: A Report on the NES Pilot Study Items." *Political Behavior* 12, no. 3: 289–314.

Dalla, Rochelle L., Amy Ellis, and Sheran C. Cramer. 2005. "Immigration and Rural America: Latinos' Perception of Work and Residence in Three Meatpacking Communities." *Community Work and Family* 8, no. 2: 163–85.

Dawson, Michael C. 2001. *Black Visions: The Roots of Contemporary African-American Political Ideologies*. Chicago: University of Chicago Press.

De Genova, Nicholas P. 2002. "Migrant 'Illegality' and Deportability in Everyday Life." *Annual Review of Anthropology* 31, no. 1: 419–47.

De La Garza, Rodolfo O., Angelo Falcon, and F. Chris García. 1996. "Will the Real Americans Please Stand Up: Anglo and Mexican-American Support of Core American Political Values." *American Journal of Political Science* 40, no. 2: 335–51.

DeSipio, Louis. 2011. "Immigrant Incorporation in an Era of Weak Civic Institutions: Immigrant Civic and Political Participation in the United States." *American Behavioral Scientist* 55, no. 9: 1189–213.

De Souza Briggs, Xavier. 2013. "Conclusion: Rethinking Immigrant Political Incorporation: What Have We Learned, and What Next?" In *Outsiders No More? Models of Immigrant Political Incorporation*, ed. Jennifer Hochschild, Jacqueline Chattopadhyay, Claudine Cay, and Michael Jones-Correa. New York: Oxford University Press.

Dion, Kenneth L. 2002. "Immigrants' Perceptions of Housing Discrimination in Toronto: The Housing New Canadians Project." *Journal of Social Issues* 57, no. 3: 523–39.

Djupe, Paul A., and Jacob Neiheisel. 2012. "How Religious Communities Affect Political Participation among Latinos." *Social Science Quarterly* 93, no. 2: 333–55.

Doerschler, Peter, and Pamela Irving Jackson. 2012. "Do Muslims in Germany Really Fail to Integrate? Muslim Integration and Trust in Public Institutions." *International Migration & Integration* 13, no. 4: 503–23.

Donato, Katharine, Charles Tolbert, Alfred Nucci, and Yukio Kawano. 2008. "Changing Faces, Changing Places: The Emergence of New Nonmetropolitan Immigrant Gateways." In *New Faces in New Places: The Changing Geography of American Immigration*, ed. Douglas Massey. New York: Russell Foundation.

Dovidio, John F., Agata Gluszek, Melissa-Sue John, Ruth Ditlmann, and Paul Lagunes. 2010. "Understanding Bias toward Latinos: Discrimination, Dimensions of Difference, and Experience of Exclusion." *Journal of Social Issues* 66, no. 1: 59–78.

Downs, Anthony. 1957. *An Economic Theory of Democracy*. New York: Harper.

Duany, Jorge. 1998. "Reconstructing Racial Identity: Ethnicity, Color, and Class among Dominicans in the United States and Puerto Rico." *Latin American Perspectives* 25, no. 3: 147–72.

Durand, Jorge, Douglas Massey, and Fernando Charvet. 2000. "The Changing Geography of Mexican Immigration to the United States: 1910–1996." *Social Science Quarterly* 81, no. 1: 1–15.

Easton, David. 1965. *A Systems Analysis of Political Life*. New York: John Wiley and Sons.

Ellis, Mark. 2006. "Unsettling Immigrant Geographies: U.S. Immigration and the Politics of Scale." *Tijdschrift voor economische en sociale geografie* 97, no. 1: 49–58.

Espenshade, Thomas J. 1995. "Unauthorized Immigration to the United States." *Annual Review of Sociology* 21, no. 1: 195–216.

Espinal, Rosario, Jonathan Hartlyn, and Jana Morgan Kelly. 2006. "Performance Still Matters: Explaining Trust in Government in the Dominican Republic." *Comparative Political Studies* 39, no. 2: 200–223.

Evett, Sophia R., Anne Marie G. Hakstian, Jerome D. Williams, and Geraldine R. Henderson. 2013. "What's Race Got to Do with It? Responses to Consumer Discrimination." *Analysis of Social Issues and Public Policy* 13, no. 1: 165–85.

Farmland. n.d. "Monmouth Plant." Http://monmouthfarmland.com.

Feagin, Joe R. 2014. *Racist America: Roots, Current Realities, and Future Reparations*. 3rd ed. New York: Routledge.

Federal Electoral Commission. n.d. "Citizens' Guide." Http://www.fec.gov/pages/brochures/citizens.shtml.

Fekete, Liz. 2001. "The Emergence of Xeno-Racism." *Race and Class* 43, no. 2: 23–40.

Fennelly, Katherine. 2008. "Prejudice toward Immigrants in the Midwest." In *New Faces in New Places: The Changing Geography of American Immigration*, ed. Douglas Massey. New York: Russell Foundation.

Fennelly, Katherine, and Helga Leitner. 2002. "How the Food Industry Is Diversifying Rural Minnesota." JSRI Working Paper #29. Julian Samora Research Institute, Michigan State University.

Foner, Nancy, and Richard Alba. 2008. "Immigrant Religion in the U.S. and Western Europe: Bridge or Barrier to Inclusion?" *International Migration Review* 42, no. 2: 360–92.

Frank, Reanne, Ilana Redstone Akresh, and Bo Lu. 2010. "Latino Immigrants and the U.S. Racial Order: How and Where Do They Fit In?" *American Sociological Review* 75, no. 3: 378–401.

Freeman, Gary P., Luis F. B. Plascencia, Susan Gonzalez Baker, and Manuel Orozco. 2002. "Explaining the Surge in Citizenship Applications in the 1990s: Lawful Permanent Residents in Texas." *Social Science Quarterly* 83, no. 4: 1013–25.

Fryberg, Stephanie A., Nicole M. Stephens, Rebecca Covarrubias, Hazel Rose Markus, Erin D. Carter, Giselle A. Laiduc, and Ana J. Salido. 2012. "How the Media Frames the Immigration Debate: The Critical Role of Location and Politics." *Analyses of Social Issues and Public Policy* 12, no. 1: 96–112.

Gerstle, Gary. 2010. "Historical and Contemporary Perspectives on Immigrant Political Incorporation: The American Experience." *International Labor and Working-Class History* 78 (Fall): 110–17.

Gidengil, Elisabeth, and Dietlind Stolle. 2009. "The Role of Social Networks in Immigrant Women's Political Incorporation." *International Migration Review* 43, no. 4: 727–63.

Gill, Stephen. 1995. "The Global Panopticon? The Neoliberal State, and Democratic Surveillance." *Alternatives: Global, Local, Political* 20, no. 1: 1–49.

González-Barrera, Ana, Mark Hugo Lopez, Jeffrey S. Passel, and Paul Taylor. 2013. "The Path Not Taken: Two Thirds of Legal Mexican Immigrants Are Not U.S. Citizens." Pew Research Center. Http://www.pewhispanic.org.

Goodwin, Lin A. 2002. "Teacher Preparation and the Education of Immigrant Children." *Education and Urban Society* 34, no. 2: 156–71.

Goto, Sharon G., Gilbert C. Gee, and David T. Takeuchi. 2002. "Strangers Still? The Experience of Discrimination among Chinese Americans." *Journal of Community Psychology* 30, no. 2: 211–24.

Gouveia, Lourdes, and Rogelio Saenz. 2000. "Global Forces and Latino Population Growth in the Midwest: A Regional and Subregional Analysis." *Latino/Latin American Studies Faculty Proceedings & Presentations*, Paper 1:305–28.

Green, Tristin K. 2003. "Discrimination in the Workplace Dynamics: Toward a Structural Account of Disparate Treatment Theory." *Harvard Civil Rights-Civil Liberties Law Review* 38:91–110.

Guterbock, Thomas, and Bruce London. 1983. "Race, Political Orientation, and Participation: An Empirical Test for Four Competing Theories." *American Sociological Review* 48, no. 4: 439–53.

Hagan, Jacqueline, Nestor Rodriguez, Randy Capps, and Nika Kabiri. 2003. "The Effects of Recent

Welfare and Immigration Reform on Immigrants' Access to Health Care." *International Migration Review* 37, no. 2: 444–63.

Halpern, David. 2005. *Determinants of Social Capital*. Cambridge: Polity Press.

Haverluk, Terrence W., and Laurie D. Trautman. 2008. "The Changing Geography of U.S. Hispanics from 1990–2006: A Shift to the South and Midwest." *Journal of Geography* 107, no. 3: 87–101.

Hersch, Joni. 2011. "The Persistence of Skin Color Discrimination for Immigrants." *Social Science Research* 40, no. 5: 1337–49.

Hetherington, Marc. 1998. "The Political Relevance of Political Trust." *American Political Science Review* 92, no. 4: 791–808.

———. 1999. "The Effect of Political Trust on the Presidential Vote, 1968–96." *American Political Science Review* 93, no. 2: 311–26.

Hiemstra, Nancy. 2010. "Immigrant 'Illegality' as Neoliberal Governmentality in Leadville, Colorado." *Antipode* 42, no. 1: 74–102.

Hill, Nancy, and Kathryn Torres. 2010. "Negotiating the American Dream: The Paradox of Aspirations and Achievement among Latino Students and Engagement between their Families and Schools." *Journal of Social Issues* 66, no. 1: 95–112.

Hirschman, Charles, and Douglas S. Massey. 2008. "Places and Peoples: The New American Mosaic." In *New Faces in New Places: The Changing Geography of American Immigration*, ed. Douglas S. Massey. New York: Russell Foundation.

Hochschild, Jennifer. 2013. "Moving Up and In: Two Dimensions of Immigrant Political Incorporation." In *Outsiders No More? Models of Immigrant Political Incorporation*, ed. Jennifer Hochschild, Jacqueline Chattopadhyay, Claudine Cay, and Michael Jones-Correa. New York: Oxford University Press.

Hochschild, Jennifer L., and John H. Mollenkopf. 2009. "Modeling Immigrant Political Incorporation." In *Bringing Outsiders In: Transatlantic Perspectives on Immigrant Political Incorporation*, ed. Jennifer L. Hochschild and John H. Mollenkopf. Ithaca, NY: Cornell University Press.

Huntington, Samuel P. 2004. *Who Are We? The Challenges to America's National Identity*. New York: Simon and Schuster.

Immigration Direct. 2013. "Strict Immigration Laws in Alabama Ruled Unconstitutional." Http://www.immigrationdirect.com.

Inda, Xavier J. 2013. "Subject to Deportation: IRCA, 'Criminal Aliens,' and the Policing of Immigration." *Migration Studies* 1, no. 3: 292–310.

Jackson, Robert A. 2009. "Latino Political Connectedness and Electoral Participation." *Journal of Political Marketing* 8, no. 3: 233–62.

Jacoby, W. G. 2003. "Ideology in the 2000 Election: A Study of Ambivalence." In *Models of Voting in Presidential Elections: The 2000 Election*," ed. Bernard Bailyn and Patricia L. Denault. Stanford, CA: Stanford Law & Politics.

Jang, Seung-Jin. 2009. "Get Out on Behalf of Your Group: Electoral Participation of Latinos and Asian Americans." *Political Behavior* 31, no. 4: 511–35.

Jensen, Leif. 2006. "New Immigrant Settlements in Rural America: Problems, Prospects, and Policies." *Carsey School of Public Policy at the Scholars' Repository*. Paper 17. Http://scholars.unh.edu.

Jeong, Gyung-Ho, Gary J. Miller, Camilla Schofield, and Itai Sened. 2011. "Cracks in the

Opposition: Immigration as a Wedge Issue for the Reagan Coalition." *American Journal of Political Science* 55, no. 3: 511–25.

Jiménez, Tomas R. 2011. "Immigrants in the United States: How Well Are They Integrating into Society?" Washington, DC: Migration Policy Institute. Http://www.migrationpolicy.org.

Johnson, Kenneth M., and Daniel T. Lichter. 2008. "Population Growth in New Hispanic Destinations." *Carsey School of Public Policy at the Scholars' Repository*. Paper 42. Http://scholars.unh.edu.

Johnson, Kevin R. 1998. "Race, the Immigration Laws, and Domestic Race Relations: A 'Magic Mirror' into the Heart of Darkness." *Indiana Law Journal* 73, no. 4: 1111–35.

Jones-Correa, Michael. 2004. "Understanding Immigrant Politics: Lessons from the U.S." *Migration Policy Institute's Migration Information Source*. August 1. Http://migrationinformation.org.

Joppke, Christian. 1999. *Immigration and the United States: The United States, Germany, and Great Britain*. New York: Oxford University Press.

———. 2001. "The Legal-Domestic Sources of Immigrant Rights: The United States, Germany, and the European Union." *Comparative Political Studies* 34, no. 4: 339–66.

Junn, Jane. 1999. "Participation in Liberal Democracy: The Political Assimilation of Immigrants and Ethnic Minorities in the United States." *American Behavioral Scientist* 42, no. 9: 1417–38.

Kam, Cindy D., Elizabeth J. Zechmeister, and Jennifer R. Wilking. 2008. "From the Gap to the Chasm: Gender and Participation among Non-Hispanic Whites and Mexican Americans." *Political Research Quarterly* 61, no. 2: 205–18.

Kandel, William, and John Cromartie. 2004. *New Patterns of Hispanic Settlement in Rural America*. U.S. Department of Agriculture, Economic Research Service.

Kanstroom, Daniel. 2004. "Criminalizing the Undocumented: Ironic Boundaries of the Post–September 11th 'Pale of Law.'" *North Carolina Journal of International Law and Commercial Regulation* 29:639–70.

Kaufmann, Karen M. 2003. "Cracks in the Rainbow: Group Commonality as a Basis for Latino and African-American Political Coalitions." *Political Research Quarterly* 56, no. 2: 199–210.

Kennedy, Deseriee A. 2001. "Consumer Discrimination: The Limitations of Federal Civil Rights Protection." *Missouri Law Review* 66:275–339.

Kilty, Keith M., and María Vidal de Haynes. 2000. "Racism, Nativism, and Exclusion: Public Policy, Immigration, and the Latino Experience in the United States." *Journal of Poverty* 4, no. 1/2: 1–25.

Kobach, Chris W. 2008. "Attrition through Enforcement: A Rational Approach to Illegal Immigration." *Tulsa Journal of Comparative and International Law* 15, no. 2: 155–63.

Korhonen, Marjaana. 2006. "Discovering Keys to the Integration of Immigrants: From Human Capital to Social Capital." Master's thesis, University of Tampere.

Kuperminc, Gabriel P., Adam J. Darnell, and Anabel Álvarez-Jiménez. 2008. "Parent Involvement in the Academic Adjustment of Latino Middle and High School Youth: Teacher Expectations and School Belonging as Mediators." *Journal of Adolescence* 31, no. 4: 469–83.

Langford, Anne E. 2004. "What's in a Name? Notarios in the United States and the Exploitation of a Vulnerable Latino Immigrant Population." *Harvard Latino Law Review* 7:115–36.

Law, Anna O. 2002. "The Diversity Visa Lottery: A Cycle of Unintended Consequences in United States Immigration Policy." *Journal of American Ethnic History* 21, no. 4: 3–29.

Leach, Mark A., and Frank D. Bean. 2008. "The Structure and Dynamics of Mexican Migration to New Destinations in the United States." In *New Faces in New Places: The Changing Geography of American Immigration*, ed. Douglas Massey. New York: Russell Foundation.

Leal, David L. 2002. "Political Participation by Latino Non-Citizens in the United States." *British Journal of Political Science* 32, no. 2: 353–70.

Leighley, Jan E., and Jonathan E. Nagler. 1992. "Individual and Systemic Influences on Turnout: Who Votes? 1984." *Journal of Politics* 54, no. 3: 718–40.

Leighley, Jan E., and Arnold Vedlitz. 1999. "Race, Ethnicity, and Political Participation: Competing Models and Contrasting Explanations." *Journal of Politics* 61, no. 4: 1092–114.

Levi, Margaret, and Laura Stoker. 2000. "Political Trust and Trustworthiness." *Annual Review of Political Science* 3, no. 1: 475–507.

Lichter, Daniel T. 2012. "Immigration and the New Racial Diversity in Rural America." *Rural Sociology* 77, no. 1: 3–35.

Lichter, Daniel T., and Kenneth M. Johnson. 2006. "Emerging Rural Settlement Patterns and the Geography of Redistribution of America's New Immigrants." *Rural Sociology* 71, no. 1: 109–51.

Lien, Pei-te. 1994. "Ethnicity and Political Participation: A Comparison between Asian and Mexican Americans." *Political Behavior* 15, no. 2: 237–64.

Lim, Chaeyoon. 2008. "Social Networks and Political Participation: How Do Networks Matter?" *Social Forces* 87, no. 2: 961–82.

Longworth, Richard C. 2009. *Caught in the Middle: America's Heartland in the Age of Globalism*. New York: Bloomsbury.

López, Ann A. 2011. "New Questions in the Immigration Debate." *Anthropology Now* 3, no. 1: 47–53.

Luckstead, Jeff, Stephen Devadoss, and Abelardo Rodríguez. 2012. "The Effects of North American Free Trade Agreement and United States Farm Policies on Illegal Immigration and Agricultural Trade." *Journal of Agricultural and Applied Economics* 44, no. 1: 1–19.

Mahler, Sarah J., and Myer Siemiatycki. 2011. "Diverse Pathways to Immigrant Political Incorporation: Comparative Canadian and U.S. Perspectives." *American Behavioral Scientist* 55, no. 9: 1123–30.

Marchevsky, Alejandra, and Beth Baker. 2014. "Why Has President Obama Deported More Immigrants Than Any Other President in US History?" *The Nation*, March 31. Http://www.thenation.com.

Marshall, Melissa J. 2001. "Does the Shoe Fit? Testing Models of Participation for African-American and Latino Involvement in Local Politics." *Urban Affairs Review* 37, no. 2: 227–48.

Martin, Philip L. 2004. "The United States: The Continuing Immigration Debate." In *Controlling Immigration: A Global Perspective*, 2nd edition, ed. Wayne A. Cornelius, Takeyuki Tsuda, Philip L. Martin, and James F. Hollifield. Stanford, CA: Stanford University Press.

Martínez, Lisa. 2008. "The Individual and Contextual Determinants of Protest among Latinos." *Mobilization: An International Quarterly* 13, no. 2: 189–204.

Mason, Patrick L. 2004. "Annual Income, Hourly Wages, and Identity among Mexican-Americans and Other Latinos." *Industrial Relations* 43, no. 4: 817–34.

Massey, Douglas. 1995. "The New Immigrants and Ethnicity in the United States." *Population and Development Review* 21, no. 3: 631–52.

Massey, Douglas S., and Chiara Capoferro. 2008. "The Geographic Diversification of American Immigration." In *New Faces in New Places: The Changing Geography of American Immigration*, ed. Douglas Massey. New York: Russell Foundation.

Masuoka, Natalie. 2006. "Together They Become One: Examining the Predictors of Panethnic Group Consciousness among Asian Americans and Latinos." *Social Science Quarterly* 87, no. 5: 993–1011.

Maxwell, Rahsaan. 2010a. "Trust in Government among British Muslims: The Importance of Migration Status." *Political Behavior* 32, no. 1: 89–109.

———. 2010b. "Evaluating Migrant Integration: Political Attitudes across Generations in Europe." *International Migration Review* 44, no. 1: 25–42.

———. 2013. "Assimilation and Political Attitudes Trade-Offs." In *Outsiders No More? Models of Immigrant Political Incorporation*, ed. Jennifer Hochschild, Jacqueline Chattopadhyay, Claudine Cay, and Michael Jones-Correa. New York: Oxford University Press.

McCabe, Kristen, and Doris Meissner. 2010. "Immigration and the United States: Recession Affects Flows, Prospects for Reform." *Migration Policy Institute's Migration Information Source.* January 20. Http://www.migrationinformation.org.

McClain, Paula D., and Joseph Stewart Jr. 2006. *"Can We All Get Along?": Racial and Ethnic Minorities in American Politics.* Boulder, CO: Westview Press.

McKenney, David H. 2013 "'Operation Stone Garden': A Case Study of Legitimation of Violence and the Consequences for Mexican Immigrants in Chaparral, New Mexico." *ETD Collection for University of Texas, El Paso.* Paper AAI1545182.

Michelson, Melissa R. 2003. "The Corrosive Effect of Acculturation: How Mexican Americans Lose Political Trust." *Social Science Quarterly* 84, no. 4: 918–33.

———. 2007. "All Roads Lead to Rust: How Acculturation Erodes Latino Immigrant Trust in Government." *Aztlán: A Journal of Chicano Studies* 32, no. 2: 21–46.

Mickelson, Roslyn A. 2003. "When Are Racial Disparities in Education the Result of Racial Discrimination? A Social Science Perspective." *Teachers College Record* 105, no. 6: 1052–86.

Miller, Arthur H. 1974. "Political Issues and Trust in Government: 1964–1970." *American Political Science Review* 68, no. 3: 951–72.

Miraftab, Faranak. 2012. "Emergent Transnational Spaces: Meat, Sweat and Global (Re) Production in the Heartland." *International Journal of Urban and Regional Research* 36, no. 6: 1204–22.

Mishler, William, and Richard Rose. 2001. "What Are the Origins of Political Trust? Testing Institutional and Cultural Theories in Post-Communist Societies." *Comparative Political Studies* 34, no. 1: 30–62.

Mollenkopf, John, and Jennifer Hochschild. 2010. "Immigrant Political Incorporation: Comparing Success in the United States and Western Europe." *Ethnic and Racial Studies* 33, no. 1: 19–38.

Mossakowski, Krysia N. 2003. "Coping with Perceived Discrimination: Does Ethnic Identity Protect Mental Health?" *Journal of Health and Social Behavior* 44 (September): 318–31.

Municipal Research and Services Center (MRSC). 2014. "Open Public Meetings Act." Http://www.mrsc.org.

National Conference of State Legislatures. 2011. "Arizona's Enforcement Immigration Laws." Http://www.ncsl.org.

Nevins, Joseph. 2007. "Dying for a Cup of Coffee? Migrant Deaths in the US-Mexico Border Region in the Neoliberal Age." *Geopolitics* 12, no. 2: 228–47.

Ngai, Mae M. 2003. "The Strange Career of the Illegal Alien: Immigration Restriction and Deportation Policy in the United States, 1921–1965." *Law and History Review* 21, no. 1): 69–107.

Ogletree, Charles J., Jr. 2000. "America's Schizophrenic Immigration Policy: Race, Class, and Reason." *Boston College Law Review* 41, no. 4: 754–70.

Olivas, Michael A. 2007. "Immigration-Related State and Local Ordinances: Preemption, Prejudice, and the Proper Role for Enforcement." *University of Chicago Legal Forum,* 27–56.

Ondrich, Jan, Stephen L. Ross, and John Yinger. 2000. "How Common Is Housing Discrimination? Improving on Traditional Measures." *Journal of Urban Economics* 47, no. 3: 470–500.

Ondrich, Jan, Alex Stricker, and John Yinger. 1999. "Do Landlords Discriminate? The Incidence and Causes of Racial Discrimination in Rental Housing Markets." *Journal of Housing Economics* 8, no. 3: 185–204.

Open Secrets. 2012. "2012 Election Spending Will Reach $6 Billion, Center for Responsive Politics Predicts." Http://www.opensecrets.org.

Oxman-Martínez, Jacqueline, Anneke J. Rumens, Jacques Moreau, Ye R. Choi, Morton Beiser, Linda Ogilvie, and Robert Armstrong. 2012. "Perceived Ethnic Discrimination and Social Exclusion: Newcomer Immigrant Children in Canada." *American Journal of Orthopsychiatry* 82, no. 3: 376–88.

Padilla, Amado M. 2006. "Bicultural Social Development." *Hispanic Journal of Behavioral Sciences* 28:467–97.

Padilla, Amado M., and William Pérez. 2003. "Acculturation, Social Identity, and Social Cognition: A New Perspective." *Hispanic Journal of Behavioral Sciences* 25, no. 1: 35–55.

Paral, Rob. 2009. *Mexican Immigration in the Midwest: Meaning and Implications.* Chicago Council on Global Affairs. Heartland Papers 1.

Park, Robert E. 1928. "Migration and the Marginal Man." *American Journal of Sociology* 33, no. 6: 881–93.

———. 2000. "The Nature of Race Relations." In *Theories of Race and Racism: A Reader,* ed. Les Black and John Solomos. New York: Routledge.

Park, Robert E., and Ernest W. Burgess. 1969. *Introduction to the Science of Sociology.* Chicago: University of Chicago Press.

Parrado, Emilio A., and William Kandel. 2008. "New Hispanic Migrant Destinations: A Tale of Two Industries." In *New Faces in New Places: The Changing Geography of American Immigration,* ed. Douglas S. Massey. New York: Russell Foundation.

Pereira, Cícero, Jorge Vala, and Rui Costa-Lopes. 2010. "From Prejudice to Discrimination: The Legitimizing Role of Perceived Threat in Discrimination against Immigrants." *European Journal of Social Psychology* 40, no. 7: 1231–50.

Pérez Rosenbaum, Rene. 1997. *Migration and Integration of Latinos into Rural Midwestern Communities: The Case of "Mexicans" in Adrian, Michigan.* Research Report 19. East Lansing, MI: Julian Samora Research Institute.

Pew Hispanic Center. 2007. "The 2007 Survey of Latinos: As Illegal Immigration Issue Heats Up, Immigrants Feel the Chill." Http://www.pewhispanic.org.

———. 2013. "Unauthorized Immigrants: How Pew Research Counts Them and What We Know about Them." Http://www.pewresearch.org.

———. 2014. "Record Number of Deportations in 2012." Http://www.pewresearch.org.

Phinney, Jean S., Tanya Madden, and Lorena Santos. 1998. "Psychological Variables as Predictors of Perceived Ethnic Discrimination among Minority and Immigrant Adolescents." *Journal of Applied Social Psychology* 28, no. 11: 937–53.

Plous, Scott. 2003. "The Psychology of Prejudice, Stereotyping, and Discrimination." In *Understanding Prejudice and Racism*, ed. Scott Plous. New York: McGraw Hill.

Portes, Alejandro. 1998. "Social Capital: Its Origins and Applications in Modern Sociology." *Annual Review of Sociology* 24:1–24.

Portes, Alejandro, and Jozsef Böröcz. 1989. "Contemporary Immigration: Theoretical Perspectives and Its Determinants and Modes of Incorporation." *International Migration Review* 23, no. 3: 606–30.

Portes, Alejandro, and Dag MacLeod. 1999. "Educating the Second Generation: Determinants of Academic Achievement among Children of Immigrants in the United States." *Journal of Ethnic and Migration Studies* 25, no. 3: 373–96.

Portes, Alejandro, Robert Nash Parker, and José A. Cobas. 1980. "Assimilation or Consciousness: Perceptions of U.S. Society among Recent Latin American Immigrants to the United States." *Social Forces* 59, no. 1: 200–224.

Portes, Alejandro, and Rubén Rumbaut. 2001. *The Story of the Immigrant Second Generation: Legacies.* Berkeley: University of California Press.

Portes, Alejandro, and Min Zhou. 1993. "The New Second Generation: Segmented Assimilation and Its Variants." *Annals of the American Academy of Political and Social Science* 530, no. 1: 74–94.

———. 1994. "Should Immigrants Assimilate?" *The Public Interest* (Summer): 18–33.

Potochnic, Stephanie, Krista M. Pereira, and Andrew Fuligni. 2012 "Fitting In: The Roles of Social Acceptance and Discrimination in Shaping the Daily Psychological Well-Being of Latino Youth." *Social Science Quarterly* 93, no. 1: 173–90.

Putnam, Robert D. 1993. *Making Democracy Work: Civic Traditions in Modern Italy*. Princeton, NJ: Princeton University Press.

———. 2000. *Bowling Alone: The Collapse and Revival of American Community*. New York: Simon & Schuster.

———. 2007. "E Pluribus Unum: Diversity and Community in the Twenty-first Century." *Scandinavian Political Studies* 30, no. 2: 137–74.

Quillian, Lincoln. 2006. "New Approaches to Understanding Racial Prejudice and Discrimination." *Annual Review of Sociology* 32, no. 1: 299–328.

Rakosi Rosenbloom, Susan, and Niobe Way. 2004. "Experiences of Discrimination among African American, Asian American, and Latino Adolescents in an Urban High School." *Youth Society* 35, no. 4: 420–51.

Ramakrishnan, S. Karthick, and Celia Viramontes. 2010. "Civic Spaces: Mexican Hometown Associations and Immigrant Participation." *Journal of Social Issues* 66, no. 1: 155–73.

Riosmena, Fernando, and Douglas S. Massey. 2012. "Pathways to El Norte: Origins, Destinations, and Characteristics of Mexican Migrants to the United States." *International Migration*

Review 46, no. 1: 3–36.

Rivera-Batiz, Francisco L. 1999. "Undocumented Workers in the Labor Market: An Analysis of the Earnings of Legal and Illegal Mexican Immigrants in the United States." *Journal of Population Economics* 12, no. 1: 91–116.

Rocha, Rene, and Rodolfo Espino. 2010. "Segregation, Immigration, and Latino Participation in Ethnic Politics." *American Politics Research* 38, no. 4: 614–35.

Romero, Mary. 2006. "Racial Profiling and Immigration Law Enforcement: Rounding Up of Usual Suspects in the Latino Community." *Critical Sociology* 32, no. 2–3: 447–73.

Romero, Victor. 2004. "Race, Immigration, and the Department of Homeland Security." *Journal of Civil Rights and Economic Development* 19, no. 1: 7.

Rumbaut, Ruben G. 1994. "The Crucible Within: Ethnic Identity, Self-Esteem, and Segmented Assimilation among Children of Immigrants." *International Migration Review* 28, no. 4: 748–94.

Saenz, Rogelio. 2011. "The Changing Demography of Latinos in the Midwest." In *Latinos in the Midwest*, ed. Rubén Martinez. East Lansing: Michigan State University Press.

Safi, Mirna. 2010. "Immigrants' Life Satisfaction in Europe: Between Assimilation and Discrimination." *European Sociological Review* 26, no. 2: 159–76.

Sainsbury, Diane. 2006. "Immigrants' Social Rights in Comparative Perspective: Welfare Regimes, Forms of Immigration and Immigration Policy Regimes." *Journal of European Social Policy* 16, no. 3: 229–44.

Salinas, Lupe S. 2005. "Latino Educational Neglect: The Result Bespeaks Discrimination." *Race, Religion, Gender & Class* 5, no. 2: 269–324.

Samers, Michael. 2001. "'Here to Work': Undocumented Immigration in the United States and Europe." *SAIS Review* 21, no. 1: 131–45.

Sánchez, Gabriel R. 2008. "Latino Group Consciousness and Perceptions of Commonality with African Americans." *Social Science Quarterly* 89, no. 2: 428–44.

Sánchez, Gabriel R., and Natalie Masuoka. 2010. "Brown-Utility Heuristic? The Presence and Contributing Factors of Latino Linked Fate." *Hispanic Journal of Behavioral Sciences* 32, no. 4: 519–31.

Sánchez, Gabriel R., and Jason L. Morin. 2011. "The Effect of Descriptive Representation on Latinos' Views of Government and of Themselves." *Social Science Quarterly* 92, no. 2: 483–508.

Sánchez, Juan, and Petra Brock. 1996. "Outcomes of Perceived Discrimination among Hispanic Employees: Is Diversity Management a Luxury or a Necessity?" *Academy of Management Journal* 39, no. 3: 704–19.

Sanderson, Matthew, and Matthew Painter II. 2011. "Occupational Channels for Mexican Migration: New Destination Formation in a Binational Context." *Rural Sociology* 76, no. 4: 461–80.

Sassen, Saskia. 1996. *Losing Control? Sovereignty in an Age of Globalization.* New York: Columbia University Press.

Saucedo, Leticia M. 2004. "The Browning of the American Workplace: Protecting Workers in Increasingly Latino-ized Occupations." *Notre Dame Law Review* 80, no. 1: 303–32.

Schildkraut, Deborah J. 2005. "The Rise and Fall of Political Engagement among Latinos: The Role of Identity and Perceptions of Discrimination." *Political Behavior* 27, no. 3: 285–312.

Schleef, Debra J., and H. B. Cavalcanti. 2009. *Latinos in Dixie: Class and Assimilation in*

Richmond, Virginia. Albany, NY: SUNY Press.

Schwartz, Seth J., Jennifer B. Unger, Byron L. Zamboanga, and José Szapocznik. 2010. "Rethinking the Concept of Acculturation: Implications for Theory and Research." *American Psychologist* 65, no. 4: 237–51.

Segura, Gary. 2013. "Behavioral and Attitudinal Components of Immigrant Political Incorporation." In *Outsiders No More? Models of Immigrant Political Incorporation*, ed. Jennifer Hochschild, Jacqueline Chattopadhyay, Claudine Cay, and Michael Jones-Correa. New York: Oxford University Press.

Setzler, Mark, and Nick McRee. n.d. "Prospects for Political Incorporation among Young Mexican American Immigrants." Http://acme.highpoint.edu/~msetzler.

Shah, Paru. 2009. "Motivating Participation: The Symbolic Effects of Latino Representation on Parent School Involvement." *Social Science Quarterly* 90, no. 1: 212–30.

Shaw, Randy. 2008. *Beyond the Fields: Cesar Chavez, the UFW, and the Struggle for Justice in the 21st Century.* Berkeley: University of California Press.

Shorey, Hal S., Gloria Cowan, and Mary P. Sullivan. 2002. "Predicting Perceptions of Discrimination among Hispanics and Anglos." *Hispanic Journal of Behavioral Sciences* 24, no. 1: 3–22.

Staton, Jeffrey, Robert A. Jackson, and Damarys Canache. 2007. "Dual Nationality among Latinos: What Are the Implications for Political Connectedness?" *Journal of Politics* 69, no. 2: 470–82.

Stein, Gabriela L., Laura M. González, and Nadia Huq. 2012. "Cultural Stressors and the Hopelessness Model of Depressive Symptoms in Latino Adolescents." *Journal of Youth and Adolescence* 41, no. 10: 1339–49.

Stephan, Walter G., Oscar Ybarra, and Guy Bachman. 1999. "Prejudice toward Immigrants." *Journal of Applied Social Psychology* 29, no. 11: 2221–37.

Stoll, Michael A., and Janelle S. Wong. 2007. "Immigration and Civic Participation in a Multiracial and Multiethnic Context." *International Migration Review* 41, no. 4: 880–908.

Stowell, Jacob I., Ramiro Martínez Jr., and Jeffrey M. Cancino. 2012. "Latino Crime and Latinos in the Criminal Justice System: Trends, Policy Implications, and Future Research Initiatives. *Race and Social Problems* 4, no. 1: 31–40.

Suro, Roberto, and Audrey Singer. 2002. *Latino Growth in Metropolitan America: Changing Patterns, New Locations.* Brookings Institution, Center on Urban and Metropolitan Policy, in collaboration with the Pew Hispanic Center.

Tam Cho, Wendy K. 1999. "Naturalization, Socialization, Participation: Immigrants and (Non-) Voting." *Journal of Politics* 61, no. 4: 1140–55.

Teske, Raymond H. C., and Bardin H. Nelson. 1974. "Acculturation and Assimilation: A Clarification." *American Ethnologist* 1, no. 2: 351–67.

U.S. Census Bureau. 1983. 1980 Census of Population. Washington: U.S. Census Bureau.

———. 2011. "The Hispanic Population: 2010." *U.S. Census Bureau.* Http://www.census.gov.

———. 2012a. American FactFinder. Census 2000. Http://factfinder2.census.gov.

———. 2012b. American FactFinder. Census 2010. Http://factfinder2.census.gov.

———. 2013a. American FactFinder. *U.S. Census Bureau.* Http://factfinder2.census.gov.

———. 2013b. "Nativity and Citizenship Status by Sex, Hispanic Origin, and Race." *U.S. Census Bureau.* Http://www.census.gov.

———. 2013c. "Nativity and Citizenship Status by Sex, and Hispanic Type." *U.S. Census Bureau.* Http://www.census.gov.

U.S. Citizenship and Immigration Services (USCIS). 2006. "Temporary Migration to the United States: Nonimmigrant Admissions under U.S. Immigration Law." Federal Depository Library Program Electronic Collection (FDLP/EC) Archive. Http://permanent.access.gpo.gov.

———. 2011. "Green Card through Self Petition." *Department of Homeland Security.* Http://www.uscis.gov.

———. n.d. "National Interest Waiver." *Department of Homeland Security.* Http://www.uscis.gov.

Valdivia, Corinne, Pedro Dozi, Stephen Jeanetta, Lisa Y. Flores, Domingo Martínez, and Anne Dannerbeck. 2008. "The Impact of Networks and the Context of Reception on Asset Accumulation Strategies of Latino Newcomers in New Settlement Communities of the Midwest." *American Journal of Agricultural Economics* 90, no. 5: 1319–25.

Valdivia, Corinne, and Lisa Y. Flores. 2012. "Factors Affecting the Job Satisfaction of Latino/a Immigrants in the Midwest." *Journal of Career Development* 39:31–49.

Valentine, Eric. 2005. *Uniting Two Cultures: Latino Immigrants in the Wisconsin Dairy Industry.* San Diego: University of California, San Diego.

Varsanyi, Monica W. 2011. "Neoliberalism and Nativism: Anti-Immigrant Policy Activism and an Emerging Politics of Scale." *International Journal of Urban and Regional Research* 35, no. 2: 295–311.

Varsanyi, Monica W., Paul G. Lewis, Doris Marie Provine, and Scott Decker. 2012. "A Multilayered Jurisdictional Patchwork: Immigration Federalism in the United States." *Law & Policy* 34, no. 2: 138–58.

Varsanyi, Monica W., and Joseph Nevens. 2007. "Introduction: Borderline Contradictions: Neoliberalism, Unauthorized Migration, and Intensifying Immigration Policing." *Geopolitics* 12, no. 2: 223–27.

Vega, Arturo, Rubén Martínez, and Tia Stevens. 2011. "Cosas Políticas: Politics, Attitudes, and Perceptions by Region." In *Latinos in the Midwest*, ed. Rubén Martinez. East Lansing: Michigan State University Press.

Verba, Sidney, and Norman H. Nie. 1972. *Participation in America: Political Democracy and Social Equality.* Chicago: University of Chicago Press.

Verba, Sidney, Kay Lehman Schlozman, and Henry Brady. 1995. *Voice and Equality: Civic Voluntarism in American Politics.* Cambridge, MA: Harvard University Press.

Verkuyten, Maykel. 2008. "Life Satisfaction among Ethnic Minorities: The Role of Discrimination and Group Identification." *Social Indicators Research* 89, no. 3: 391–404.

Viruell-Fuentes, Edna A., Patricia Y. Miranda, and Sawsan Abdulrahim. 2012. "More than Culture: Structural Racism, Intersectionality Theory, and Immigrant Health." *Social Science & Medicine* 75, no. 12: 2099–116.

Walker, Kyle E., and Helga Leitner. 2011. "The Variegated Landscape of Local Immigration Policies in the United States." *Urban Geography* 32, no. 2: 156–78.

Wals, Sergio C. 2011. "Does What Happens in Los Mochis Stay in Los Mochis? Explaining Post-Migration Political Behavior." *Political Research Quarterly* 64, no. 3: 600–611.

Wampler, Brian, María Chávez, and Francisco I. Pedraza. 2009. "Should I Stay or Should I Go? Explaining Why Most Mexican Immigrants Are Choosing to Remain Permanently in the United States." *Latino Studies* 7, no. 1: 83–104.

Waters, Mary. 1994. "Ethnic and Racial Identities of Second-Generation Black Immigrants in New York City." *International Migration Review* 28, no. 4: 795–820.

Waters, Mary, and Tomás R. Jiménez. 2005. "Assessing Immigrant Assimilation: New Empirical and Theoretical Challenges." *Annual Review of Sociology* 31, no. 1: 105–25.

Weisberg, Herbert F. 2002. "Partisanship and Incumbency in Presidential Elections." *Political Behavior* 24, no. 4: 339–60.

Wenzel, James. 2006. "Acculturation Effects on Trust in National and Local Governments among Mexican Americans." *Social Science Quarterly* 87, no. 5: 1073–87.

White House. n.d. "Creating an Immigration System for the 21st Century." Http://www.whitehouse.gov.

Wilkes, Rima. 2015. "We Trust in Government, Just Not in Yours: Race, Partisanship, and Political Trust, 1958–2012." *Social Science Research* 49:356–71.

Williams, David R. 2006. "Race, Socioeconomic Status, and Health: The Added Effects of Racism and Discrimination." *Annals of the New York Academy of Sciences* 896, no. 1: 173–88.

Williams, Jerome D., Geraldine R. Henderson, and Anne-Marie Harris. 2001. "Consumer Racial Profiling: Bigotry Goes to Market." *The New Crisis* (November/December): 22–24.

Williamson, Vanessa, Theda Skocpol, and John Coggin. 2011. "The Tea Party and the Remaking of American Conservatism." *Perspectives on Politics* 9, no. 1: 25–43.

Wolfinger, Raymond E., and Steven J. Rosenstone. 1980. *Who Votes?* New Haven, CT: Yale University Press.

Woods, Joshua. 2011. "The 9/11 Effect: Toward a Social Science of Terrorist Threat." *Social Science Journal* 48, no. 1: 213–33.

Woods, Joshua, and Damien Arthur. 2014. "The Threat of Terrorism and the Changing Public Discourse on Immigration after September 11." *Sociological Spectrum* 34, no. 5: 421–41.

Woolcock, Michael, and Deepa Narayan. 2000. "Social Capital: Implications for Development Theory, Research, and Policy." *World Bank Research Observer* 15, no. 2: 225–49.

Yinger, John. 1998. "Housing Discrimination Is Still Worth Worrying About." *Housing Policy Debate* 9, no. 4: 893–927.

Zick, Andreas, Thomas F. Pettigrew, and Ulrich Wagner. 2008. "Ethnic Prejudice and Discrimination in Europe." *Journal of Social Issues* 64, no. 2: 233–51.

Index

crime, 2–3, 17, 18, 63, 110; violent, 20, 67, 73

cultural incorporation: 30–33, 36–38, 46–48, 74–75, 116–21; in Central Illinois, 38, 46; factors for, 30, 35, 38, 40, 116, 119, 123

culture: connectedness with other, 46–47; identity and, 37–41; incorporation and, 74–75; among Latinos, 118, 119, 120, 122; linked fates and, 32, 38–42; solidarity and, 43, 121. *See also* acculturation; English language

D

Deferred Action for Childhood Arrivals (DACA), 15, 22

Deferred Action for Parents of Americans (DAPA), 15, 22

democracy, 97, 99–100, 118

demonstrations: on immigration reform, 91; by Latinos, 75, 79–80, 85, 88, 91–92, 126

deportation, 5, 9, 16; avoiding, 15, 27, 30–31, 74, 98, 121, 126; Border Patrol and, 13, 19, 20; Hispanic, 98, 110; numbers, 17; Operation Wetback and, 65; raids and, 30; stopping, 91; traffic violations and, 18, 67

destinations: Illinois, 1, 2–4, 6, 10; Beardstown, 98, 115; immigrant, 11–12, 20, 56, 110; Midwest, 21, 61; North, 17; South, 17, 21; Southwest, 13; West, 115

Dillingham Commission on Immigration, 13

discrimination: in Beardstown, 7, 49–50, 54–56, 59, 61–71, 98, 123; context of reception and, 19, 51, 117, 123–25;

derogatory language and, 65; group identity and, 70; host population and, 64; labor market, 60; Latinos and, 40, 47, 58, 70, 112; measuring, 52, 58–59; in meatpacking plants, 60–62, 98, 110; in Monmouth, 7, 10, 49, 53–56, 59–61, 64–71, 75, 121–26; newcomers and, 4, 53, 101; in public places, 59, 62–63, 71, 124; regional, 14; by skin color, 53; wages and, 61, 69. *See also* prejudice

driver's license, 22, 23, 67

dual-language education, 6, 64, 65, 71, 124, 125

Durbin, Dick, 91

E

Easton, David, 103

economics: consequences of immigration and, 16, 49, 53, 116; government policies and, 102; of host community, 4; language skills and, 119; Mexican, 50; naturalization rates and, 24; racism and, 52, 69; SES Model and, 44, 81; U.S. status and, 104–6

education, 8; CASA promotes, 126; citizenship and, 14–15, 24, 26; college degree benefits and, 61, 74, 90, 109, 127; connectedness and, 39; curricula in, 64; discrimination and, 52, 56–58; immigrants pursue, 4; participation and, 81, 86, 94; trust in government and, 101, 102, 105, 111, 119. *See also* language

El Paso-Ciudad Juarez, 19, 98

empathy, 39, 40, 42, 120

employment: employers and, 5; Latino, 6, 8, 60; social class and, 35; status,